Topographies of Suffering

TOPOGRAPHIES OF SUFFERING

Buchenwald, Babi Yar, Lidice

Jessica Rapson

berghahn
NEW YORK · OXFORD
www.berghahnbooks.com

Published in 2015 by
Berghahn Books
www.berghahnbooks.com

Library of Congress Cataloging-in-Publication Data

Rapson, Jessica, 1982– author.
Topographies of suffering: Buchenwald, Babi Yar, Lidice / Jessica Rapson.
    pages cm
Includes bibliographical references and index.
ISBN 978-1-78238-709-1 (hardback: alk. paper) —
ISBN 978-1-78238-710-7 (ebook)
  1. World War, 1939–1945—Europe—Atrocities—Case studies. 2. Holocaust, Jewish
(1939–1945)—History—Case studies. 3. Collective memory—Europe—Case studies.
4. Historical geography—Europe—Case studies. 5. Europe—Ethnic relations. I. Title.
D804.E85R37 2015
940.53'18 — dc23
                                                                      2014039954

British Library Cataloguing in Publication Data

A catalogue record for this book is available from the British Library

Printed on acid-free paper

ISBN: 978-1-78238-709-1 hardback
ISBN: 978-1-78238-710-7 ebook

For Eva Margaret Rapson (1912–2012)
and
Virginia Elizabeth Rapson (1980-2014)

CONTENTS

FIGURES

PREFACE

On Tuesday, 7 June 2011, Jorge Semprun, Spanish writer, political activist and survivor of the Nazi concentration camp Buchenwald, died at his home in Paris.[1] Semprun's writing about his time in Buchenwald encapsulates the key principles, desires and frustrations which characterize this book, and his death brought them home anew. A heartfelt requiem, by the French philosopher Bernard Henri-Lévy (2011), isolates the unique pull of Semprun's work:

> I loved this beautiful idea of the writer, the post-Proustian idea that memory feeds upon itself and is increased by what it spits out and what is gleaned from it. I loved, and still love, the idea that books do not drain the memory but arouse it; I loved that he thought, and proved, that digging into one's memories does not exhaust them, rather it fertilizes them. I loved his rejection of this popular assumption of a massive, passive memory, waiting in limbo for one to come along and inventory its stock so it can be stored, once and for all, in the false light of a reliquary.

Henri-Lévy's obituary honours Semprun's approach to writing, the way he fed upon his own memories, fertilized them, rendered them productive and dynamic. Upon first reading, however, it struck me forcefully that Henri-Lévy's description is applicable beyond Semprun's oeuvre; for it resonates with how I understand collective memory; that is, the memories we gather and recreate. Such memories are not, as memory studies in the wake of Pierre Nora (1989) would have us believe, fixed in historical time and frozen in nation-place. As increasingly reflexive practitioners (Confino and Fritzsche 2002; Erll and Rigney 2009) have hinted, memory is always in production and never produced. It is always a journey and never a destination.

The Holocaust is frequently described in scholarly discourse as unrepresentable, and a corresponding assumption that the experiences of Nazi victims deny, evade or transcend communication and comprehension has become prevalent as a result (see Weissman 2004).[2] Yet Semprun explicitly disrupts these delimitations:

you can always say everything. The 'ineffable' you hear so much about is only
an alibi. Or a sign of laziness. You can always say anything: language contains
everything ... You have merely to think about it. And to set to it. And have
the time, of course, and courage, for a boundless and probably never-ending
account (1997: 13–14).

Just as experience, with time and courage, can be represented, this book
suggests that it can also be communicated. This is not to imply that someone else's memories can become my own; interaction is not osmosis, and
the 'memories' I produce will not be the same those of someone else. It is
not possible, or desirable, for the Holocaust to become 'real' for those who
confront it as history; we cannot enter into 'the Holocaust universe' as a lived
experience (see Langer 1993). What can be done, with time and courage, is
to confront the memories of another in a way which means something, which
is worth doing (see Weissman 2004: 112), which is not akin to the vicarious
appropriation of so-called 'unclaimed' experience (see Caruth 1996), and in
doing so we participate in a dialogue which fuels memory's dynamism.

But what is the nature of this productive, processual dynamism? How
does it happen? I explore one possible answer to these questions in this book,
in interrogating the potential of the encounters we may have with memory
texts: be they literary forms from testimony to fiction, or specific landscapes,
from memorials to unmarked mass graves. Beyond gaining an improved understanding of the dynamic between memory, literature and landscape, this
book highlights the ethical potential of such encounters. As such it is inspired by Emmanuel Levinas's suggestion that the impossibility of knowing
the other resides in the nature of the desire for this knowledge; a desire
'beyond everything that can simply complete it. It is like goodness – the
Desired does not fill it, but deepens it' (Levinas 1969: 34). This creates 'a
relationship whose positivity comes from remoteness, from separation, for
it nourishes itself, one might say, with its hunger' (Levinas 1969: 34). In
Levinasian terms it is through this dialogic relation that it becomes possible
to avoid the 'self-centred totalistic thinking that organizes men and things
into power systems, and gives us control over nature and other people' (Wild
2007: 17). The approach to the Holocaust I pursue here is one which pur-
posefully avoids this totalizing objectification of others of the past, whilst
maintaining a reflexive refusal of complete identification. Despite stemming
from this philosophical premise, this is not a philosophical book in disciplinary terms, nor is it intended as a reconsideration of the work of Levinas.
Rather, fuelled by his notion of relationships nourished by hunger, I suggest
a way of entering into a dialogue with others of the past without assuming a
sense of mastery: in encounters which deepen but do not fill us, which touch
but do not complete us.

Notes

1. Semprun's name is spelt throughout this book without the diacritic ('ú'), following works published in English translation.
2. The term 'Holocaust' is deployed in this book to describe the murder and persecution of Jews and others by the National Socialist regime, a broad use of a term with a complex history of application. My decision to employ it as such is made in line with widespread academic and popular usage.

ACKNOWLEDGEMENTS

This book is the product of six years of research, travelling and writing. It would not have been possible without the guidance, support and friendship of a number of amazing people. Thanks are due to a veritable plethora of people and institutions: to the Department of English and Comparative Literature at Goldsmiths, University of London; the Morris Leigh Foundation; and the Arts and Humanities Research Council for their generous financial contributions towards my fieldwork costs; to Professor Gill Rye and the staff and students of the MA in Cultural Memory at the Institute of Germanic and Romance Studies, where the seeds of the project germinated. Innumerable people have supported and encouraged me throughout my travels: Charlotte Rea, an inspiring photographer, who accompanied me to Buchenwald in 2008; perceptive and supportive Anna Phillips, with whom I visited Lidice in 2010; and my father, without whose company in Kiev in 2011 I would have (literally) been lost. To those whom I have encountered on my journeys, and who have generously shared their experiences with me, I am also indebted.

I have been lucky enough to benefit from the perceptive guidance of a number of fantastic scholars throughout the process of writing this book, including Astrid Erll, Padraig Kirwan, Stef Craps and Robert Eaglestone, and my anonymous reviewers. I am grateful for their keen insights, acumen and time. For inspirational dialogue over related material at conferences, seminars and publications throughout this process, I am also indebted to Dirk Moses, Susannah Radstone, Anna Reading, Michael Rothberg and Pieter Vermeulen. I would also like to thank Chris Lloyd and Helen Palmer for their support, enthusiasm and academic acumen.

Last, but certainly not least, heartfelt gratitude is due to the following individuals: to Rick Crownshaw, whose critical rigour, encyclopaedic knowledge, generosity and patience I have relied upon throughout the process of writing this book; to Lucy Bond, who lived this project with me every step of the way, and without whose continuous support, encouragement and phenomenal intellect this monograph would never have seen the light of day; to Arthur McVey, who has never given up on me; and to my parents Nick and Caroline Rapson who have supported me so generously in so many ways and never expected anything in return.

INTRODUCTION

As the Holocaust passes out of living memory, there is a new urgency to formulate ways in which its narratives may yet be encountered and attended to. This book turns to landscape to offer one possible solution. Three case studies are explored: the Buchenwald Concentration Camp Memorial near Weimar, Germany; the Babi Yar Ravine in Kiev, Ukraine, where a mass grave holds the remains of victims of an *Einsatzgruppen* massacre; and the site of the mass grave and razed village of Lidice, in the Czech Republic, also the result of an *Einsatzgruppen* operation. These landscapes are considered, initially, as intensely localized and geographically rooted, and in turn as co-ordinates in larger, often globally constituted networks of commemoration. Across these landscapes and networks, I suggest, encounters with topographies of suffering – landscapes formerly inhabited by those from the past with whom they may attempt to empathize – are significant co-ordinates in the formation of contemporary Holocaust cultural memory.

Why landscape? The complexity and significance of the relationship between the violence of war and the physical environment has been established (Russell and Tucker 2004; Russell 2001; Closmann 2009), as has the notable impact of military processes on landscape features; militarization 'operates through landscape which it changes or maintains, in both a physical and cultural sense' (Coates, Cole and Pearson 2010: 3). The fundamentally geographical nature of many of the events of the Holocaust in particular has furthermore been recognized (Cole et al. 2009), as has the idea that 'narrative of extermination' of the concentration camp is best expressed in geographical terms (Koonz 1994: 258–80). The 'Nazis' appropriation of the trope of landscape in their genocidal redefinitions of nation, home and Heimat' (Baer 2002: 77), and their practical harnessing of topography in processes of mass killing and burial, affected the way victims experienced the Holocaust as it happened. Furthermore, the Holocaust demands a positioning of the self in relation to this history (Baer 2002: 68–69). I suggest that the examples of Holocaust landscapes discussed in this book provoke within the viewer what Mitch Rose and John Wylie (2006: 477) have called 'the tension of regarding at a distance that which enables one to see'. This tension is an issue for everyone who encounters these commemorative places with what Amy Hungerford (2003: 105) has described as an 'intense concern' for the victims of the past.

Landscape invites scholarship from many different disciplines across the social and natural sciences and humanities (see Thompson 2009: 7). For the purposes of this investigation into contemporary encounters with Holocaust history, approaches from two of these disciplines are particularly significant: cultural memory and cultural geography. As will become clear, there is a notable confluence in the way scholars from these disciplines have approached 'landscape' in recent years. Alongside these influences from cultural memory and geography, this book also draws on elements of ecocritical thinking. My interrogations of Holocaust literature – from testimony to fiction – pay particular attention to representations of encounters with the specifically 'natural' elements of the landscapes discussed. Ecocritical thinking is fundamentally concerned with the nature and representation of the relationship between human beings and the world they inhabit, and maintains faith in the potential of universal environmental sensibility.

One might well question the relevance of this environmental sensibility to a book concerned with Holocaust memory. Genocide scholar Mark Levene (2004: 440) usefully articulates the justification for this focus when he claims that '[a] world without genocide can only develop in one in which principles of equity, social justice, *environmental stability* – and one might add genuine human kindness – have become the "norm"' (my emphasis). Indeed Levene (2010) nominated climate change as 'the elephant in the room' of genocide scholarship. The audience responded with concerns about the intentions of actors; in the case of genocide, the destruction of people is an explicit goal. Climate change, even anthropogenic, may have lethal consequences but, they suggested, it should not be seen in the same light. Yet such a distinction is compellingly disrupted in Rob Nixon's (2011: 2) recent discussion of poverty and activism in the 'global South', in which the definition of what constitutes violence and perpetration is opened up. Nixon promotes awareness of slow, 'attritional violence that is typically not viewed as violence at all', encompassing climate change, deforestation, and the radioactive aftermath of war. He simultaneously broadens the category of victimhood; his focus is not necessarily on the targets of genocidal attacks, but on the poor who have few tools to combat the violence of capitalism, a capitalism that writes 'land in a bureaucratic, externalising and extraction driven manner that is often pitilessly instrumental' (2011: 17). This broadening of what constitutes violence underscores the comparative frameworks into which the Holocaust is drawn throughout this study. The victims of slow violence, the poor, are rendered 'dispensable citizens', akin to those who, in Holocaust discourse, Giorgio Agamben (1995) describes as 'bare life'; life that does not deserve to live. Examples of this rendering are visible in each part of this book, both within and beyond the context of the Holocaust.

The interaction between local, national and global environments fundamental to an ecocritical perspective is a central concern throughout this book, and one of its fundamental organizing principles. Each section begins with a consideration of a site-based memorial as a geographically specific space, with due attendance to local and national histories and associated discourse. I trace ideological heritages and the shaping of memorial topographies by particular regimes and 'memorial entrepreneurs' (see Jordan 2006: 11). With this fundamental platform in place, I move on to consider various mediations and remediations of each place, with a focus on literary texts. The final chapters of each part of the book all consider globally dispersed mediations of these sites beyond their original geographical locations. This structure was in part determined by the sites themselves, which were selected for the unique ways in which they are all deeply rooted and simultaneously de-territorialized, but it is also influenced by recent developments in the disciplines of memory studies and cultural geography which will be explored briefly in this introduction.

The first chapter on Buchenwald examines the past and present landscapes of the camp itself and the surrounding area, which includes the historic city of Weimar and the picturesque, forested, Ettersburg slopes. Tracing a series of landscape ideologies and redefinitions I harness existing scholarship to provide a comprehensive overview of Buchenwald's journey from idyllic hunting land to concentration camp memorial. Close attention is then dedicated, in Chapter 2, to the literary work of Semprun, who experienced Buchenwald as an inmate from 1943 to 1945. Three of Semprun's texts, *The Long Voyage* [*Le Grand Voyage*] (1963), *What a Beautiful Sunday!* [*Quel beau Dimanche!*] (1980), and *Literature or Life* [*L'écriture ou la vie*] (1994), discuss his memories of Buchenwald in detail. These texts are ideally suited to a consideration of process and mediation; he returns to particular moments over and over again, revising and reimagining his past, laying bare the fundamentally metamorphic nature of memory. The chapter exposes the potential of Semprun's literature to animate the landscapes of Buchenwald for those who encounter them. Guided by Semprun, the investigation is grounded in the specific cultural history of this locale, allowing for an interrogation of the relationship between humanity and the natural world specific to the German context. The overall discussion of Semprun's Buchenwald proposes that a fundamentally affective form of memory-work may be prompted by encounters with literature and landscape, and concludes that landscape can and will continue to play a role in interpreting atrocious pasts and providing a platform for ethically driven response.

The final chapter of part one undertakes a transcultural comparison between the Holocaust and Southern U.S. legacies of racial inequality, based on analysis of journalist Mark Jacobson's travel memoir *The Lampshade: A Holocaust Detective Story from Buchenwald to New Orleans* (2010). Probing potential shared ground between very different forms of human and 'natural' violence, this chapter traces Jacobson's journey from a flooded post-Katrina New Orleans – where a lampshade apparently made from human skin drifts to the surface in an abandoned house – to the Ettersburg slope and Buchenwald, the original home of this particular piece of Nazi iconography. The resulting narrative, I suggest, calls for a reconsideration of racial boundaries commensurate with emerging discourse on genocide and environmental disaster.

Part two begins with an exploration of Babi Yar in Kiev, which considers the atrocity that took place at the ravine, and the landscape of the ravine itself as a microcosm of the larger topography of the Holocaust in Ukraine. Commemoration at Babi Yar has been extremely slow to appear and is still emerging only hesitantly against a backdrop of political and cultural marginalization of the Holocaust in Ukraine, particularly in comparison to a recent official focus on the suffering of the Ukrainian people under Stalin. Both Hitler's and Stalin's campaigns in Ukraine resulted in a similar disruption of landscape and landscape experience; an increased acknowledgement of such similarities, I argue, might go some way to countering the marginalization of Holocaust memory in Ukraine. Chapter 5 then moves on to focus on what has become an alternative commemorative medium for Babi Yar itself: the mediation and remediation of the atrocity in literature. I trace a journey through text, beginning with a testimonial account of Babi Yar by Ukrainian survivor Dina Pronicheva. I then track the integration of this account into Anatoli Kuznetsov's biography of his life in Kiev as a witness to the German invasion (*Babi Yar: A Document in the Form of a Novel*, 1972), and its subsequent mobilization in the fiction of the English writer D.M. Thomas (*The White Hotel*, 1981). This literary trajectory was instrumental in creating the international awareness of the atrocity that prompted the creation of a commemorative landscape thousands of miles away on the Colorado plains: the Babi Yar Memorial Park in Denver, the subject of the final chapter in part two.

Inaugurated in 1982, the park represents the efforts of community groups in Denver to draw attention to continued marginalization of minority groups in Soviet territories during the Communist era. Landscaping at the park aims to highlight certain distinctive geographical features that resonate with the specific environment of the site in Kiev, including a natural ravine on which the park is centred and a similar grassland ecosystem. The park is currently undergoing a process of reorientation. Chapter 6 examines the new design's integration of the Holocaust into a nationalized narrative concerning the War on Terror.

Part three explores commemoration and activism surrounding the attempted annihilation of the Czech village of Lidice. As in the preceding parts, the investigation begins with the place itself. Chapter 7 thus considers the significance of the Nazis' attempt to remove Lidice from history and memory by re-landscaping the area and covering it with German soil. The international reaction to this act has had notable results: both places and people around the world were named 'Lidice' in memory of the village, which was itself rebuilt as a result of a community fundraising project based in Stoke-on-Trent almost immediately after the end of the war. The new Lidice is both living space and memorial complex, comprising a museum, one of the largest commemorative rose gardens in the world, and a large area of open landscape where the original village stood, and where faint traces of former structures are visible. I provide an overview of this complex environment, paying close attention to the particular methods of landscaping that have been employed there.

Chapter 8 moves on to examine the various textual representations of Lidice that emerged in the years following its destruction. I isolate a tendency to frame it within a narrative of the disrupted pastoral; a nostalgic vision which demonstrably resonates with people across many cultures. The final chapter focuses in particular on inscriptions of Lidice into local contexts via cosmopolitan memory processes, again demonstrating a variety of trans-cultural forms of engagement. I finally turn to the mobilization of Lidice in recent years: the chapter examines two particular cases of town twinning, as proposals for the Czech village to be officially linked to Khojaly, Azerbaijan (announced February 2011) and Stoke-on-Trent, UK (planning underway since September 2010) take shape. In looking closely at the dynamics of twinning, the final chapter evaluates the potential cosmopolitanism of this emerging network.

Before embarking on the three journeys that comprise the main part of this book, this introduction unpacks recent scholarly trajectories on landscape and memory, considers ways in which nature and literature may mediate memory, and interrogates the ethical potential of associated encounters with the Holocaust. I outline a theoretical confluence between cultural memory and cultural geography, demonstrating landscape's fundamental role in shaping memory and experience. Whilst an explosion of work on memorials and monuments (see Confino and Fritzsche 2002: 1; Young 1994: 1–16) has resulted in a climate of 'memory fatigue' (Huyssen 2003: 3), refocusing attention on the larger landscapes which contain these structures and the processes that shape them may revitalize the study of commemorative spaces and the encounters they facilitate. At the nexus of cultural memory and cultural geography lies scholarship on 'difficult heritage' (MacDonald 2009; Logan and Reeves 2009), 'dark tourism' (Lennon and Foley 2000; Sharpley and Stone 2009) and 'tourists of history' (Sturken 2007). A plethora of related work has considered both the experiences of visitors at sites of former atrocities and the challenges faced by those who curate and manage these places. My own contribution to this body of work will be considered in further detail later in this introduction.

Lieux to Landscape

Founding texts on cultural memory and cultural geography – the study of how groups engage with and make sense of the landscapes around them (D. Atkinson et al. 2005: xiv) – bear significant similarities. By 'cultural memory', I refer to the diverse and ever-expanding body of scholarship which has developed since a model of collective memory was propounded by French sociologist Maurice Halbwachs ([1925] 1992 and [1950] 1980). Since Halbwachs's innovation, memory scholars have considered ways in which individual memories become part of larger social and cultural frameworks, and vice versa. Halbwachs's work rendered 'the boundaries between [the collective and the individual] permeable' (Crownshaw 2010: 2), prompting a tendency to see personal memories as existing in an inevitable dialogue with associated cultural texts, representations and media. Examinations of the interplay between memory and varied cultural frameworks, then, fall into the category of 'cultural memory'. Halbwachs (1980: 156–7) implicitly prompts us to consider memory's relationship to landscape by affirming the centrality of space and place to the way people think about the past; his discussion of 'implacement' posits groups and their environments as 'mutually responsive' (Browne and Middleton 2011: 40) and essential to stabilizing collective memory (Halbwachs 1980: 140).

The cultural turn in geography left behind 'spatial science' to achieve more holistic considerations of 'humanized space', notably echoing Halbwachs's model of implacement. As Todd Samuel Presner (2007: 11) notes, 'while the discipline of cultural geography lies primarily outside of literary and cultural studies, there are a number of significant points of contact … not the least of which is the idea that culture is spatially constituted'. Early cultural geographers frequently conceptualized landscapes as 'indigenous' spaces in which identity and place were organically connected (Wylie 2007: 23), often through a nostalgic lens which mourned the post–World War II loss of romantic rural vistas and ways of life (see Hoskins [1954] 1985). This markedly nostalgic nationalism led to a distinct research focus on remnants that seemed to fix or embody particular pasts. In memory studies these tendencies can be traced to Pierre Nora (1989: 7), whose attempt to stay the 'acceleration of history' resulted in an exhaustive seven volume essay assemblage of French *lieux de mémoire,* including texts and sites from 'true memorials – monuments to the dead [to] objects as seemingly different as museums, commemorations, archives, heraldic devices or emblems' (Nora 2001: xix). Whilst dealing with a broader spectrum of social collectives, even Halbwachs (1950: 50) originally conceived of collective memory as taking place within 'the theatre' of his national society. It is crucial to note, particularly in relation to the first section of this book on the camp at Buchenwald, that both disciplinary trends have been traced back to nineteenth century German romanticism, 'from whence ideas about the particularity, value, and vitality of certain "cultural groups" ... first emerged', later to 'culminate in twentieth-century cultural nationalism' (Wylie 2007: 22). Implied here is a 'superorganic' understanding of culture (Duncan 1980) as existing 'both above and beyond the participating members' of that culture; 'an entity with a structure, set of processes, and momentum of its own' (Zelinsky 1973: 40–1). The analyses in this book are wary of assuming these 'naturalized affiliations between subject and object' (see Campbell 2008: 3) that reify culture, granting it autonomy beyond individual or even group human participation and endeavour.

Awareness of landscape's memorative preservation of 'the order of things' (Yates 2001: 17) is implicit in both Halbwachs's notion of implacement and Nora's (1989: 7) crystallization of the 'history of France through memory' (2001: xx), a text which assumes that symbols and sites can 'embody' memory. These texts can thus be read as 'specific representations' *of* that memory (2001: xviii), a logic which set in motion a tendency in others to overlook the way in which memorial sites are subject to continuous evolution.[1] Much 1980s US cultural geography echoed Nora's notion of embodied memory, in examinations of 'repositories of myth, imagination, symbolic value and cultural meaning' (Wylie 2007: 44–5). The influential Berkeley School privileged a focus on the 'ordered presentation' of visible objects as they exist in relation to one another (Sauer 1963: 97–98), extending to material manifestations in landscape, rather than associated processes (Mikesell and Wagner 1962). Reading landscapes as text undeniably results in rich, highly textured works (see Schama 1995; Iles 2003). However, this turn cast landscape as an archive from which stable meanings may be retrieved and recuperated. A similar tendency has been prevalent in discussions of the 'sites and events' of 'dark tourism' which are often seen as 'products' (Lennon and Foley 2000: 3), a term implying both fixity and homogeneity, and, furthermore, casting the tourist as consumer. Recent scholarship continues to define sites of 'difficult heritage' as *lieux de mémoire* (Logan and Reeves 2009: 2), reinforcing a dominant assumption that such places 'harbour' memory, and echo Nora's connection between site and nation-state (see MacDonald 2009: 2). Certainly such places have often become visitor attractions because of their perceived role in the construction – or destruction – of nations and national identity, but this is by no means the only way in which they are encountered, as the transculturally grounded explorations in this book demonstrate; for 'the meanings of landscape, either historically or for the future, are never simply there, inherent and voluble' (Dorrian and Rose 2003: 17). Buchenwald, Babi Yar and Lidice are, therefore, not read here as representations *of* memory, but as co-ordinates in the dialogue that fuels memory's dynamism and evolution.

Early cultural geographers also generated the understanding that perceiving the world *as* landscape (either those we dwell in or travel through) is itself an objectifying 'way of seeing' (Cosgrove and Daniels 1988), drawing attention to the questionable ethics of landscape traditions. Perhaps rightly, the landscape mode has frequently been seen to function as a duplicitous vehicle for transcendent redemption. This possibility is interrogated in my consideration of the difficult relationship between Buchenwald and the ideological heritage of nearby Weimar in part one; Semprun positions Johann Wolfgang von Goethe as a figure who 'see[s] with landscape' and in doing so assumes the privilege and mastery of a detached vision germane to European elite consciousness (see Cosgrove [1984] 1998: 1).

It should be noted at this stage that the fundamental viability of representation in itself is one which haunts discourse surrounding the Holocaust. The perceived extremity of original victim experience has generated a sense that it remains 'unclaimed' (Caruth 1996: 4) and accordingly cannot find adequate representation, whether in literature, the visual arts, or in place.[2] We are warned that aestheticizing the Holocaust in representation risks redeeming it (Adorno 1965: 125–7), even through the act of writing its history (Friedlander 1993: 61). We are left with the delimitation that 'neither acts of remembrance or ethical action' can 'provide a sense of what it was like to be there' (Bernard-Donals and Glejzer 2001: 2). In this context, it seems that promoting landscape as a way of seeing, or at least as a platform for encountering, the Holocaust, risks replicating a perspective which has been linked to its perpetrators; the object of the gaze – including the human subject – is evaluated and classified, deemed other and objectified (see Milchman and Rosenburg 1998: 229–232). Following this logic, Zygmunt Bauman (2000: 92) argues that the modern culture that made the Holocaust possible is a 'garden culture': 'If the Jews are defined as a legitimate problem, if the garden needs weeding, then there is a surely a "rational" way to proceed' (Markle 1995: 128). This perspective is explored in my discussion of landscaping practices at Lidice in section 3, where I suggest that the nationalistic, superorganic bounded nationhood central to Nazi ideology, explicit in *Blut und Boden* [blood and soil] rhetoric, must be acknowledged but not reinscribed as the genocide is remembered and commemorated. Bauman's gardening metaphor takes on an uncomfortable literality in Holocaust landscapes, which were often implicated in genocidal processes, a notion probed in my discussion of Ukrainian topography in Part 2.

Each case study in this book, then, attends to earlier cross-disciplinary conceptualizations of landscape and associated ethical concerns. However, beyond this, I promote a new way of perceiving landscape influenced by more recent scholarship which has acknowledged that monuments and memorials are constantly subject to 'shifting social frameworks' (Rigney 2008: 94), and performative and dynamic processes (Rigney 2008: 94; Parr 2008: 1). Understanding memory as 'embedded in social networks', as a set of 'practices and interventions' rather than a textual or representational medium (Confino and Fritzsche 2002: 5) grounds a turn 'from "sites" to "dynamics" parallel to a larger shift of attention within cultural studies from products to processes, from a focus on discrete cultural artefacts to an interest in the way those artefacts circulate and interact with their environment' (Erll and Rigney 2009: 3). Memory is never static, as the texts around which it circulates are continuously involved in processes of mediation and remediation (Erll and Rigney 2009: 1–14). Attention to movement and process led cultural geographer W.J.T. Mitchell (1994: 1) to proclaim that landscape 'circulates as a medium of exchange', in other words, that landscape itself 'travels: [is] not just literally transported, but that values, beliefs and attitudes that work through and emerge from specific landscape practices and "ways of seeing" can be seen to migrate through spaces and times' (Wylie 2007: 122). This book sees both landscape and memory as created through social processes, evolutionary in a way that defies the fixity of Nora's *lieux*. Landscapes 'are always in the process of "becoming," no longer reified or concretized – inert and there – … always subject to change, and everywhere implicated in the ongoing formulation of social life' (Schein 1997: 662). Furthermore, as Dorrian and Rose (2003: 17) argue, 'landscapes are always perceived in a particular way at a particular time. They are mobilized, and in that mobilization may become productive: productive in relation to a past or to a future, but that relation is always drawn with regard to the present.' Such mobilizations are clearly demonstrated in my discussion of Lidice's twinning with Khojaly and Stoke, highlighting the extent to which landscape and memory are fundamentally realms of the present. Thus, whilst Confino and Fritzsche (2002: 5) take memory 'out of the museum and away from the monument', I return to these 'sites' of memory as *landscapes*; not as places which embody memory, but as co-ordinates in dialogue with others that produce it. Where 'site' implies stasis (Rigney 2008: 93), 'landscape' implies metamorphosis.[3] I focus, then, not only on 'sites' as they can be seen to represent political and institutional agendas, but as experiential frameworks.

As indicated above, these landscapes are considered both as geographically rooted territories, determined by specific local national polemics and co-ordinates in global memory trajectories. In relating Buchenwald to New Orleans and observing the mobilization of Babi Yar in Denver and Lidice in Azerbaijan and the United Kingdom, I follow Neil Campbell (2008: 8) in thinking space 'rhizomatically', 'beyond its function as national unifier', as 'unfinished multiple, and 'open" in order to 'trac[e] divergent, entangled lines of composition that both interconnect and split apart constantly'. Probing the way in which memory may appear simultaneously locally determined and geographically uncontainable, Presner (2007: 12) advocates a focus on how 'language and the places of encounter … have become deterritorialized and remapped according to new constellations, figures and sites of contact'. This cultural-geographical approach fruitfully maps historical events in nexuses, rather than marked points on a chronological line, allowing 'a new topology of concepts and problems to surface' (Presner 2007: 14). Crucially, rhizomatic geography is one of 'becoming' (Campbell 2008: 34), not 'arboreal' rootedness or completion, a notion explored in relation to Semprun's testimonial literature in part one. As I will also propose throughout each section of this book, such geographies facilitate what Michael Rothberg (2009: 3) calls memory's multidirectionality, its subjection 'to ongoing negotiation, cross-referencing and borrowing'; each section closes with a consideration of ways in such multidirectional work is performed in the respective public sphere discussed, and to whose benefit or detriment.

Similarly, whilst I explore ways in which landscapes have historically been perceived as organically linked to particular national identities in the service of both genocide and memory, I am mindful that such perceptions have all too often led to a focus on 'roots' rather than 'routes', on 'dwelling' rather than travel (Campbell 2008: 4). I therefore embrace Campbell's 'mobile genealogy', 'a cultural discourse constructed through both national and transnational mediations, of roots and routes, with its territories defined and redefined (deterritorialized) from both inside and outside' (2008: 8). As such, I place each of my three case study sites in transcultural context. Pioneered by Wolfgang Welsch (2009) as a methodological premise for literary analysis, transculturalism moves beyond the kind of intercultural delimitation fundamental to the *lieux de mémoire*. Astrid Erll (2011a: 7), echoing other key thinkers in a move beyond the *lieux* (see Confino and Fritzsche 2002: 1–24; Rigney 2008: 93–4), has argued that Nora's binding of nation-state and ethnicity constitutes an 'old-fashioned concept of national culture and its puristic memory', which refuses the multiethnic, multicultural reality of contemporary life. A transcultural view allows for this reality, provides a lens through which we may comprehend 'the sheer plethora of shared lieux de mémoire that have emerged through travel, trade, war, and colonialism' (Erll

2011a: 8). Accordingly Erll (2011a: 11) conceives of transcultural memory 'as the incessant wandering of carriers, media, contents, forms, and practices of memory, their continual "travels" and ongoing transformations through time and space, across social, linguistic and political borders'. Key to the transcultural turn is the opening up, or transcendence of, national borders, and a cosmopolitan outlook characterized by a reluctance to lose sight of or universalize cultural specificities (see Bond and Rapson 2014), an approach maintained in each section of this book as I navigate between local sites and transcultural networks.

The transcultural lens facilitates a focus on deterritorialization, a term which, as noted above, can generally be used to describe the 'definition and redefinition of territory' (Campbell 2008: 8). In introducing the notion of cosmopolitan memory, Daniel Levy and Natan Sznaider (2006) utilize the term *hyphenated*[4] to highlight the way in which site-specific atrocities may become 'de-territorialized' from their original locations via related mediatory, commemorative and social processes. Accordingly, the potential exists for a variety of memory texts to become more accessible to people from diverse cultural backgrounds and geographic locations, as new global links place them at the centre of a dynamic creation of 'new connections that situate … political, economic, and social experiences in a new type of supranational context' (Levy and Sznaider 2006: 10). The limitations and potential of this theoretical model will be discussed in relation to the twinning of Lidice with Stoke-on-Trent and Khojaly in Part 3. Levy and Sznaider's use of the term 'de-territorialization' resonates with its conceptualization by Dorrian and Rose (2003: 16), who propose the de-territorialization of landscape as 'up-rooting it from its location within fixed webs of signification and transporting it, trailing a set of potentialities which can produce effects in new domains. This is certainly not an argument for evacuating … the "content" of the term'. Thus when I suggest the de-territorialization of memory from landscape at various points in *Topographies of Suffering,* I similarly maintain that neither landscapes nor the memories connected with them are necessarily evacuated in the process. As theories of transculturalism, cosmopolitanism and multidirectionality have developed, the inherently processual, travelling nature of both memory and landscape has come to the fore. Yet as Susannah Radstone's (2011) summary of the emergence of transcultural and multidirectional theories insists, locatedness remains central to the experience, practice and theory of memory. Thus in drawing attention to the many ways in which Holocaust memories may travel across Europe and beyond, this book also recognizes the geographical specificity of their origins in Germany, Ukraine and the Czech Republic.

The local-global dynamic recognized by the transcultural turn is also fundamentally resonant with the ecocritical sensibility maintained throughout

the analyses offered here. As Lawrence Buell (2005: 12) notes, 'environmental criticism's working conception of "environment" has broadened ...
to include ... the interpenetration of the global by the local'. Ecocritical attachment to the earth functions at these two interconnected levels. That we
feel intensely for the local environments we inhabit and consequently strive
to protect them may lead to a concern for the world in its entirety, for each
local environment is a part of that larger whole. Ecocritical logic is sceptical
towards:

> mythographies of national landscape ... intensified both by mounting critique
> of the perceived ethnocentricity of all such myths and by the increasing aware-
> ness that the environmental problems the world now faces 'are quite unaware
> of national and cultural boundaries' (Claviez 1999: 377). National borders by
> no means regularly correspond with 'natural' borders (Buell 2005: 81–2).

Accordingly, my discussions of various textual mediations – the work of Semprun, Jacobson, Thomas, Kuznetsov and Millay, amongst others – are undertaken from a broadly ecocritical perspective.

Concurrent with the embrace of transcultural dynamism, memory studies
scholars have increasingly drawn attention to the processes of mediation and
remediation that keep memory moving. The introduction now moves on to
briefly highlight the potential of the key mediating factors of commemorative dynamism I explore in this book: the shaping of natural processes and
elements by heritage professionals, and literary representations of the landscapes in question.

'Natural' and Literary Mediation

Within the context of Holocaust memorials, a 'return to nature' may seem
conceptually appropriate as a way to lay the victims of industrialized processes (see Bartov 1996: 3–4) to rest, yet extended studies of visitor engagement with natural materials in these landscapes are surprisingly rare.
Nonetheless, work on commemorative landscape in general offers some useful insights. The apparent vulnerability, mutability and regenerative capacity
of many 'natural' materials renders them powerfully affective, leading John
Dixon Hunt (2001: 16) to argue that landscape will always enjoy 'a fundamental advantage' over other commemorative forms. Much existing discussion of memory and landscape tends to echo official discourse surrounding
commemorative practice at Holocaust memorials; that is, nature is frequently
designated as a witness to human violence (see Schama 1995: 24). This anthropomorphic pre-mediation of nature is clearly illogical – 'culture perpet-
uates itself though the power of the dead, while nature, as far as we know,

makes no use of this resource except in a strictly organic sense' (Pogue Harrison 2003: ix) – but affective nonetheless. As Elaine Scarry (1985: 288–9) explains, whilst '[t]he naturally existing external world … is wholly ignorant of the "hurtability" of human beings … [t]he human imagination reconceives the external world [by] quite literally, "making it" as knowledgeable about human pain as if it were itself animate and in pain'. Whilst the natural world 'cannot be sentiently aware of pain', 'its design, its structure, is the structure of a perception'. Thus we grant nature perception, and likewise memory, for its design, structure and dynamism are akin to those of perception and memory. Whilst this book pays due attention to the affectivity, I also keep in mind nature's intrinsic amorality and its purely organic response to human violence and death.

To say that natural regeneration consoles us does not rely so completely on the anthropomorphic logic that grounds an assumption of sympathy, for we can be consoled by something without any agenda of its own. In this book the affectivity of regenerative growth is considered alongside the rhetoric of ruins. Ruins are the remains of deliberately constructed human structures, worn down by the encroachment of natural elements, but they are not to be conflated with them; ruins are constantly diminishing, whilst nature 'grows'. Yet the two together have affective impact: 'inert matter is made increasingly meaningful by its juxtaposition to living forms … we are pleased by the contrast between the fixity of the inert and the mutability of its natural frame' (Stewart 1998: 111–112). This juxtaposition, and the affectivity of natural regeneration, is considered in detail in relation to Semprun's mediation of Buchenwald, the work of memorial entrepreneurs at the Babi Yar Park in Denver, and landscaping practices at Lidice. Michael Roth et al. (1997: 5) argue that ruins 'embody the dialectic of nature and artifice'; ruins are often the 'work' of nature. It is often suggested that ruins take us closer to the events of history,[5] but in actuality ruins, precisely in their visible dialogue with nature, force us to realize the unbridgeable gap between the present and the past, a gap which my own discussions of sites strives to recognize. Charles Merewether (1997: 25) has argued that 'ruins collapse temporalities', when in fact they may *reassert* them. Natural materials are central to this reassertion, unique in their ability to record the passing of time; nature, that which exists both before us and around us, forces a recognition of the impossibility of collapsing temporal distance between the past and the present. In fact, nature presents us with the stark reality of this distance in a way that cannot be avoided or glossed over in the commemorative environment. Our sentimental anthropomorphism may render it affective, but it is in its indifferent growth – its very *lack* of agenda – that it situates us in relation to history.

This book also highlights the frequently pastoral sensibility fundamental to the affectivity of nature at commemorative sites. No longer simply an invocation of an 'lived harmony between people and place' which was only ever imagined, yearned for rather than lived (Gifford 1999: 31), the term 'pastoral' has itself evolved to describe a particular state of mind which reduces the complex to the simple (Peck 1992: 75). Always-already elegiac, the pastoral 'takes the form of an isolated moment, a kind of island in time, and one which gains its meaning and intensity through the tensions it creates with the historical world' (Lindenberger in Peck 1992: 75; also see Young [1994: 120] on the 'unexpected, even unseemly beauty' of concentration camp landscapes). In my discussions of the mediation of the memory of landscape in literature (and film, in Part 3), I demonstrate the way in which Western associations of rural nature with an ideal past have shaped a range of mediatory texts and processes. In such texts, nature, like the ruin, becomes a link to a past to which we might long to return and avert catastrophe ahead, a spatial and temporal marker – for natural growth records the passing of time – inherently tied up in Western cultural consciousness with a sense of belated responsibility (Soper 1995) similar to that which inspires the retrospective creation of memorials.

In a departure from the study of memorial spaces as realms of representational fixity, then, I pay particular attention throughout this book to 'natural' elements of landscape which are constantly in flux: plants, soil, topographical contours, weather and climate. I also isolate the processes of mediation that shape the affectivity of these natural forms in memorial landscapes – processes to which I now turn attention. Perhaps unsurprisingly in light of the above discussion of nature's affective potential, despite the increase in the use of technology in Holocaust museums the 'natural' areas of memorial landscapes continue to capture curatorial and visitor imaginations. Camps and mass graves were often located away from urban centres, and with the passing of time they increasingly lend themselves to integration with their surrounding natural environments. Their management, as several examples in this book demonstrate, reveals a distinctive curatorial reliance on nature's commemorative value, as something that can both sympathize and console. However, and not unlike its museum counterpart, the memorial landscape raises ethical issues for curators which warrant an attention that has so far been largely lacking in scholarship on the subject. Perhaps this is because theorists assume, as Sarah Farmer (1995: 98) does, that '[u]nlike the writer of a book or the director of a museum, the custodian of a memorial site is not free to select what to tell and what to leave untold'. This is a suggestion largely refuted in this book, as I demonstrate the extent to which commemorative curation is also a process of subjective history-writing much the same as that which occurs within the walls of museums and which similarly mediates visitor experience (see Baruch Stier 2003: 126).

Whilst museum spaces are often subject to intense scrutiny, and even unintended echoes of perpetrator ideology are subject to critique (see Crownshaw 2010: 208), such rigorous interrogation of representative strategy has infrequently been applied to the natural landscapes that exist in dialogue with museal structures. A rare exception can be found in Michael Addis and Andrew Charlesworth's (2002) study of Auschwitz and Plaszow, which takes into account the effect human intervention, or its lack, may have on visitor experience. In considering the extent to which management practices may constitute an unwitting parallel with Nazi ideology, they note that '[u]niform lawns are more likely [than meadows] to let us regard the victims as the authorities did, as "Figuren", objects, a mass' (2002: 246). This study reminds us that, outside as well as inside, curators are polemically motivated, and they create meaning as well as simply organizing objects which are in themselves perceived as meaningful. In doing so they narrativize visitor performance (see Patraka 1999: 122 and Young 1994: vii), a practice considered in relation to the specific topography of each memorial site in this book. Finally, as Chris Pearson (2009: 152) argues, '[t]he environment as natural entity' is frequently overlooked in investigations into the construction of memorials and the way they are experienced, as is the way in which 'memorials actively engage with their environment and in turn the environment naturally engages with them'. Inspired by such gaps, this book examines how both curatorial polemics and environmental factors contribute to contemporary landscaping of Holocaust memory.

The final mediating co-ordinate I rely on is literature, a representational form which has been embraced by scholars of memory (see Erll 2011b: 144–71), and, more recently, cultural geography (see Wylie 2007: 206–7), for whom it 'brings to the fore the possibility of sharing stories via landscape experience' (Lorimer 2006). Landscape writing, in particular, may provide a way into understanding experiences of 'mobility, exile, distance and non-belonging' (Wylie 2007: 211), 'to reintroduce … questions of subjectivity and the self' (2007: 213). Attention to landscape is often notable as a component of Holocaust writing, not least because victim experiences were frequently diasporic; new landscapes were encountered through deportation and internment, and subsequent descriptions often foreground testimonial accounts.

However, as noted previously, all representative forms meet a challenge in the context of the Holocaust. In the case of literature by original witnesses, there are undoubtedly problems of translation: how can experiences belonging to the past – experiences which only exist in memory – be effectively translated into language? This question is particularly central to my discussion of Semprun's work. The perception that literature is an aestheticizing form that inevitably transforms experience into linear narrative, and the idea that personal narratives invite personification (see Lang in Levi and Rothberg 2003: 330 and Hungerford 2003) – also plague discussion of literary representation, concerns which become more explicit and divisive with regard to literature about the Holocaust created by those who did not experience it (see Vice 2000: 1; Wiesel in Lewis and Appelfeld 1984: 155). Analyses of Holocaust literature in this book do not aim to advance the debate over which genres are appropriate or acceptable, but focus instead on the capacity of these texts to animate Holocaust in the reader's imagination; for '[w]hat is remembered of the Holocaust 'depends ... on the texts now giving them form' (Young in Levi and Rothberg 2003: 335).

I am, then, less concerned with discrepancies between history, memory and representation, than with the intricate and intimate relationship between these co-ordinates. Thus I focus not solely on the texts themselves, but on their relationship with the imaginative work of memory they may potentially provoke. As Huyssen (1995: 2–3) reminds us, '[r]e-presentation always comes after ... The past is not simply there in memory, but it must be articulated to become memory.' Literary mediations of Holocaust memory by visitors to commemorative sites are therefore examined alongside those produced by those originally persecuted at them, for the journeys taken by all inform the way a site can be interpreted and understood. As Kathryn Jones (2007: 36) suggests, many survivors 'use the familiarity of the journey in order to engage with the uninitiated reader's everyday experience[s]', and furthermore that the experiences of travellers to Holocaust sites are structured by their recollection of related literary material (2007: 60). Thus these authors 'contribute to the interactive, dialogical relationship between Holocaust memorial and visitor' (2007: 61). However, crucially, Jones (2007: 51) concludes her discussion of visitor engagement by underlining the way in which, at times, metaphors of travel may be 'evoked solely in order to be negated', serving only 'to underline the irreducible gulf constructed by the authors between the reality they experienced in the camps and the knowledge of their addressees and readers who did not enter this world'. Thus she advocates the use of metaphorical associations as a way into accessing the experience of victims, but not as a way to take ownership of this experience. The particular form of 'becoming' implied in Jones's descriptions of the productive interplay between memorial environments, literature and memory, and the gulf that is nonetheless maintained between victim and visitor, are key characteristics of the model of memory proposed in this book.

Encountering Past Others: Visitors and Victims

The notion that landscape experience has played an inherent role in the acquisition of power recurs in postcolonial discourse (see Tolia-Kelly 2010). Correspondingly, travel is sometimes seen to be superficial, vicarious and fundamentally self-serving, 'a way of having the encounter [with the other] while keeping it in the realm of otherness and fantasy' (Clark 1999: 167). A similar logic casts tourists as consumers (Urry 1990), a notion endorsed by Lennon and Foley's model of dark tourism.[6] Yet travel should not necessarily be interpreted as a claim to ownership, either of place or the experience of others. Susan Sontag (2007: 228) reminds us that '[t]o be a traveller ... is to be constantly reminded of the simultaneity of what is going on in the world, your world and the very different world you have visited ... it's a question of sympathy ... of the limits of the human imagination'. Self-other engagement may indeed be confined to certain limits, but some sense of limitation – certainly an avoidance of total identification – is ethically desirable for reasons which will be discussed shortly.

There are understandable ethical concerns about the integration of sites of atrocity into tourist itineraries which may potentially normalize atrocious histories and provide a form of entertainment, concerns exemplified in debates surrounding the inclusion of Auschwitz-Birkenau to 'stag' weekend itineraries in Krakow;[7] the seriousness demanded by the concentration camp sits ill within a category predominantly embedded in concepts of leisure, pleasure and relaxation. However, binary opposition between touristic states such as pilgrimage (commonly understood as a sacred endeavour) and leisure (aligned with secularity and comparative profanity) can be disrupted: 'The notion of leisure contains elements of purposefulness and dedication, while pilgrimage, the pursuit of the transcendent, also carries with it senses of travel, excitement and adventure' (Keil 2005: 480). Furthermore, '[m]any forms of contemporary tourism can be said to be guided by a self-consciousness about the potential superficialities of everyday tourism' (Sturken 2007: 11). Tourism is too complex to be understood merely as a means to a straightforward and predictable end; rather, it 'instantiates, a hermeneutics ... based on the interpretation of a multiplicity of texts and markers, all oriented to producing knowledge of Self and Other" (Koshar 2000b: 103). Rudy Koshar follows Michel de Certeau (1988: xiii) in emphasizing the potential of everyday activities to transgress prescribed limits of meaning, returning autonomy to consumers; rendering them 'unrecognised producers, poets of their own acts', creators of 'sentences' or 'trajectories' which, whilst 'composed with the vocabularies of established language ... trace out the ruses of other interests and desires that are neither determined nor captured by the systems in which they develop'. This recognition of consumer autonomy is not fully embraced in studies of dark tourism, but a valuable precedent can be seen in MacDonald's (2009: 147) in-depth review of tourism to Nuremburg, which recognizes audiences as 'active rather than passive'. MacDonald's methodology also accommodates 'the gloriously unavoidable nature of human interaction' (2009: 21). Such unavoidable interactions similarly shape my handling of each case study site in this book, an aspect of my own methodology which is mainly explored in the concluding chapter.

Victims and visitors are capable of forging their own paths through landscapes, and mark out trajectories between them, a phenomenon particularly evident in my discussion of Jacobson's navigation between Buchenwald and New Orleans. The terms in which I consider the potential of the sites to facilitate engagement with difficult pasts is grounded in a phenomenological strain of cultural geography (Tilley 1994; D. Abrams 1996; Ingold 2000; Cloke and Jones 2001; Wylie 2005, 2006) influenced by Maurice Merleau-Ponty (1962: 303–4): 'the system of experience is not arrayed before me as though I were God, it is lived by me from a certain point of view; I am not the spectator, I am involved'. Leaving behind models of place as 'decentred from agency and meaning' and 'equivalent to and separate from time' (Tilley 1994: 9), phenomenological studies of landscape recognize varied modes of perception, such as smell, hearing, and touch, 'releas[ing] the visual gaze from its detention as the accomplice of Cartesian spectatorial epistemology' (Tilley 1994: 9). Hence the potential of the phenomenological approach in the context of the Holocaust as understood by Bauman; that is, as an event resulting from an excess of Cartesian rationalism. This strain of scholarship sees landscape as a participatory platform, a space of engagement; something with which we are 'intertwined' (Wylie 2007: 152). Ingold (2000: 207) similarly proposes that a phenomenological approach renders landscape a space for 'attentive involvement', a phrase which places the subject in an intimate relationship with the world around us without 'making it' the same. Furthermore, whilst pure phenomenology is focused on bodily experience in the world, the 'lived immediacy of actual experience' (Thrift 2008: 6), there is a cognitive dimension to phenomenological immersion which prompts discussion, analysis, reflection and theorization of that bodily experience. In this way, immersion in landscape retains an element of essential reflexivity which my studies of Buchenwald, Babi Yar and Lidice hope to maintain. These places are always guided by personal memories, but also 'replete with social meanings' due to the 'constant process of production and reproduction through the movement and activities of members of a group' (Tilley 1994: 16). Thus landscape, like memory, is conceptualized as a production, 'both constituted and constitutive' (Tilley 1994: 17).

Phenomenological cultural geography has also set a precedent in the embrace of nonrepresentational perspectives, or in Hayden Lorimer's (2005: 84) phrasing 'more-than-representational' theory:

> The focus falls on how life takes shape and gains expression in shared experiences, everyday routines, fleeting encounters, embodied movements, precognitive triggers, practical skills, affective intensities, enduring urges, unexceptional inter-

actions and sensuous dispositions. [This] offers an escape from the established
academic habit of striving to uncover meanings and values that apparently await
our discovery, interpretation, judgement and ultimate representation.

Influenced by Deleuzian thought, a relational approach to geography has
been increasingly popular since the late 1990s (Wylie 2007: 199). Relational
geography presents 'a topological picture of the world' more concerned with
'networks, connections, flows and mobilities' (Wylie 2007: 199) than with
the specificities of particular spaces and how they are experienced. In privi-
leging 'connective properties' over the traditional geographical denominators
of 'distance and position' (Wylie 2007: 204), relational topology presents a
challenge to conventional ways of thinking about landscape. Whilst it can
be argued that in such an approach 'a certain topographical richness is being sacrificed for the sake of topological complexity' (Wylie 2007: 205), it is
worth looking for memory both as it is forged within memorial spaces and
as it creates new ones. Accordingly, whilst each part of this book opens with
a topographical reading of the site in question, topological networks, flows
and mobilities emerge throughout each one, connecting Buchenwald to New
Orleans, Babi Yar to Denver, and Lidice to Stoke-on-Trent, Khojaly and beyond. There may be tensions between these spaces, but this can be seen
as contributing to, rather than negating, the discourse that both surrounds
them and constitutes their dynamism.

The cultural geographic model of phenomenology as discussed here has
fruitful implications for the contemplation of the Holocaust and its victims,
if we consider what a phenomenological inhabitation of the past might be.
Clearly such a model implies the breakdown of formerly assumed delimiting
borders between victim and witness, just as landscape might collapse the
divide between the world and the self. Such a breakdown is visible in trauma
theory; according to Dori Laub (in Felman and Laub 1992: 57), for example,
witnesses who view traumatic testimony become not only 'participants' but
'co-owners' of the experiences described therein, in a troubling conflation
of self and other. This overextension could similarly be seen to characterize
some variations of Marianne Hirsch's model of 'postmemory' (1997). Developed to describe 'the second generation response to the trauma of the first'
(2001: 8), postmemory usefully articulates the way memories of events we
have never lived through are both intensely powerful and intensely mediated;
a form of 'imaginative investment and creation' (Hirsch 1997: 22), an 'encounter with another, an act of telling and listening ... to another's wound,
recognizable in its intersubjective relation' (Hirsch 2001: 12). Postmemory's
potential for reciprocity – for a meaningful encounter between the self of the
present and the other of the past – is appealing. However, this compelling
concept has been overapplied, often without sufficient critical distance, in

subsequent studies of memory, not least because Hirsch herself places few limitations upon it;[8] indeed she posits postmemory as 'a space of remembrance' open to those who care enough to inhabit it (1999: 8). As Weissman (2004: 17) has argued, the very idea 'that a deep personal connection to the Holocaust is enough to transform its learned history into inherited, lived memory' is 'dubious at best'. According to this logic Alison Landsberg's (1997: 82) 'spaces of transference' – film or museum spaces which give the participant 'a kind of experiential relationship' that 'might actually install in us "symptoms" or prosthetic memories through which we didn't actually live' – also raise questions.

Whilst both Hirsch and Landsberg are arguably uncritical of an empathy unconstrained by the limitations of a bounded self, Dominic LaCapra's (2001: 102) notion of 'empathic unsettlement' provides an approach to secondary witnessing which avoids the 'extreme identification' (LaCapra 2001: 103) implicit in some variations of post- and prosthetic memory. Covering a number of loosely defined modes of response in which an individual is significantly affected by exposure to a traumatized other, the empathically unsettled subject remains aware of the caesura inherent to an ethical self/ other relation. LaCapra (2001: 102) redefines the limits of traumatic transference, suggesting that, whilst secondary trauma cannot be discounted as a potential response, 'it is blatantly obvious that there is a major difference between the experience of camp inmates or Holocaust survivors and that of the viewer'.[9] Thus he remains keen to restrict the use of the term trauma to '"limit cases" that pass a certain threshold' (Bennett 2005: 9). Furthermore, LaCapra (2004: 41) recognizes that 'empathy is an affective relation to the other recognized as other, while identification involves acting out [their] problems'. Empathic unsettlement, then, might characterize an onlooker whose genuine concern for the others of the past leads them to attempt to imagine others' past suffering whilst simultaneously acknowledging their bounded selves. Such a possibility is implied in Derek Dalton's (2009) exploration of a visit to Birkenau, in which the author identifies himself with Amy Hungerford's model of an onlooker who shows 'an intense concern with the subject despite that they are not themselves survivors' (2009: 188). Reassured by evidence of many small acts of performative commemoration, 'responses ... as unique and personal as the thousands of people who visit Auschwitz Birkenau each year' (2009: 211) Dalton concludes that whilst '[t] he experience of visiting Auschwitz-Birkenau as a dark tourist must entail an experiential failure' (2009: 211), the site nonetheless provides 'a powerful backdrop – a type of mise en scène – that helps animate the imagination'. This is a 'small paradoxical triumph ... worth celebrating ... whilst I cannot 'live [the] loss' [of victims] ... I can pause to imagine their suffering' (Dalton 2009: 218). Dalton's 'out-of-wartime temporality' (2009: 218) refuses the extremity of empathic overidentification, and the metamorphosis of the landscape itself is essential in this realization of difference. His imagination is also animated through an on-site consideration of relevant literary material that was fundamental to his experience at Birkenau, for his visit was mediated by both 'the exhibits and sights' he encountered there and 'the memory of … representations that are evoked by being there' (2009: 118). The three case studies discussed in this book demonstrate the diversity of the mediatory co-ordinates that ground our encounters with past suffering, envisioning how our relations with the others of the past may be founded upon a fundamentally ethical premise; demonstrating intense concern, yet avoiding complete identification.

Throughout these case-based explorations, I rely on the notion that visits to sites of atrocious histories are rooted in complex personal motivations as well as previous encounters with diverse media, both literary and visual. The same factors inevitably shape academics who work on these landscapes. In some cases, as in Dalton's essay, the resulting work takes into account the personal experiences of the writer alongside a consideration of theoretical or conceptual concerns. In turn, this adds to the rich archive of existing work by survivors, travel writers and even authors of fiction, all of whom contribute to the mediation and remediation of memorial landscapes. As Lucy Bond (2011: 749) notes, some 'testimony-criticism' of this nature risks 'engendering a conflation of biography and analysis' to produce 'a form of theory that draws upon the author's own experiences as its principle frame of reference' (Bond 2011: 749). Critiqued in the particular context of 9/11 literature, Bond notes that an overemphasis on personal experience risks the despecification of the event's larger sociopolitical context. Clearly a similar risk may be extended to the Holocaust context, but some examples of what we might call Holocaust testimony-criticism, notably those which avoid the inclusion of the self within an extended traumatic paradigm,[10] are enriched by the integration of an author's personal response to the landscapes in question (see Bartov 2007; MacDonald 2009). Such authors are most successful when they maintain a separation between themselves and the others of the past, focussing reflexively on their encounters as secondary witnesses. Thus the final challenge, perhaps, of work such as this, must be to situate not only the self but also *myself*, in relation to the Holocaust and its landscapes. Beneath the theoretical models explored in this book lies my own sense of unsettlement in the face of historical suffering. More explicitly personal codas complete each chapter, and this separation of analysis and biographical recollection is deliberate, for my own experience is but a small part of my frame of reference. I optimistically maintain that both the specificity of past suffering and the unique contexts in which it occurred are thrown into relief, rather than obscured, by my own involvement.

Notes

1. Nora himself was aware of the necessarily evolutionary nature of memory sites, stating that their capacity for metamorphosis is central to their existence (1989: 19), but memory is still seen to be 'attached' to such sites.

2. See Elie Wiesel's commonly cited remark that the Holocaust is '[t]he ultimate event, the ultimate mystery, never to be comprehended or transmitted' (in Roth and Berenbaum 1989: 3).

3. As Ann Whiston Spirn argues, 'dictionaries must be revised, and ... older meanings revived'; '[O]lder meanings' – based on the etymology of 'scape' from the Danish *skabe* and the German *schaffen* ('to shape') – imply both the association between people and place which creates landscape and their 'embeddedness in culture' (1998: 17).

4. In order to maintain a clear usage, when I discuss 'de-territorializations' of memory from landscape I adopt their spelling. When referring to an attempt to attach a fixed meaning to a particular landscape, I employ the term 'territorialization'.

5. Young, for example, remarks on the common habit of 'mistaking the piece [the artefact or ruin] for the whole, the implied whole for unmediated history' (1994: 127).

6. In certain contexts this has been illuminating. Marita Sturken (2007), for example, demonstrates how a culture of fear and paranoia in the wake of specific acts of terrorism – the Oklahoma City bombings in 1995 and the destruction of the World Trade Center in 2001 – resulted in particular consumer behaviours motivated by desire for security, comfort and the consolidation of specific forms of North American national identity. This analysis serves to articulate ways in which tourism, memory production and identity are deeply related, but does not advance understanding of the tourist beyond existing assumptions about their susceptibility to manipulation by capitalist systems.

7. For example, the head of the Holocaust Educational Trust Karen Pollock stated that the advertisement of Auschwitz visits 'alongside nights of drinking and clubbing' was 'entirely inappropriate (NineMSN 2010), and subsequent defence by an associated tour operator ('Denzil', NineMSN 2010). Whether or not one agrees with the inclusion of Auschwitz in such an itinerary, the motivations of and behaviour exhibited by the tourists in question are undoubtedly worthy of note. Outrage is understandable, but too frequently results in dismissal, which rarely advances discourse. Whilst '[c]onsensus ... leads to invisibility', '[c]ontroversy ... may be the most important factor in keeping memory alive' (Rigney 2008: 94).

8. Whilst originally a term to describe 'second-generation memories of cultural or collective traumatic events and experiences' (1997: 22), Hirsch's definition of the second generation ('those who grew up dominated by narratives that preceded their birth, whose own belated stories are evacuated by the stories of the previous generation shaped by traumatic events that can be neither understood not recreated') (1997: 22) – is somewhat loose.

9. The viewer in the context of LaCapra's discussion is someone exposed to Holocaust testimony videos, but the principle can arguably be applied to those who contemplate the suffering of others in various other mediums.

10. For example the 'travelling' of trauma implied by Caruth: 'In a catastrophic age ... trauma may provide the very link between cultures: not as a simple understanding of the pasts of others but rather ... as our ability to listen through the departures we have all taken from ourselves' (1996: 11). The potential of listening through shared departures is arguably undermined by the overextension of the trauma itself.

PART I

BUCHENWALD

There is no knowing or sensing a place except by being in that place, and to be in a place is to be in a position to perceive it.
— Edward Casey, 'How to Get from Space to Place in a Fairly Short Stretch of Time: Phenomenological Prolegomena'

This section examines the Buchenwald Concentration Camp Memorial and related memorial discourse.[1] Relying on literary works alongside cultural-geographic analysis of landscape, the section overall reveals literature's capacity to provoke a form of future-oriented consciousness in the wake of past atrocity. Academic commentary on Buchenwald has, to date, considered both the site and relevant literature primarily within the discourse of commemorative politics (see Young 1994: 72–99; Farmer 1995; Kattago 1998; Azaryahu 2003; Niven 2007), frequently neglecting a detailed consideration of the dialogue that exists *between* literature and landscape (although see Brodzki 2007). This part of the book provides such an exploration.

Chapter 1, 'Defining and Redefining Buchenwald' examines the present-day concentration camp memorial as a *lieu de mémoire* caught between two poles of German history: Weimar classicism and Nazi atrocity. This dialectic will also be seen to shape recent configurations of Buchenwald in global perspective, evidenced in the ways in which the camp and memories of the Holocaust were integrated into the celebration of Weimar's selection as a European City of Culture in 1999 and the 2012 nomination of Weimar-Buchenwald as a UNESCO World Heritage Site. The same poles of history are explored in Chapter 2, 'Semprun's Buchenwald', which reads Spanish Holocaust survivor Jorge Semprun's testimonial project as a nuanced, and often scathing, negotiation of the camp's dichotomous history. I focus on the phenomenological potential of Buchenwald as a site-specific memorial space, arguing that landscapes of past suffering may present us with a platform for an ethical model of immersive and dynamic memory work. The particular way in which Semprun negotiates the spaces of his internment enables a critique of National Socialist culture, challenging the notion that

access to the particular cultural capital 'embedded' in Buchenwald's landscape is organically determined by an exclusive 'blood and soil' connection.
Effectively, Semprun immerses himself in this landscape in a way that refuses the Nazis' claims on it. I highlight both his engagement with and sense
of emplacement within landscape and the implications of his oeuvre for contemporary visitors as they traverse the landscapes of Weimar-Buchenwald.
Charting Semprun's return to Buchenwald as a visitor in the 1990s, I finally
consider the universal ecocritical implications of his response to the camp as
memorial space, suggesting that his Buchenwald oeuvre ultimately functions
as both a form of resistance against totalitarian logic and a call for heightened
environmental consciousness in the wake of atrocity.

Chapter 3, 'Buchenwald to New Orleans', examines an investigative travel
memoir that draws Buchenwald and the Holocaust into comparison with
natural disaster: Mark Jacobson's *The Lampshade: A Holocaust Detective
Story from Buchenwald to New Orleans* (2010). Jacobson, a Brooklyn Jew and
a journalist for *New York* magazine, takes on the task of tracing the history of
a lampshade apparently made from human skin, looted from a flooded house
in New Orleans in the days following Hurricane Katrina. This investigation,
which takes two years and spans three continents, leads Jacobson to the
Buchenwald memorial, and to engage with Semprun's accounts of the camp.
Ultimately, I argue, Jacobson's quest can be read as an attempt to provide
restitution for Buchenwald's anonymous dead which opens up into a broader
project to identify how different forms of violence are connected and might
be prevented.

Notes

1. Abbreviations: Semprun texts: *LV: The Long Voyage* (1963); *WBS: What a Beautiful
    Sunday!* (1983); *LL: Literature or Life* (1997).
        Gedenkstätte Buchenwald Publications: *BTM: Buchenwald: A Tour of the Memo-
    rial Site* (1993); *BGE: Buchenwald Concentration Camp 1937–1945: A Guide to the
    Permanent Historical Exhibition* (2004); *KLB: K.L. Buchenwald, Post Weimar: The
    Former Buchenwald Concentration Camp, photographed by Jürgen M. Pietsch in 1998
    and 1999* (2006).

ONE

DEFINING AND REDEFINING BUCHENWALD

Buchenwald lies 8km from the small city of Weimar, perched on the slopes of the Ettersburg and surrounded by Thuringian forestland. This area is home to one of Germany's most prized literary and cultural legacies: Weimar classicism. Weimar's notable residents have included Goethe, Herder, Friedrich Schiller, Franz Liszt and Johann Sebastian Bach. Goethe famously strolled on the Ettersburg slopes, hunting land for the dukes of Saxony-Weimar from the sixteenth century, with his friends and lovers, and many of his plays were enacted in an amateur theatre in the forest. The homes and tombs of these internationally recognized figures attract tourists to Weimar from all over the world. Many sites, including parks and buildings from the classical and Bauhaus periods, are listed by the United Nations Educational, Scientific and Cultural Organization (UNESCO). Amongst these are both Goethe's home and garden house. From as early as 1900 the forests, too, have been popular with tourists (*BGE* 2004, 27).[1] Forests such as those found in Thuringia have long been 'quintessential symbol[s] of Germanness' (Lekan 2004: 9); they play a central role in national literature and have traditionally been integrated into the everyday life of its people.[2] Furthermore, they have been key co-ordinates in the concept of *Heimat,* the superorganic attachment of the German people to their native land. When this landscape was taken over by the Nazis, it was dramatically altered, generating a new layer of symbolic meaning. After liberation, the East German authorities re-landscaped the camp to celebrate the triumph of Communist resistance over Nazi fascism; these three phases of the camp's history are now juxtaposed in the present-day landscape of Weimar-Buchenwald. The series of territorializations described in this section have created a landscape in which memories of traditional German classicism, Nazism, and Communism continue to jostle against one another for space.[3]

National Socialist Landscaping

Along with Sachsenhausen, north Berlin, and Dachau, Munich, the camp near Weimar was originally planned to 'optimally combine the organisational, political and economic interests of the SS in a single complex' (BGE 25) in addition to its functions as a detention facility. With an enormous complex of labour subcamps and extensive SS accommodation and training facilities, by the end of World War II Buchenwald was the largest concentration camp in existence. Over six thousand SS men and women, and often their families too, were housed in the area directly around the main camp. From an initial allotment of 46 ha, 190 ha were eventually deforested (BGE 31). The selection of this site, which would require extensive deforestation, is incommensurate with Nazis' advocation of forest protection in the early years of the Third Reich. Ecologically speaking, 'no German government had ever taken the protection of the German forests more seriously' than the Nazis (Schama 1995: 119); their arboreal policies was based on the exemplary *Dauerwald* (perpetual or eternal forest) philosophy which was designed to improve the long-term health of woodland ecosystems (Imort 2005: 5). However, as the demands of warfare clashed with the original ecological principle of forest protection (Lekan 2004: 14) the traditional, reverent relationship between the Germans and their trees was gradually subverted.[4] The deforestation of nationally treasured forestland was but one example of this trend, as the Nazis territorialized German land within a new ideological framework.

In ecocritical discourses, deforestation is a both a fall from attunement with nature and a historical precursor to war and the expansion of empire (Bate 2000: 28). The laws of civilization have constantly been defined 'against the forests' (Pogue Harrison 1993: 2): 'Human beings have by no means exploited the forests only materially; they have also plundered its trees in order to forge their fundamental etymologies, symbols, analogies, structures of thought, emblems of identity, concepts of continuity, and notions of systems' (Pogue Harrison 1993: 7–8). Deforestation is the 'mastery and possession of nature' in practice (Bate 2000: 87; Pogue Harrison 1993: 107). In plundering the Thuringian forest – even the barracks at Buchenwald were built by inmates using wood from the forest – the Nazis forged a powerful symbol, a space constituted by and constitutive of the structure of National Socialist thought.

Buchenwald appeared in the homeland of Germany's cultural elite for practical and ideological reasons. The Land of Thuringia was known as the heart of Germany; it would thus need protection from 'subversive' elements (these could be detained in the camp) and invading forces (to be held off by the SS stationed there) (BGE 25). The Nazis were also attracted by the potential gains of exploiting nearby land with the forced labour the camp could provide; there were minable loam deposits and turnip fields in the near vicinity. Furthermore Weimar, home to National Socialist rallies, parties and parades and with a record of loyal Nazi citizenship, was ideologically prepared for Buchenwald. The sole protest raised concerned the first proposed name, 'K.L. Ettersburg'. The local chapter of the NS Cultural Community objected that this would associate the traditional home of Weimar classicism with a forced labour camp (see *BGE* 29; *KLB* 64). Thus they named the camp KL [*Konzentrationslager*] Buchenwald/Weimar. However, the change in name did not sufficiently disguise the formation of a new cultural dichotomy. 'Buchenwald' [*beech wood*] was a self-evident reference to the camp's idyllic forest setting.[5] As former Buchenwald inmate Eugen Kogon (*BTM* 29) has identified, Nazi sentimental-brutal ideology – not dissimilar to that which grounded their appropriation of the German forests – found representation in the 'new connection' between Weimar ('formerly the city of the German classical writers who had given German emotion and intellect their highest expression') and the camp at Buchenwald ('a raw piece of land on which the new German emotion was to flower').

In a stark embrace of the new connection, the only tree left standing in the main area of the camp after deforestation was a large oak, under which Goethe reputedly sat to write poetry (Gorra 2004: 16). In 1944, the tree was reduced to a stump during an Allied bombing attack; however, the attempt to preserve it continued as the camp authorities filled the centre of the stump with concrete to prevent erosion (Kattago 1998: 275).

Whilst the camp's proposed name was changed to avoid implicating Goethe's cultural legacy, Young's (1994: 73–4) discussion of Buchenwald suggests that the Nazis built the camp on the Ettersburg 'precisely because it already had a mythological past … when Himmler cynically designated Goethe's oak as the centre of the camp … he hoped to neutralize the memory of Goethe even as he invoked the philosopher's cultural authority'. Nonetheless, what Buchenwald survivor Ernst Thape referred to as the 'Weimar-Buchenwald' dichotomy was created: 'Weimar meant Wieland and Herder, meant Schiller and Goethe, meant Liszt and Friedrich Nietzsche, and now it also meant Buchenwald … the negative pole of German culture after Goethe had so long been the positive pole. Weimar became the symbol of Germany's moral dichotomy' (Thape in *WTT* 135).

Goethe, this positive pole, reappears frequently in Semprun's work, as will be seen in the next chapter. Indeed the two writers share a preoccupation with ways of seeing and experiencing landscape and, in particular, its 'natural' elements. Goethe advocated the human encounter with nature as an enriching experience, and the natural world as a realm to be approached with reverence (Seamon 1978: 239). He promoted immersion in nature, yet his approach was grounded in a scientific perspective which demanded nat-

Figure 1.1. Stump of Goethe's Oak © Charlotte Rea

ural phenomena be studied, categorized and objectified. In this respect, his thinking can be seen to have informed and coalesced with the evolution of *Heimat* ideology in German culture; in books, 'Heimat nature was a mixture of geology, climate, flora and fauna, and geography' yet 'for all its ... regulation, local and national nature remained for Heimatlers a territory replete with beauty and memories' (Confino 1997b: 114). *Heimat* was later appropriated by National Socialist writers to shore up the notion of a national identity rooted in the territory of the nation state, and was instrumental in legitimizing the Nazis' construction of an 'organic' German identity. Like Goethe's name, 'Heimat became simply one term among many that revolved around the central themes of race, blood and German identity'; 'stripped of its provincial particularities' (Applegate 1990: 18), the local dimension of *Heimat* was submerged by the nationalizing narratives of Nazi ideology. Goethe's reverence for nature may seem to fit uneasily with his particular cosmopolitanism, which was underpinned by a 'totalizing, transcendental view of the world'; 'As an object to be surveyed, the landscape is an orderly and encompassable panorama able to be observed, structured and known as a totality ... [Goethe's] synthesizing vision allows a mastery of objects in the world'

(Presner 2007: 76). This uneasy marriage of inhabitation and reverence, taxonomy and mastery anticipated the contradictory sentimental-brutal dualism of National Socialism that shaped the creation of Buchenwald.

Ideologies of Commemoration

The camp's topography changed immediately upon liberation in spring, 1945, when survivors erected a temporary wooden obelisk monument on the main muster ground (Young 1994: 75). It operated as a prison for Soviet prisoners of war before being turned into an official memorial site by the authorities. Over seven thousand prisoners died in the Soviet camp as a result of disease and malnourishment (Buchenwald.de 2012). The landscape entered into a new phase accompanied by a new layer of rhetoric which mobilized it as a symbol of Communism's triumph over the Nazi regime. As *Heimat* was reborn in postwar Germany, with a restored focus on the relationship between the local and the national (Applegate 1990: 18), classic German literature too was again appropriated, this time to repair a country destroyed by Nazi brutality:

> Goethe was revived to represent the 'other,' humanistic and spiritual Germany, which became all the more vital with the destruction of the political Germany. Friedrich Meinecke [1946] suggested that Germany identity be renewed by the spirit of German classicism and that the moral rebirth of the nation be promoted by hours set aside each Sunday to celebrate Goethe. (Kaes 1992: 13)

Nonetheless, as Richard Alewyn (in *WTT* 137) warned, 'It will not do … to pride oneself on Goethe and deny Hitler. There is only Goethe *and* Hitler, humanity *and* bestiality.'[6] The complexities of this duality will be considered further in relation to Semprun's memoirs.

As previously noted, scholarly work on Buchenwald to date has provided a full exposition of the political undercurrents that shaped the landscape during the Communist period, and has contextualized this fully as part of a dominating trend in East German memorial culture. I provide a brief overview here in order to map the series of attempts to territorialize the landscape which feature in my later discussion of Semprun's works. Young (1994: 72–79) features the Buchenwald memorial, along with those at Dachau and Bergen-Belsen, as paradigmatic of Holocaust commemoration throughout the German Democratic Republic (GDR); as a self-defined antifascist state, the GDR's approach to Buchenwald pointedly celebrated its Communist resistance. Whilst surviving prisoners initially instigated the 'cult' of anti-fascist rhetoric that was to shape the site's development, 'exaggerating the extent, effectiveness, and probity of communist resistance' at the camp

(Niven 2007: 2), it was the SED and GDR authorities that took control of its re-landscaping (Niven 2007: 3, 53). A central component of this was the addition of Fritz Cremer's bronze statue group entitled *Revolt of the Prisoners,* 'a spreading victory wedge of dignified, fighting figures unbent by their travails in the camps ... a monument to triumph and resistance, to triumph *in* resistance' (Young 1994: 78). The resulting collaboration, comprising Cremer and landscape gardener Reinhold Lingner amongst others, created a 'memorial complex' on the Ettersburg slope between 1955 and 1958. This included three mass graves encircled in concrete, transformed into 'ring tombs', linked by a concrete strip dubbed the 'Road of Nations'. Cremer's vast sculpture group overlooks the landscape, and is still the first monument visible to visitors approaching from Weimar. As Koshar (2000a: 215) notes, 'like national war monuments of the German past, [it] was to be seen from miles around and surrounded by a huge space big enough for ten thousand participants ... not primarily a mournful representation of death but a German victory monument'. Jewish victims were not part of this memorial space, and the complex overall 'represents, essentially, a journey from pain to triumph that transcends any victimhood' (Niven 2007: 59). Notably, the memorial was in part located in this position overlooking Weimar because, for much of the planning period, the camp itself was still being used a prison for enemies of the new regime. Thus the landscape was, at this point, effectively divided into two halves (Azaryahu 2003: 5).

After the Soviet camp was closed, the barracks of the main camp area were marked out for perpetuity. Razed not long after liberation, their foundations were demarcated with coloured stones and gravel.

Other buildings in this area, including the crematorium, were left to stand as evidence of Nazi barbarism. These have been persevered for perpetuity, whilst the former SS living quarters, stables and leisure spaces were abandoned and are now covered with layers of moss and broken up by trees.

The stump of Goethe's oak has remained a key co-ordinate which has attracted an ever-evolving range of interpretations; in the GDR phase, Young (1994: 74) argues,

> Buchenwald was chosen as the centre of ... commemorative activity for some of the same reasons the Nazis had chosen to build a camp there in the first place: this stunningly beautiful region seemed in both cases to exemplify the heart of German culture. As the nearby Ettersburg mountain range and city of Weimar would suggest the majesty of German culture, the charred and withered remains of Goethe's oak would symbolize the depths to which the culture had sunk.

As Bill Niven (2007: 4) notes, the way in which Communism's official memory discourse transformed the camp 'confirms Halbwachs's argument that the past is being continually molded to fit the exigencies of the present'.

Figure 1.2. Gravelled former barrack spaces © Charlotte Rea

Figure 1.3. Former SS riding house © Charlotte Rea

Buchenwald had become a *lieu de mémoire* of the GDR, representing not the suffering of those interned there under the Nazis, but the political appropriation of that suffering.

After the reunification of Germany in 1989 the landscape of Buchenwald was again territorialized, or 'reoriented', in Maoz Azaryahu's (2003: 6) phrasing, as heroic narratives lost 'credibility and authority' when the East-German management team were replaced with western Germans in 1990 (Farmer 1995: 104) and the use of the camp as a Soviet prison in the years after the war was uncovered. Heated discussions between memorial authorities and the local public went eventually resulted in the 'recasting' of the commemorative landscape (Farmer 1995: 11). Plans were made to commemorate the German victims of Soviet rule alongside those of fascism, although it was made clear that the Nazi era of the camp should remain the dominant narrative. The original Cremer monument was to be preserved to signify 'a chapter of Buchenwald's history and evidence for its political instrumentalization for propaganda purposes' (Azaryahu 2003: 10). The landscape, effectively, was divided into three 'cultural geographies of memory' (Azaryahu 2003: 11): the main camp with its barrack foundations and crematoria to represent the Nazi regime; the Soviet camp exhibition and mass graves commemorating the 1945–1951 period; and the GDR memory complex with Cremer's sculpture group directing attention to the Communists' triumphant mobilization of Buchenwald's history from 1951 to 1989. On the periphery of these three spaces lay areas, such the aforementioned former SS accommodation buildings, for which minimal official interpretation was offered (and which are now little more than overgrown ruins).

The myth that Buchenwald had been completely self-liberated was firmly discredited during the World War II fiftieth anniversary celebrations at Buchenwald in 1995 when the prime minister of Thuringia thanked U.S. veterans for their part in the events of April 1945 at Buchenwald (Azaryahu 2003: 13). New guidebooks and route maps of the site were published in 1993 (Azaryahu 2003: 10), and in 1997 an exhibition opened in a specially commissioned block, narrating the history of Special Camp No. 2, although as Farmer notes, the objects displayed create an 'incomplete, fragmentary, almost cryptic' impression in comparison to the 'fully elaborated and institutionalized historical narrative' provided in the Permanent Historical Exhibition on the main camp (Farmer 1995: 104). Despite discrepancies in the way the two histories were presented, there was some sense that the landscape was taking on a more democratic face; the way the entrances to the respective exhibits were positioned meant that '[v]isitors could, if they chose, see the exhibits at the Soviet camp or the Nazi camp, without having to see both' (Farmer 1995: 107). In this, the most recent phase of curation, the aim was to use different parts of the landscape to reflect the camp's multiple histories in order to 'avoid encouraging simplistic parallels between the Nazi and the Soviet camps' (Farmer 1995: 108). After much discussion, the mass grave pits containing the bodies of the German victims of the Soviet camp were marked out by brushed steel pillars.

Conveniently, the graves were geographically distanced from the main commemorative area. The oak that seemed such a powerful symbol of the coincidental spatial overlap between Goethe's realm and Buchenwald remains a prominent feature at the memorial site today. Signposted, discussed in the museum guidebooks, and integrated into the most frequented walking tour of the site, the monumentality of the stump continues to endure.

Weimar-Buchenwald's sentimental-brutal dichotomy is central to the tourist experience of this area to date. As Young (1994: 7) has argued, monuments are always fixed points of reference amongst others; together they create meaning, orientation and linear narratives for the memorial landscape visitor. As a result 'any memorial marker in the landscape, no matter how alien its surroundings, is still perceived in the midst of its geography' (Young 1994: 7). The composite memorial landscape of Weimar-Buchenwald bears out this dialogical relationship. As travel writer Michael Gorra (2004: 16) noted when visiting the camp, 'any student of German culture' at Buchenwald must

Figure 1.4. Graveyard of Special Camp No. 2 © Charlotte Rea

'worry at the question of how one might get from the poet [Goethe] to the prison ... of their coincidence in something more than space'. Certainly, Hitler's rhetoric frequently implicated Goethe in National Socialist ideology.[7] But whilst Goethe's oft-cited rejection of the emancipation of the Jewish people in his own time has generated accusations of anti-Semitism, it has also been described as a rejection of emancipation in general (Berghahn 2001: 6), rather than nascent discrimination against the Jewish race.[8] As will be seen, in the following chapter, Semprun dubs Goethe 'a good beginning' to an account of Buchenwald. To fully comprehend this statement, I argue that we must look beyond Goethe's racial politics to the particular nature of his humanism. Humanism's 'positive affirmation that human beings can find within themselves the resources to live a good life' (Norman 2004: 18) initially seems to have no place in the dehumanizing zone of the concentration camp. Yet as Norman (2004: 8) has also suggested, humanism raises questions, one of which is central to this context: 'Does a belief in the idea of 'man' function to exclude groups of people who do not match this favoured model of what it is to be human?' Semprun's work, as will be seen, forges a response to this question.

Weimar 1999 to UNESCO 2012

The positive and negative poles of German history and culture were notable in the way the local topography was mapped for visitors in 1999, when Weimar became the first former Eastern bloc city, and the smallest to date, to be awarded the title of Europe's City of Culture. An associated conference (*Why Weimar? Questioning the Legacy of Weimar from Goethe to 1999*, McGill University) aimed to address the issues surrounding the complexities of the city's culture. Weimar was described as an important *lieu de mémoire* for German national identity, a cultural and political homeland for numerous important movements in history, including romanticism, classicism, the Bauhaus, the Weimar Republic, and National Socialism (Roth 2003). In an assessment of the events organised throughout the year known as Weimar 1999, Silke Roth (2003: 95) observed that, whilst many of these histories were downplayed, classicism and National Socialism emerged as clear priorities in the schedule. An opening speech by then president of the Federal Republic of Germany (FRG) Roman Herzog glossed over the reunification of Germany and East/West relations, stressing a model of German culture defined by a 'contrast between Enlightenment and National Socialist terror'.[9] Of the 370 events organized for Weimar 1999, Roth argues that whilst those celebrating Weimar classicism, and in particular Goethe, were most predominant (perhaps unsurprisingly, as 1999 was the 250th anniversary of his birth).

Buchenwald and National Socialism were also highly visible. Indeed there was an emphasis, in some events, on the connection between the two; an art exhibition, *Marked Site*, even featured anachronistic drawings of Goethe at Buchenwald. Although only 12 of the 370 events made direct references to Buchenwald, Roth maintains that these were prioritized in the overall schedule; they were opened by celebrities and politicians, and were given particularly prominent media coverage. The accompanying speeches were characterized by the advocation of a 'never again' philosophy with regards the Holocaust, and a small protest was held against contemporary right-wing activities in Weimar (Roth 2003: 99).

One of the events in the programme was a walking route around the town. Entitled *Walking through Time in Weimar: A Criss-cross Guide to Cultural History: Weaving between Goethe's House and Buchenwald* (1999), it encompassed twenty-three 'stations in time'; visitors would walk from place to place and consider the rich histories behind these points on the map. Gerd Schuchardt (Thuringian Minister of Science, Research and Culture) (*WTT* 1999: 6) prefaced the exhibition catalogue with a statement which suggests the potential of Weimar-Buchenwald to become more than a static site when approached in such a way:

> Some towns convey the impression of being particularly alive with their own history. Weimar is surely one of them … It depends … on how history seems to live on in the people of a town. For many visitors and also many residents of Weimar, probing into this history, encountering the personalities and the spirit of other ages, tracing the oft-sung Weimar myth, will be an exciting enterprise. The time traveller is carried into different layers of the past, experiencing the complexity of this history. It is today's town which provides the stage, with all its stone vestiges of yesterday.
>
> The dimension of the weft and warp between Goethe's house and Buchenwald shows whoever sets out in Weimar what it means to embark on time travel in a German town.

The stations on the tour included all the likely cultural highlights of the city, such as the houses that had belonged to its cultural heroes, the squares posthumously named after them, and the graveyard where many of them were buried. Although it did not include the site of Buchenwald itself (the camp lies outside the city lines), the Nazi past was represented in an exhibition at the city train station (the closest point in the city to the camp, and once linked to it by rail). The former Ducal stables on Kegelplatz, used as Gestapo headquarters from 1937 to 1945, was also included to represent the 'darker' side of Weimar's history. Classicism and Nazism again emerged alongside one another in this curatorial mapping of the city. The dual territorialization of the landscape was laid bare.

Somehow, then, despite Weimar's many legacies, Buchenwald and Goethe took precedence in the cultural landscape of Weimar 1999. Visitors were confronted with the dialectical opposites of creativity and destruction, sentimentality and brutalism that seem embedded in the fiercely territorialized landscape of today's Weimar-Buchenwald. And yet the problem remains, despite Schuchardt's optimistic description of the area as a platform for travelling in time; how does one get from the poet of Enlightenment humanism to the prison in the forest? The dichotomy identified by Thape and Kogon, and the polarities of Goethean humanism and Hitlerian brutality structures visitors' experience in the present day. This dichotomy was a central concern for Semprun, a phenomenon that both captivated him as an inmate and shaped his literary representations of his time in Buchenwald; I will go on to argue that his writing places Buchenwald's polarities in dialogue, staking his own claims on the landscape and, in his own engagement with it, opening it up as space of possibility for new phenomenological encounters.

In 2004, UNESCO announced an action plan entitled 'Filling the Gap', designed to introduce 'sites representative of the ambivalences of mankind's heritage' (Buchenwald.de 2012a) to its portfolio of protected sites. Member states were asked to nominate such sites, and since the call several have been added to their catalogue of landscapes of destruction, which already included Auschwitz-Birkenau (since 1979) and the Hiroshima Peace Memorial (since 1996). These sites form part of the World Heritage Programme, 'a unique global placemaking endeavor fostering "peace in the minds of men" through the ritual reappropriation of tangible monuments, which are juxtaposed against one another to create a worldwide imagined community' (Di Giovine 2009: 33). On 31 August 2012, Christoph Matschie, the Thuringian Minister of Education, Science and Culture, announced that the Free State of Thuringia would be nominating the grounds of Buchenwald as a UNESCO site in addition to their application for Erfurt's Medieval Jewish heritage. Matschie (Buchenwald.de 2012b) explained the desire behind the nomination as follows:

> We would … like to give prominence to the overall significance of the double location Weimar-Buchenwald: on the one hand the spirit of German poets and thinkers, on the other hand National Socialism as the darkest chapter in German history. As contrary as these two epochs are, they are also inseparably linked in Weimar and Buchenwald. With the World Heritage application, we acknowledge this responsibility.

This was a clear acceptance of Weimar-Buchenwald's coincidence in something more than space, despite its clear allocation of 'contrary' natures to German poets and thinkers and National Socialism. Volkhard Knigge, director of the Buchenwald and associated Mittelbau-Dora memorials, made a statement which exhibited more resistance to clear cut separation:

> The Buchenwald survivor and author Ivan Ivanji … expresses the chief message of this double location as follows: 'The time has come for humanity to understand that barbarianism does not fall from the sky. It is always bred in culture, but not in every culture. And it is bred in culture under specific political, societal, social and legal conditions. It does not fall from the sky overnight, knock at the door and say "here I am".' (Knigge 2012)

After listing the ways in which negative poles of history were as important to the definition of cultural identity as their positive counterparts, Knigge concluded: 'What remains when culture and barbarianism can no longer be thought of as inevitable antitheses? Presumably nothing but to persist in this antagonism in a second act of naivety – a naivety which is enlightened about itself' (2012).

Such recognition of the close affinity between culture and barbarism was established in philosophical and critical discourse by the Frankfurt School, in most forceful terms by Theodor Adorno in essays on the culture industry, and with Max Horkheimer (2002: xiv) in *Dialectics of Enlightenment*; a book which set out to 'explain why humanity, instead of entering a truly human state, is sinking into a new kind of barbarism'. Knigge's acknowledgement of this dialectic is evidence of the filtration of theoretical discourse into the management of memorial space. His speech also flagged a related aim of the nomination as 'to take the double location Weimar-Buchenwald seriously to the entire extent of its capacity to move the conscience, the heart and the mind in Germany and beyond Germany's boundaries' (Knigge 2012). Given the World Heritage's Programme's global remit and focus on the achievement of peace, Knigge makes a strong case for Buchenwald's inclusion. As the next chapter demonstrates, taking Weimar-Buchenwald's 'double location' seriously is a significant characteristic of Semprun's writing. In the third chapter of this section, I consider connections between Buchenwald and another landscape beyond Germany's boundaries, in which 'specific political, societal, social and legal conditions' also came to play a part in the creation of barbarism: New Orleans after Hurricane Katrina.

Notes

1. Baedeker's guides from the period describe the Thuringian Forest as 'full of interest for the pedestrian' (1925: 266), and grant the area an asterisk designating it as of notable interest to the traveller.

2. Throughout the twentieth century, the German people made regular pilgrimages on Sundays to see the older trees in their region (Mauch 2004: 2). Forests are also seen by some as monuments to German history, places that told the people 'more about the life of [their] forebears than ramparts and walls' (Mauch 2004: 3).

3. Throughout this section I make extensive use of official Gedenkstätte Buchenwald Publications, including site guide books, as a way into interrogating its history. In doing so, I approach the analysis with a view to demonstrating the extent of the material made available by the memorial as an institution, which plays a key role in mediating the experience of visitors to the landscape. These sources are inevitably grounded in the agenda of the institution, and vigilance should be maintained concerning their potentially selective composition.

4. By the end of the war, new trees were often planted to cover the traces of Nazi crimes. After prisoners escaped from Sobibór in 1943, the Nazis razed it to the ground, buried prisoners' remains, and planted trees to disguise the remnants. The mass graves were eventually discovered by a research team in 1991 (BBC News 2001). Firs and lupines were planted over mass graves and foundations at Belzec (O'Neil and Tregenza 2007). Attempts to screen the activities of functioning camps are also documented; poplar trees were planted to mask the crematoria at Birkenau early in 1944 (Gilbert 1997: 152). It should be noted too that even in the early days of the Reich forest protection was selective; it did not extend to non-native trees: 'the unwanted foreigners and bastards that have as little right to be in the German forest as they have to be in the German *Volk*' (Willi Parchmann, head of the Nazi Party forestry unit, 1934, cited in Imort 2005: 44).

5. Ernst Weichart's memoir *The Forest of the Dead [Der Totenwald]* (1947) recalls how this 'lovely' name sparked an immediate mistrust to those familiar with the Nazis' use of misleading signifiers (1947: 59).

6. Professor Alewyn, an exiled Jewish Germanist who was 'forcibly retired' from Heidelberg in 1933 (Wilson 2001: 156), was perhaps ideally situated to press this point. Although, as Wilson – who also cites Alewyn on this point, albeit a slightly divergent translation which substitutes 'humaneness' for 'humanity' – argues, to set these two figures up as polar opposites, with Goethe standing in for 'humaneness' and Hitler for 'bestiality' is to overlook the former's 'disdain for human and civil rights' and his 'regressive attitude to Jewish emancipation' (2001: 156).

7. The 'spirit of Weimar' was a lofty but useful device; it could legitimize anything', and Thomas Mann was 'appalled at the mixture of Goethe worship and Hitlerism' he encountered on his journey to Weimar in 1932 to give a speech for the hundredth anniversary of Goethe's death (Lepenies 2006: 158). Throughout Hitler's *Mein Kampf* ([1925] 2004), Goethe's name was invoked to emphasize the superiority of German culture. Hitler's participation at ceremonial occasions such as the opening of the first Reichstag of the Third Reich, at which the memories of Goethe, Friedrich Schiller and Kant were openly celebrated, aligned the new Führer with the 'noble and lofty heritage' of German classicism (Glaser 1978: 41).

8. Klaus L. Berghahn (2001: 7), for example, noting Hitler's comment in *Mein Kampf* that even Goethe had 'been disgusted by the thought that, in the future, marriages of Christians and Jews should no longer be forbidden by law,' argues that Goethe was in fact opposed to mixed marriages 'because they offend the religious beliefs of both parties and lead to religious conflicts between spouses', a perspective from which prejudice against either group involved was largely irrelevant.

9. Roth also highlights that one of the reasons for the choice of Weimar as 1999 Capital of Culture was its former identity as an Eastern Bloc city; selecting Weimar was an attempt to celebrate the success of the process of German reunification. Despite this, references to the former GDR and to reunification were downplayed. Although eleven related events took place – only one less than those on the subject of Buchenwald – they were all held towards the end of the programme, in winter, when tourist numbers had dropped dramatically. They were given only marginal attention by the media.

SEMPRUN'S BUCHENWALD

The first chapter provided an overview of the original camp at Buchenwald and the various stages of commemorative landscaping that have since taken place. This chapter continues to examine the Buchenwald landscape in order to destabilize certain delimitations concerning the relationship between subject and space in the concentration camp, via an examination of the testimonial project of former inmate Jorge Semprun (whose approach to memory I have already touched upon). Foremost amongst these delimitations is Ulrich Baer's (2002: 65) statement that Holocaust sites 'failed to accommodate human experience' for victims in the past, and that, in the present they are 'radically inhospitable'; accordingly 'attempts to inhabit them through empathic identification and imaginary projection via transferential bonds, [are] illusory at best' (Baer 2002: 83). Baer (2002: 72) argues that disorientation of deportation, for the camp subject, destroys the 'symbolic notion of a place that could hold experiences together'. Geoffrey Hartman, in an interview with Cathy Caruth (Caruth and Hartman 1996: 648) on 'traumatic' place memory similarly suggested that it is 'difficult to think of the camps as being ... memory places'.[1] Yet whilst at times Semprun arguably presents a 'traumatic,' or 'blocked' response to time and place,[2] the spatial experience recalled in his work indicates a complex and intimate relationship between subject, landscape and history, one which implies a sustained and ultimately recollectable form of engagement; place, it seems, *does* hold his experiences together. I will argue that Semprun's narratives, which cover the full spectrum of his Buchenwald experience – including deportation and arrival (1942), internment (1942–3), and return to the camp as survivor (1990) – provide evidence of this.

This chapter undertakes an ecocritical examination of Semprun's work, with particular focus on the principle that '[o]ur identities are constituted in time and place ... always shaped by both memory and environment' (Bate 2000: 109); Semprun's work offers receptive readers 'a sense of being-at-home-in-the-world' (Bate 2000) on the Ettersburg slopes. Landscape is thus

presented as habitable, and potentially able to facilitate the imaginative projection Baer dismisses as illusory. Semprun's multilingual abilities almost
certainly helped him maintain an administrative role at Buchenwald which
allowed access to several areas of the camp he might otherwise have struggled to enter; amongst them the infirmary where Halbwachs lay 'rotting' (*LL*
17). His involvement with Buchenwald's underground Communist resistance also allowed him a little more privilege and better living conditions
than, for example, the majority of Jewish prisoners. Furthermore, his writing
– that of a Spaniard, composed in French and frequently utilizing German,
and now widely available in English translation – is testament to his trans-
nationally constructed identity. In combination with this, in demonstrating
ecocritical sensibilities in his approach to documenting Buchenwald – an
approach which dislocates the notion that identities are always territorialized
and organically rooted in national landscapes – this chapter suggests that
Semprun's work both constitutes and encourages a transculturally grounded
response to the Holocaust. He effectively lays the landscape open for new
encounters, de-territorializing the Ettersburg terrain from the regimes of history and memory in which it is implicated. He does this through the constant
repetition and re-negotiation of his Buchenwald memories, rendering his literary oeuvre what Bella Brodzki (2007: 172) has described as 'the strongest
argument for conceptualising "survival" not as a unique and completed event,
but rather as "survivorship" – an ongoing, inconclusive, shifting experience
whose finality comes only with death'. Revisions in Semprun's narratives are
forms of translation; no account is ever final, authoritative or finished. Instead, like memorial space, his memory is constantly subject to metamorphosis. Collapsing history to bring pertinent characters and texts together
in the landscape of the Ettersburg in 1944, Semprun creates a Huyssian
palimpsest: 'put[s] different things in one place', placing 'memories of what
there was before' alongside 'imagined alternatives to what there is' (Huyssen
2003: 7).

   Both the politically driven re-landscaping of Buchenwald as a memorial
and Semprun's narrative re-draftings of his experiences result, according to
Brodzki, in overarching losses of meaning. Whilst loss underpins Semprun's
work – the initial loss of his Spanish homeland, and later of his political and
social beliefs (his eventual rejection of Communism) – I interpret his writing as connotive of the evolution, rather than the evacuation, of meaning.
His reconsideration of German literary culture and related signification of
nature and landscape suggests that the Holocaust may have disrupted frequently perceived meanings, but these are mediated and remediated rather
than rendered void. Furthermore, Semprun's work is uniquely suited to an
interrogation of past-present engagement because, against the grain of much
Holocaust scholarship, he believed in writing as something that could com-

municate experience and facilitate understanding; that 'the essential truth of the [camp] experience' could 'be imparted only ... through the artifice of a work of art' (*LL* 125), through fiction. Wishing to 'avoid a recital of suffering and horror', he drew on his experience and moved beyond it, 'opening the narrative to ... [f]iction that would be as illuminating as the truth' (165). His determination to overcome such obstacles stems from his resistance to the concept of representational failure in the wake of extreme experience, that 'the "ineffable" ... is only an alibi' (*LL* 13–14). It is this perspective on how the past may be represented that I take forward here as I consider the encounters that potentially facilitate access to that past and prompt humane and democratic reason in the future.

A Good Beginning

Semprun was deported to the camp on the hill in 1943, as a result of his association with the Communist resistance (he was eventually expelled many years later for divergent beliefs). His testimonial project combines philosophical enquiry (in the years before his arrest he had been studying philosophy at the Sorbonne) and autobiography into three narrative journeys, all shaped by his knowledge of German language, literature and culture. Each of his three Buchenwald memoirs revisit his concentration camp internment from a different perspective: *The Long Voyage* describes the experience of deportation; *What a Beautiful Sunday!* combines detailed accounts of the camp itself juxtaposed with later memories from his time in the French Communist Party; and *Literature or Life* deals primarily with his memories of liberation and his eventual return to Buchenwald as a visitor. As Susan Suleiman points out, it was a strange, 'one is almost tempted to say happy, coincidence, for a writer concerned with testimony and memory to have been present at the deathbed of Maurice Halbwachs' (2006: 154). And indeed, all Semprun's memoirs evidence engagement with the kind of implacement so central to Halbwachs's formulation of collective memory.

When embarking on an account of his internment at Buchenwald, Semprun faced one obstacle in particular: he needed to decide where to start. He debates the point in some depth, primarily via accounts of his conversations with an American liberating soldier, Lt. Rosenfeld. Whilst acknowledging that '[t]here are all sorts of beginnings,' he decides that '[o]ne ought to begin with the essential part of [the] experience ... to go beyond the clear facts of this horror to get at the root of radical Evil' (*LL* 87). It is with the essence of experience, he insists, not its horrific semblance, that an account must begin. 'Goethe wouldn't be a bad beginning,' he muses a little later (94). In invoking the name of this bulwark of German culture as the essence of an experience of internment endured over a hundred years after his death, Semprun begins his critique of Nazism's sentimental brutality. The backdrop to this conversation is a picturesque riverside scene, a cottage on the banks of the river Ilm in Weimar: Goethe's retreat. Buchenwald is a mere 8km away. At issue for Semprun, I suggest, is that Goethean humanism did little more than legitimate the exclusion of 'groups of people who do not match [a] favoured model of what it is to be human' (see Norman 2004: 8). In presenting what is arguably an ecocritical inhabitation of space, he provides an alternative perspective that corrects this exclusion. The Ettersburg again becomes Goethe's stage, in Semprun's writing, in a negotiation of German culture which oscillates between playful affection and mocking condemnation. Whilst Wolf Lepenies argues that Goethe 'became a beacon of hope for many inmates of the Nazi camps, even if they were not German' (2006: 159), and cites Semprun's imaginary conversations with Goethe on the Ettersburg as an example of this, a close examination of these episodes reveals Semprun's Goethe as representative of something far more complex and less reassuring. Unlike Lepenies' other example – Dutch Communist Nico Rost's memoir/diary *Goethe in Dachau,* in which the experience of reading the German classics is uplifting and sustaining for the author – Semprun uses Goethe to foreground a bitter critique of Nazi ideology's sentimental-brutalism, its contradictions and complexities.

Semprun's critique begins in *The Long Voyage,* a combination of autobiography and fiction which works through the experience of his five-day deportation to Buchenwald in the goods wagon of a train. The narrative voice switches throughout the text,[3] as Semprun revisits the same events over again, prompting critical interpretations of his Buchenwald texts as driven by traumatized temporal disruption (see Tidd 2005, 2008; Suleiman 2004). However, of more relevance to this enquiry is the critical acknowledgement that *LV* is undoubtedly also a form of travel writing, albeit distinct from the usual form in that it relates the tale of a forced, as opposed to elected, journey (Silk 1992: 54). Particularly notable is the parallel structure of travel and memory revealed in *The Long Voyage.* Jones (2007: 35–36) also argues that Semprun exposes 'the importance of travel and its metaphors to memory discourses concerning the Holocaust'. According to this argument, in the work of Semprun, 'metaphors of travel play a central role [as he uses] the familiarity of the journey in order to engage with the uninitiated reader's everyday experience of travel as a frame of reference for understanding the experience of deportation and internment' (Jones 2007: 36). Crucially, Semprun is creating a *relatable* framework for readers via his utilization the travel motif.

Commenting on *The Long Voyage* as travel narrative, Sally M. Silk introduces a series of points, particularly about spatial experience, which can be taken further, both in the context of *The Long Voyage* and in Semprun's other Buchenwald texts. *LV* emerges from her analysis as a subversion of tradi-

tional travel writing; contra the Enlightenment understanding of the journey as broadening the mind, Gerard's narrative leads only inwards: 'travel ...
narrows Gerard's world to such a degree that ... only the space of interiority
can be explored' (Silk 1992: 3). Silk's contrast between *LV* and the travel narratives of the Enlightenment is worthy of further scrutiny; indeed, this is the
first point in the Buchenwald texts that underscores the significance of Semprun's engagement with issues of landscape, experience and Goethe's legacy
in German culture. Goethe's *Italienische Reise* (1816–17) gave him 'the status of German traveller par excellence' (Hachmeister 2002: 1). Despite the
fact that Semprun and Goethe write at different times in different contexts,
both authors seem subject to 'the travel writer's desire to mediate between
things foreign and things familiar, to help us understand that world which
is other to us' (Blanton 2002: 2). The crucial difference between them, for
the purposes of this chapter, is their assumed subject position in relation to
worlds of otherness. Goethe's worldview in *Italienische Reise* is:

> totalizing, transcendental ... the landscape is an orderly and encompassable
> panorama able to be observed, structured and known as a totality. Even when
> the landscape is moving ... his embodied subject position is never compro-
> mised because his observations are always systematically oriented in a mappa-
> ble space and emplotted ... in cyclical time ... His observations ... are often
> made from either the highest perspective he can find ... or from the slow and
> methodical accumulation of details on the ground. In both cases, his synthe-
> sizing vision allows a mastery of objects in the world ... The geographic totality
> is organized by the visual clarity of the cardinal directions, mapped according
> to geography, and oriented according to his body in the centre of the space.
> (Presner 2007: 76–77)[4]

Semprun, as Silk's argument implies, subverts this paradigm of Enlightenment objectivity, in his retreat to an interior world. His refusal, or perhaps
his inability, to plot events in cyclical time, highlights the compromise of
his subject position. This does not mean, however, that landscapes of the
exterior world are of no interest or significance to him; indeed, I will demonstrate, they ground his interior explorations. As Silk (1992: 54) also notes,
'awareness of spatial existence plays an important role in the narration' of the
text, even if Semprun 'comes to equate the term "outside" with "life before"
and the journey itself as "being inside"'. My own analysis will demonstrate a
continued awareness of spatial existence throughout Semprun's internment,
an awareness which substantially foregrounds and shapes his time in Buchenwald. Whilst some of his landscape descriptions appear to continue the
pattern identified by Silk – outside as 'before', or somehow other from his internal world – others suggest an immersive involvement with landscape as an
inhabitable realm. In all cases space is discursive and constantly mediated.

There is a final point to be drawn from Silk's analysis which merits further exploration both in and beyond *The Long Voyage*; Semprun's reliance on 'a troping of space to define the position from which he writes many years after his experience' (Silk 1992: 63). This troping can be extended to include diverse dimensions of phenomenological experience, including the impact of seasonal changes, weather conditions and encounters with animal life; the significance of this will be scrutinized in discussions of *Literature or Life* and *What a Beautiful Sunday!* Close scrutiny of these texts alongside *The Long Voyage* indicates a sense of experiential continuity between deportation and internment, evidenced in Semprun's recurring habit of positioning himself emotionally within landscape. For example, in recollecting the journey to the camp, Semprun describes his reaction to the view of the Moselle Valley from the train:

> I close my eyes, savoring this darkness which unfolds within me, savoring this certainty of the Moselle valley, outside there beneath the snow … There it is. It's simply there … I could die right now, standing here in the boxcar crammed with future corpses, and it would still be there … beneath my lifeless gaze, sumptuously beautiful, like a Breughel winter scene. We could all die … it would still be there … I close my eyes, I open my eyes. My life is nothing more than this blinking of my eyes which reveals the Moselle valley to me … The valley unfolds … The Moselle comes in to me through my eyes, inundates my gaze, gorges my soul, which is like a sponge, with slow waters. I am nothing but this Moselle which invades me through the eyes. I have to concentrate on this savage pleasure (*LV* 11–13).

> I don't want to lose sight of this fundamental certainty … the valley, fashioned by the work of centuries (*LV* 15).

This passage suggests another element of Semprun's approach to landscape which reappears in later works: a consistent awareness of his geographical location, exhibited in his tendency to rarely mention a place without also thinking about its past and cultivation. His sense of the Moselle Valley as a 'fundamental certainty' suggests that in times of disruption and dislocation – at this stage Semprun can only guess at his destination – landscape equals continuity. However, the harmony of the Moselle, a harmony created through centuries of wine growing – man and nature in a productive relation – is implicitly disrupted later in the journey when the train stops at Trier – the birthplace of Marx.

> Was I blind, my God, deaf, dumb and blind, an oaf, an utter idiot, not to have realized sooner where it was I had heard of the Moselle valley? … The Moselle winegrowers, the Moselle woodcutters, the law about stealing wood in the Moselle. It was in the 'Mega', of course. It's a childhood friend, dammit, this damned Moselle is a childhood friend of mine. (*LV* 36)

The 'Mega,' a common name for the collected works of Marx and Engels, contains Marx's essays of 1842 in defence of Moselle peasants found guilty of stealing wood from recently privatized land. In arriving at Trier, this recalled knowledge forces a re-evaluation of the apparently timeless harmony between man and nature the landscape had seemed to represent. The always-already disrupted nature of pastoral nostalgia permeates the narrative. The following day Semprun's character is 'sunk into a sort of dull somnolence' and the scenery outside the train no longer interests him: 'It's simply that yesterday it was beautiful, and today the scenery's not beautiful' (*LV* 122). Implied, rather that stated, is that the disruption caused by the recollection of Marx's connection to the Moselle – the recognition of the pastoral as an unstable fable of harmony – undermines his pleasure in it.

There are also hints in these passages of an experience of the sublime, if that experience can be considered a 'rape' of the onlooker as he positions himself in relation to the external world (Shaw 2006: 10); Semprun is gorged, inundated and invaded, resonant with Goethe's Young Werther's description of 'Nature' as 'a monster, forever devouring regurgitating, chewing and gorging' ([1774] 1989: 66), and his response to a valley landscape whose 'power and magnificence, will be [his] undoing' ([1774] 1989: 27). Yet the sublime experience presented in Semprun's text diverges from those found in Goethe's literature; for Goethe, as for his Young Werther, 'the sublime is mysterious because unknown, dangerous because untamed, and attractive because knowledge of it promises dominion over nature itself' (Gay 1992: 96). Semprun's sublime experience is emptied of the potential to dominate nature, because the possibility of his death in the box car grants the landscape a longevity and continuity he cannot promise himself. These passages introduce an approach to landscape which recurs later on in his testimonial project. As a result, his work overall suggests something of an experiential continuity throughout his deportation and internment, with both phases mediated by the same – principally environmental – co-ordinates.

Literature or Life and *What a Beautiful Sunday!* take readers beyond deportation to unravel the substance of Semprun's experiences on arrival at Buchenwald. He continues to disclose vivid memories of the natural elements, including weather conditions and natural forms on the Ettersburg, alongside his knowledge of and engagement with intellectual and cultural history associated with the landscape. In examining these texts, it becomes clear Semprun's experiences echo Christopher Tilley's description of phenomenological spatial habitation: individually determined, guided by personal memories, and oriented in landscapes loaded with affective significance. There is little of the radical decontextualization Baer proposes as the inevitable result of deportation. However, this is not to suggest that the extreme context of Semprun's experiences does not temper his spatial engagement, or his later memories of arrival. He retains a reflexive realization of the communicative limitations of these memories. One page of *LV,* enclosed in brackets, provides readers with a concise account of arrival at Buchenwald, drawn from 'the most secret, best protected recesses of memory' (*LV* 214). It is made up of 'beech trees and tall pines ... dogs barking and the blinding brightness of all the lamps and searchlights, their icy light inundating the snow-covered landscape' (*LV* 214); a 'Wagnerian' spectacle that 'explodes' in Semprun's mind in later years, 'in unexpected ways and at the most ordinary moments':

> suddenly, like a scalpel slicing cleanly into the soft tender flesh, this memory explodes ... And if someone seeing you standing there petrified, asks: 'What are you thinking about?' you have to answer 'Nothing', of course. It's first of all a memory difficult to communicate, and, besides, you have to work it out by yourself. (*LV* 214–15)

This description adds weight to the conclusion of Jones's (2007: 51) argument on the subject of the Holocaust-as-travel, that the 'journey as a metaphor for life is evoked solely in order to be negated', as the 'normality associated with travel only serves to underline the irreducible gulf constructed by the authors between the reality they experienced at the camp and the knowledge of their addressees and readers who did not enter this world'. This sense of difference, of an irreducible gulf, does not necessarily foreclose a reader's empathic endeavour; as already determined, empathic unsettlement as conceived by LaCapra depends on a reflexive acknowledgement of the impossibility – and undesirability – of total identification. Silk, whilst concentrating in part on the ways in which Semprun's journey is a perversion of the usual activity of travel, argues that all voyages, even deportation, constitute 'an accumulation of moments, a density of various situations that relate to each other metonymically' (1992: 3); fundamentally, this is true of any journey, regardless of the situation in which it is undertaken.

Internment: Semprun on the Ettersburg

Semprun's emotional reaction to landscape and his awareness of its cultural and historical heritage continue throughout his narrative representations of his life at Buchenwald. These elements contribute to his negotiation with Goethe's legacy in particular and Germanic cultural and literary approaches to landscape and nature in general. Furthermore, whilst exploring the same 'cultural geographical histories' that now structure Buchenwald as a *lieu de mémoire* (as described above), this negotiation de-territorializes these histories and draws attention to alternative ways in which the space, and the Holocaust itself, may be encountered in and through landscape.

Key to Semprun's de-territorialization of the Ettersburg is his attempt to imagine how others, including his perpetrators, would perceive the views he looks upon, as though searching for a possible alignment of perspective. Contemplating the view over the slopes from the Buchenwald site from his walks on many Sunday afternoons, at sunset (*WBS* 237), he imagines that the guards in their watch towers would sit looking over this landscape (34). This search for perspective is thrown into relief at the opening of *What a Beautiful Sunday!* as he describes an intense longing for a shared experience of the natural world which will, even temporarily, disrupt the fixed subject-object dichotomy of his position within the camp surveyed by these guards. He recalls (in third person) standing in front of a tree in Buchenwald in the December snow:

> He remembered no other tree. There was no trace of nostalgia ... no childhood memory rising up in a stirring of the blood. He was not trying to recover something inaccessible, some impression from an earlier time. No long-lost happiness nourished this present bliss. Just the beauty of a tree, whose name, even if it was in fact what it seemed to be, had no importance. A beech, probably ... Carried away by sheer joy. A tree, just that, in its immediate splendor, in the transparent stillness of the present. (*WBS* 2)

The splendour of the scene again invokes Goethe's Young Werther, a narrative also suggestive of that which Jonathan Bate (2000: 155) describes, in ecocritical terms, via Gaston Bachelard's discussion of *The Poetics of Space* ([1958] 1969): 'a willingness to look at and listen to the world ... a letting go of the self which brings the discovery of a deeper self'. For Bachelard (1969: xv), being at one with the world occurred in phenomenological moments in which 'the duality of subject and object is iridescent, shimmering, unceasingly active in its inversions'; 'Through the poetic image, oneness with the world can be experienced directly rather than yearned for elegiacally in nostalgia for the *temps perdu* of childhood or the imagined good life of primitivism' (Bate 2000: 154). The tree, for Semprun, functions in this encounter as a poetic image, offering him an encounter with the natural world which he insists is characterized, not by nostalgia, but sheer 'immediate splendour'.

Semprun is captivated by this beech, by the 'crude dialectic' of the bud that would soon negate winter. As he stands entranced by the beech, an SS warrant officer approaches him and seems to pause before challenging him.

> For a split second he had caught himself imagining that the warrant officer would see the tree as he had. The warrant officer's gaze had weakened, invaded perhaps by so much beauty. (*WBS* 3)

> There they were, side by side; they could have talked together about the miracle of beauty ... The warrant officer took a few steps back, as *he* had done a

little while ago. The warrant officer looked at the beech, the landscape, with eyes that had turned blue. Everything seemed so innocent; there was a vague possibility that it was anyway. (*WBS* 4)

In desiring the officer to share this moment of subjection to sublime experience, this 'invasion of beauty', he looks for an ethical-emotional response that would disrupt their subject-object opposition; as ecocritic Mick Smith (2005: 219) has speculated, 'talk of being "moved" by nature' may potentially operate beyond metaphorical limitations. For Smith the emotional response to nature is a mode of attachment and involvement, an 'intimate participatory [practice] that draws us closer to others ... giving us a feeling for and an understanding of our relational emplacement within [the] world' (2005: 219). Goethe was an early advocate of such encounters and, employing an empirical approach to the study of nature (Seamon 1978: 239) he aimed to 'to arrive at not only a deeper understanding but also a more reverent appreciation of nature' (Seamon 1978: 239). Goethe taught 'an alternate mode of interaction between person and environment that entails reciprocity, wonderment and gratitude' (Seamon 1978: 247). This was central to his conception of the organic link between native land and human identity. Understanding of nature – of what thrives on that land – should thus also improve man's understanding of himself, particularly as a being of 'dignity, respect and purposefulness' (Seamon 1978: 247). Significantly, Goethe argued that such encounters with nature could be 'reproducible for others'; that they could be shared. As Semprun, in his unfulfilled desire for the guard to acknowledge his humanity reveals, Goethe's notion of the 'dignity, respect and purposefulness' of man-in-nature fails in the concentration camps. This was a space in which one set of people attempted to systematically eliminate qualities such as 'dignity, respect and purposefulness' from another. The officer cannot share in the momentary sublime, cannot be moved by nature: 'Suddenly it was all over' (*WBS* 4). The illusion of a shared or reproducible encounter is shattered; as the officer points his revolver at Semprun's chest he concludes: 'Between SS Warrant Officer Kurt Krauss and No. 44904 there is all the distance created by the right to kill' (5).

The story of the beech exemplifies Semprun's experience of Buchenwald's landscape as sublime and underlines his acute awareness of the history and culture associated with the geographical location of his internment. Later in *What a Beautiful Sunday!* he continues the anecdote, implying a hidden confluence between the roots of National Socialist sentimental-brutality and Goethean humanism. The warrant officer took him back to the camp gates ('They were going to rough me up, no doubt about it' [*WBS* 128]). A *Hauptsturmführer* arrived and questioned him about why he was found standing immobile at the gates.

'Because of the tree, Hauptsturmführer!' I say ...

'The tree?' he says.

'There was a tree, by itself, a beech, a very fine tree. As soon as I saw it, I thought it might be Goethe's tree, so I went up to it.'

He looks very interested.

'Goethe!' he exclaims. 'So you know the works of Goethe?' A distinct change of tone. *Kultur* has its uses. (*WBS* 129)

Schwartz nods understandingly.

'You're quite wrong,' he says. 'Goethe's tree, the one on which he carved his initials, is inside the camp, on the esplanade between the kitchens and the clothing stores! And anyway, it's not a beech, but an oak!'

I know this already of course, but I must put on a display of great interest, as if delighted at acquiring a new piece of information.

'Oh, that's the one!'

'Yes,' says Schwartz, 'we spared it when the hill was cleared of trees, in memory of Goethe!'

And he embarks on a long speech about the respect shown by the National Socialists for good German cultural tradition ... I am no longer listening. I am thinking that Goethe and Eckermann would be very pleased if they heard him. (*WBS* 132–33)

Indeed, Semprun's Goethe, who he frequently conjures to stroll across the Ettersburg, displays the same a naive sentimentality as Young Werther who, when learning his favourite walnut trees have been cut down for wood, laments that 'there are people devoid of appreciation or feeling for that which has real value on earth' (Goethe 1989: 93). Semprun's imaginary Goethe rhapsodizes to an imaginary Eckermann:

'Did you know ... that tree in whose shade we were so fond of resting is still inside the camp? That, again, is a typically German gesture, and one that I appreciate! Despite the terrible demands of the war, that tree – which the officers and soldiers of this garrison continue to call "Goethe's tree," which, no doubt, will not fail to raise the spirits of the wretches imprisoned here for various reasons – that tree has not been cut down ... Yes, I appreciate that gesture of respect toward the memory of our history. Even in 1937, when the construction of this re-education camp was begun, I was profoundly touched by the representations made by the National Socialist Cultural Association of Weimar, demanding that the camp should not bear the name K.L. Ettersburg, due to the imperishable links between that place and my life and work. I can tell you, Eckermann, I was profoundly touched by those representations and by the decision finally made – in the highest places, I understand from a reliable source – to call the camp K.L. Buchenwald!" (*WBS* 206–7)

In these passages Semprun presents an implicit critique of Goethe's particular humanism. His irreverent portrayal shows the imaginary Goethe's reaction to the Nazi regime as one of 'understanding neutrality'; Eckermann depicts a Hitler 'radiating ... all the wisdom that the Goethean synthesis of the classical spirit and Faustian demonism can produce' (*WBS* 204). Semprun's Goethe is alarmed that Thomas Mann, 'a writer so close to Goethean thought', had famously denounced National Socialist ideology, and unsettled that Martin Heidegger, a thinker 'so removed from Goethean humanism', was infamously a member of the Nazi Party (*WBS* 205). The inadequacy of the imaginary Goethe's statement that 'the intellectual cannot be uninterested in politics' (*WBS* 205) serves to highlight the failure of the real Goethe to make any meaningful contribution to a discussion of Jewish emancipation or the larger politics of his time. The imaginary Goethe's reaction to Buchenwald, particularly to the Nazis' 'typically German' reaction to preserving the tree furthermore reflects Semprun's comprehension of National Socialistic distortion of traditional German values.[5] On walking past the zoological garden, the basic structure of which still exists today, Semprun's Goethe remarks approvingly on the excellent condition in which the animals are being kept: 'At a difficult time like ours, this respect for animal life, for the requirements of nature, seems to me to be specifically German ... as far as we are concerned, this characteristic ... seems to me ... inherent in a view of the world in which harmony between man and nature plays a determining role" (*WBS* 202–3). His naive approval of the legend '*Jedem das Seine*' [to each his due], emblazoned above the camp gates, completes Semprun's condemnatory depiction of the great German humanist:

> 'I find it most significant and most encouraging ... Is it not an excellent motto for a society organised to defend the freedom of all, of the whole society, to the detriment, if necessary, of an excessive, harmful individual freedom?' (207)

Furthermore, he boasts:

> 'Whoever the author of that inscription ... may be, I cannot help thinking that I had something to do with it, that the breath of my inspiration is to be found in it. To each his due, indeed, to each the place that is due to him, through birth or talent, in the hierarchy of individual freedom and constraints that make up the liberty of us all.' (208)

This is the Semprun's indictment: Goethean humanism is guilty of exclusion, for it advocates a paradoxical hierarchy designed to grant 'freedom for all' which can only function by constraining the liberty of particular individuals.

Literature or Life further reveals the way in which elements of the natural environment, including weather conditions and plant and animal life, became important grounding tropes for Semprun's later recollections. His descriptions suggest an application of symbolic meaning to natural elements that fits with Tilley's description of a phenomenological spatial relationship; such elements became 'reference points and places of emotional orientation for human attachment and involvement' (1994: 17). Semprun's references to birds throughout *LL,* for example, indicate sustained attention to, and a sensual awareness of, environmental factors. The text opens with Semprun's account of his encounter with three Allied soldiers in the forest on the Ettersburg immediately after the liberation of Buchenwald. The soldiers stare fearfully at Semprun. He asks one of them:

> 'What's the matter? … You're surprised to find the woods so quiet?'
> He looks round at the trees encircling us. The other men do the same. Listening. No, it's not the silence. They hadn't noticed, hadn't heard the silence. I'm what's scaring them, obviously, and nothing else.
> 'No birds left', I continue, pursuing my idea. 'They say the smoke from the crematory drove them away. Never any birds in the forest…'
> They listen closely, straining to understand.
> 'The smell of burned flesh, that's what did it!'
> They wince, glance at one another. In almost palpable distress. A sort of gasp, a heave of revulsion. (*LL* 5)

This tableau has been discussed in existing scholarship on Semprun, for it deals with the fear experienced by survivors that their testimony would 'drive away' any potential audience (see Langer 1993: 61 and Mandel 2006: 108–9). As Naomi Mandel (2006: 108) notes, there is a Levinasian implication 'in the Allied officers' inability to "face" the survivor'. Yet there is another undercurrent here which deserves attention. The disappearance of birds is an enduring herald of apocalypse in environmental literature. In the opening chapter of Rachel Carson's founding ecocritical text *Silent Spring* (1962: 22), the 'grim spectre' of human-perpetrated environmental disaster is heralded by 'a spring without voices' – the end of the dawn chorus. In Semprun's account, pastoral disruption finds a new home in the concentration camp, as the crematorium pollutes the earth anew. His repeated allusions to the month of April, when the camp was liberated, to the 'deep draught' of spring (*LL* 28), serve to reinforce the seasonal temporality of this ecocritical parallel. Furthermore, although Semprun's account attributes the birds' disappearance from the Ettersburg to the smoke produced from the cremation of human bodies, this example is also worth considering in light of Carson's argument that the industry responsible for an explosion in the invention of manmade pesticides was a 'child of the Second World War' (1962: 32); chemicals designed for warfare were initially commonly tested on insects, and such experiments resulted in the production of many new varieties of synthetic pesticide. Prewar insecticides, Carson explains, were derived from natural products, and were considerably less biologically potent than their synthetic descendants. With what Carson (1962: 42) has labelled 'a certain ironic significance', the insecticidal properties of many chemical agents were discovered by Gerhard Schrader, a German chemist, in the 1930s: 'Almost immediately the German government realized the significance of these same chemicals as new and devastating weapons in man's war against his own kind, and the work on them was declared secret. Some became the deadly nerve gases. Others, of closely allied structure, became insecticides' (1962: 42). Both Carson and Semprun recognize the significance of such allied structures of toxicity and their impact on all forms of life. Semprun's thoughts periodically return to birds: in the above passage on their absence; not long after when he visits Weimar upon liberation, and comments on their palpable presence (*LL* 93–94); and many years later when he returns as an honoured guest and they, too, have come back to Buchenwald (296, 304). The birds, in their absence and presence, become one of Semprun's environmental memory tropes, and offer him a way of speaking about what may otherwise be unspeakable.

Many of Semprun's recollections are introduced with seasonal signposts: 'this splendid April morning' (*LL* 15); 'that autumn day' (55); 'this first experience of torture. Out in the garden with its sloping lawn, the trees still bore leaves of yellow and russet gold' (54); 'every afternoon that spring' (17) – the spring that Halbwachs died. This introduces a sense of temporal stability to a text which, like *LV* and *WBS*, otherwise refuses to be pinned down to a linear narrative ('It's crazy how memory goes back and forth' [*WBS* 125]). Seasonal changes also took on new associations for Semprun after Buchenwald. The aforementioned 'deep draught' of the liberation spring; the end of winter 1945 always stays with him (*LL* 28). Years later, the advent of spring shatters Semprun's 'hard-won peace of mind': 'The anguish of former days returned to haunt me, especially in April. Various circumstances make it difficult to escape this month unscathed; the deeply affecting renewal of nature, the anniversary of the liberation of Buchenwald' (*LL* 226). Embedded in this seasonal awareness are perhaps the most pervasive of Semprun's environmental memory tropes; those of weather conditions, most particularly wind and snow. Weather, 'a prime means of linking spatiality and temporality' (Bate 2000: 109), is, for Semprun, impossible to disassociate from place memory. These elements frequently accompany the crematorium smoke in Semprun's accounts.

The Ettersburg winds and snows are, for Semprun, unique to Buchenwald, and are presented in his work as elements of continuity throughout internment, liberation and later life. Frequent references to these elements, both on his return to the camp as a visitor and in intervening years, cast them as vehicles of return, willed or unwilled; wind and snow take him back to the past and into the future, for example in this sudden memory 'snowstorm' one

May day: 'I was swept away by a staggering memory of snow on the Etters-burg. A perfectly calm giddiness, heartbreakingly lucid. I felt myself floating in the future of this memory. There would always be this memory, this loneli-ness: this snow in all the sunshine, this smoke in every springtime' (*LL* 139).

The continuity provided by weather is also projected, by Semprun, back into the Ettersburg's past; the wind is a 'wind for all seasons on Goethe's hillside' (*LL* 37). The landscape around him was 'the snowy forest where Goethe and Eckermann were fond of walking' (*WBS* 126). The seasons on the Ettersburg, too, are eternal frameworks which accommodate his experi-ence alongside that of his imaginary Goethe:

> it was April.
> Goethe would have ordered his barouche ... would have commented on the beauties of the landscape, the tiny events in the life of the birds ... it would be spring, in the fine forests of Thuringia! (*WBS* 82)

All that separates Semprun's Buchenwald from Goethe's in these passages is the crematorium smoke that sends the birds away. Distinctions collapse completely when Semprun projects an imaginary Goethe into the Buchen-wald landscape. From a man who '*would have* commented on the beauties of the landscape' (my emphasis), Goethe seems to materialize; he 'still' walks on the Ettersburg. For Semprun, coincidences of shared geographical co-ordinates across history were 'not without meaning' (*WBS* 92), although he berates himself for 'wasting ... time arguing with Goethe, catching ... bour-geois humanism in the trap of its own historical hypocrisies' (*WBS* 93). Yet he continues to imagine; an army truck becomes Goethe's sleigh, arriving 'suddenly on a cascade' of the Ettersburg snow (*WBS* 93). Indeed, Semprun 'can imagine anything on a December Sunday in that historic landscape', from the Grand Duke Charles Augustus entertaining Napoleon to Goethe and Eckermann appearing 'at the end of the avenue flanked by eagles' at Buchenwald's main entrance (*WBS* 122). The Ettersburg is a porous space, and Semprun's Goethe negotiates the same landscape, the same weather, as Semprun himself. Indeed, Eckermann's published accounts of his conversa-tions with Goethe demonstrate that the two friends were continuously con-cerned with weather,[6] echoing Semprun's narratives. Yet Goethe's approach to weather diverges notably, bearing the Cartesian hallmarks noted by Pres-ner in relation to Goethe's travel writing: he sought to 'bring order to the infinite variety of weather phenomena' (Magnus and Schmid [1906] 2004: 30).[7] He was interested in atmospheric process from the perspective of the scientist, as something to be measured with barometer and thermometer, with a view to predicting an accurate weather forecast (Rickels 2011: 95). Where Goethe was interested in measuring and documenting wind, rainfall and clouds from a distance, Semprun was concerned with the wind that blew against him and the snow that fell around him.

This phenomenological immersion in landscape is central to the way in which his narratives work to dislocate determinative territorialization of the Ettersburg by the Nazis. As suggested in the re-telling of his encounter with Karl Krauss, his engagement with the elements implies that landscape *can* become a democratic platform for empathic engagement, a space in which people may come together in a response to nature; a dialogue foreclosed in Nazism's appropriation of *Heimat* as exclusive to Germanic traditional life. Despite the failure of his attempt, the ethical intention behind it is not defeated. Indeed, his interrogation of *the idea* of Goethe, and its mobilization by National Socialism, unmoors the Nazis' territorialization of the land, undermining the implication that one racial group alone can be exclusively connected to one particular *Heimat*.

And so, Semprun tells Rosenfeld, Goethe wouldn't be a bad beginning. The deep draught of spring has arrived on the Ettersburg, and Buchenwald is liberated. Rosenfeld and Semprun stand together on a stretch of grass outside Goethe's garden house. As Semprun talks to Rosenfeld in Weimar, he enjoys a process of uncovering such connections, which seem to him to be 'quirk[s] of fate'; together they form co-ordinates in a complex yet coherent picture of Weimar-Buchenwald's duality. A few days after his visit to Goethe's house with Rosenfeld, Semprun leaves Buchenwald and Weimar behind him, travels to Paris, and returns to his work as an undercover agent for the Communist Party, not to return for nearly fifty years.

Arrivals: Memory in Place

Semprun initially abhors the notion of returning to Buchenwald in his later life: 'I had spent fifteen years trying not to be a survivor ... the trips organised for the deportees and their families to the sites of the former camps, had always filled me with horror' (*WBS* 22). He also rejected the idea that Buchenwald should one day be a memorial destination for anyone else, although his own return causes him to partially revise this opinion. At the time of liberation, he wishes for 'the camp to be abandoned to the erosion of time, to nature ... to be engulfed by the forest' (*LL* 63). This notion had first appeared in *The Long Voyage*:

> I would like to see that: the grass and the bushes, the roots and brambles encroaching as the seasons go by, beneath the persistent Ettersburg rains... obstinately encroaching, with that excessive obstinacy of natural things, among the cracks in the disjoined wood and the powdery crumbling of the cement

that would split and yield to the thrust of the beech forest, unceasingly en-croaching on this human countryside on the flank of the hill, this camp con-structed by men, the grass and the roots repossessing the place where the camp had stood. (*LV* 189)

Whilst Semprun rejects the notion that Buchenwald could become a memory site of the future, his desire for nature to overcome the camp res-onates with certain contemporary curatorial strategies at former camps, for example at Birkenau, where plants and trees are carefully controlled in order that 'lush vegetation' may lend 'peace to what was once a malevolent land-scape' (Rymaszewski 2004: 24) without interfering with ongoing efforts to preserve authentic structures. Unlike the land managers at Birkenau, how-ever, Semprun is not advocating the maintenance of a balance between ruins and nature that may soothe the spirits of a visitor. He desires the decay of the camp, not its preservation: the return of the trees, the reversal of the Nazis' deforestation of the Ettersburg.

Nonetheless, and contrary to his initial reluctance for the camp to sur-vive as a memorial, Semprun's work provides an exemplary frame of refer-ence for contemporary explorations of the Buchenwald landscape. As earlier foregrounded, Semprun's texts offer a multisensory and multidimensional spatial engagement with the landscapes of Weimar-Buchenwald. In immers-ing himself in the area's cultural history and natural environment, Semprun encounters the space on his own terms, unintentionally presenting the con-temporary explorer with an exemplary methodology which supports both reflexive critical distance and phenomenological inhabitation. Furthermore, Semprun's response to the forty years of commemorative landscaping that shaped Buchenwald between 1950 and 1990 is characterized by the same merciless condemnation that shapes his representations of Goethe's futile humanism. Readers of his work are thus exposed to the same confrontation with Germany's dichotomous history that so troubled the author himself.

Contrary to his 'old dream: that the camp should be left to the slow work of nature', the German commemorative landscape has been constructed:

a memorial, something educational, political, that's what they had built. In any case, it was Bertolt Brecht's idea. It was he who suggested that they build this majestic memorial, opposite the old concentration camp, on the slope lead-ing to Weimar. He had even wanted the figures to be larger than life, carved in stone and placed on a pediment devoid of ornament, taking in with their gaze some majestic amphitheatre. In this amphitheatre a festival would be organised each year in memory of the deportees. Oratorios, works for massed choirs would be performed there. There would be public readings and political appeals … I was well aware that Brecht had often displayed bad taste, but to such an extent, it was unbelievable! (*WBS* 22)

He describes the aforementioned Cremer monument as 'disgusting'. His objections are both aesthetic and polemic, in resonance with critique made in later years in scholarly discourse. As a member of the Communist resistance himself, Semprun was critical of the celebratory rhetoric that defined the memorial and the reality of Buchenwald. He also belies the 'self-liberation' myth presented in the site's first museum, in recollections of the American soldiers who had restored 'essential services ... in order to feed, clothe, care for, and reorganize' Buchenwald's 'several tens of thousands of survivors' (*LL* 29). Given his own later departure from the Communist Party, it is unsurprising that the one-dimensional slant of GDR commemorative architecture failed to appeal to him: 'The masses may make history, but they certainly don't write it. It is the dominant minorities – which on the left are called "vanguards" and on the right, even in the centre, "natural elites" – that write history. And re-write it, if need be, if the need is felt, and, from their dominant point of view need is often felt.' (*WBS* 40).

By 1992 Semprun had published several memoirs, and in so doing had begun the task of locating himself in relation to his past. At this point his return becomes essential to the completion of his testimony, '[t]he only way, in fact, to force me to finish the story' (*LL* 280). Upon arrival he remarks on the contrast between the two areas of the camp, one where the GDR had commissioned the vast memorial complex and the other the void where Special Camp no.2 had stood:

> On one side ... a monstrous and pompous marble monument was supposed to remind people of the misleading (since it was purely symbolic) connection of the Communist regime to the Anti-Fascist struggles of Europe's past. On the other side, a new forest had grown over the boneyards of Communism, to erase their traces in the humble and tenacious memory of the countryside, if not in that of men. (*LL* 306)

At this stage no decisive plans had been formed as to how to include a commemoration of German victims of the Soviet regime. The only commemorative markers for the prisoners of the Soviet regime in 1992 were 'a moving assembly of mismatched crosses'. On contemplating the diversity of the politics laid bare in the landscape, he finds a source of hope:

> It seems only proper to me that reunified, democratic Germany ... anchored in Europe and a possible stabilizing force for its future, should make the Weimar Buchenwald site a place of remembrance, an international centre of democratic reason ... My point is that the same political experiences that have made the history of Germany a tragic history can also allow Germany to take its place in the forefront of a democratic and universalist expansion of the idea of Europe.

And the site of Weimar-Buchenwald could become the symbol of this idea, a place of remembrance and promise. (*LL* 306–7)

Despite his reluctance that camp become a place of pilgrimage, Semprun certainly recognizes its potential as a powerful symbol; that Buchenwald might have a part to play in realizing what Brodzki (2007: 147) describes as his 'longing for freedom, justice, and international solidarity, and his multi-faceted, persistent, and principled attempts to ground a body of political convictions in real possibility'. His hopeful recognition of Buchenwald's promise is echoed in his response to the return of birdsong: 'I heard the myriad murmur of the birds. They had returned to the Ettersburg, after all. The rustle of birdsong surrounded me like the voice of the ocean. Life had returned to the slopes of the Ettersburg' (*LL* 296). He finally achieves, if not restitution for past suffering, a way to envision a future in which such suffering will not be repeated, at least not in this place, and perhaps beyond it.

He also comes to acknowledge the affective impact of the open space where the barracks had once stood (these were levelled as part of the memorial design, and their foundations marked in gravel): 'the effect was incredibly powerful. The empty space thus created, surrounded by barbed wire, dominated by the crematory chimney, swept by the wind of the Ettersburg, was a place of overwhelming remembrance' (*LL* 295). He recognizes this wind: 'The same wind, the same everlasting wind, was blowing across the eternity of the Ettersburg' (291). Indeed, Semprun's environmental memory tropes – the Ettersburg winds, snow and sunshine of his internment – structure his experience of return, just as they structured his memories of Buchenwald through the intervening years.

Place can release memories in the presence of one who remembers, memories 'which belong as much to the place' as to the 'brain or body' (Casey 1996: 25). Arriving in Weimar, Semprun becomes troubled by a vague but persistent sense of déjà vu:

I'd come here in an earlier life, one day in April 1945, with Lieutenant Rosenfeld. I'd forgotten that escapade in Weimar with Rosenfeld. I'd forgotten it so completely that in the first version of this book I hadn't said one word about it … I'd have to reinvent Rosenfeld, in a way: make him rise again from the confused obscurity of my clouded, tattered memory. (*LL* 284)

This capacity for the imaginative reinvention of memory in place is of central significance to my own advocation of Semprun's work as a guide to Buchenwald. Only he could see the reinvented memories place released for him; indeed, since his death in 2011, his seemingly ceaseless past-present remediation is finally at an end. Yet his literary legacy continues to provide a mediatory function; whilst his own endeavour was one of reinvention, in his wake we can, and should, invent anew.

Indeed, Semprun himself seems to advocate literature as a useful tool for the negotiation of space; he makes a careful selection of texts to take with him upon his return to Weimar and Buchenwald. Implicit in his choices is the notion that, beyond framing our experience of concentration camp spaces (as proposed by Jones, see the introduction), particular texts may help us negotiate the relationship between these spaces and their cultural legacies. Semprun's selection included a Thomas Mann novel, *Charlotte à Weimar* ('the Charlotte in question was Goethe's Charlotte' [*LL* 285]), and a volume of correspondence between Heidegger and humanistic German philosopher Karl Jaspers. The third book contained a selection of Paul Celan's poetry, including versions of 'Todtnauberg' – the poem in which the Romanian-Jewish author comes closest to confronting Heidegger with his silence on the Nazi destruction of European Jewry ('The Heideggerian unsaid par excellence: the unsaid of German guilt' [*LL* 290]). It is this poem which brings me to the conclusion of this chapter.

I have implied in my discussion of Semprun that his work guides us away from official commemorative monuments – or at least urges us to be vigilant to their self-referential nature – and towards the 'natural' elements of the landscape: the forest, the weather, the birds, the views over the Ettersburg valley. He is interested, likewise, not in the preserved concrete remnants of the camp but in the 'slow work' of a nature that would obliterate them. Whilst the route maps offered to visitors at Buchenwald are effective in casting 'individual experiences in the mould of shared historical themes' and translating 'the spatiality of historic sites into an itinerary based on geographical contiguity rather than historical chronology' (Azaryahu 2003: 2), Semprun, as a 'victim' who has encountered the landscape on his own terms, compels visitors to do the same, perhaps eschewing the path offered by official discourse.

So central to the official route around the site, the protection of the oak stump seems, in Semprun's work, to be little more than a symbol of 'arboreal rootedness'; I recall Campbell's (2008: 7) mobilization of Deleuze and Guattari, whereby 'the tree typifies [a] limited, rooted model, "hierarchical" and working along "pre-established paths"'. Whilst its meaning as a commemorative monument remains open to speculation, the oak can no longer effectively function simply as a monument to the Goethean era of German cultural history; it cannot but be undermined, even retrospectively, by National Socialism's lack of 'Goethean humanism' – a humanism of exclusion.[8] Semprun guides us, rather, towards a rhizomatic approach: to become 'silent discoverers of [our] own paths' (de Certeau 1988: xiii) and uncover new 'quirks of fate'. Yet there is another, more fundamental guiding premise in Semprun's work that goes beyond urging attention to the paths less travelled.

I would argue, in fact, that it is not particular points in the landscape – or which route we walk to encounter them – that matter so much as the mode of encounter we may have in and with that landscape. The overgrown SS quarters are just as likely to function affectively as all the main stops on the guide book routes.

Semprun reveals to readers his desire for a shared encounter with nature, which I have described as a form of sublime experience. This much is clear in his own ultimately frustrated desire for the SS warrant officer to be 'invaded' by the beauty of the beech. Perhaps it is such an invasion that Semprun's work prompts his readers to find on their own travels to Buchenwald. These two instances of sublime engagement – that of Semprun and that of the visitor in his wake – inevitably take their own respective forms according to the knowledge and experience that mediates the experience. Whilst postmodern re-appraisal of the sublime, particularly in the work of Jean-François Lyotard ([1983] 1988), has posited that the Holocaust itself was an instance of history as sublime and thus beyond either representation or comprehension,[9] I am wary of following such logic; it liberates us from facing the fact that history's atrocities were perpetrated and justified by human beings, legitimizing a mystification of an event 'we dare not understand, because we fear that it may be all too understandable, all too continuous with what we are –human, all too human' (Rose 1996: 43).[10] Instead the possibility may exist for an alternative experience of sublimity; an ecocritical sublime that happens in and through shared human interactions with nature. It is in finding common ground that we might break down destructive distance such as that which existed between the SS warrant officer and 'No. 44904' in 1944.

It is in elucidating the ecocritical sensibilities inherent to the experience of landscape advocated in Semprun's work that a particular reading of Celan's 'Todtnauberg' – a text Semprun himself chose to structure his own experience of return – warrants scrutiny. This interpretation, found in Bate's (2000: 271) work, presents the poem as microcosm of Holocaust territory via Heidegger (who gained 'his sense of identity from his forest dwelling-place') and Celan ('the archetypal wandering Jew, [who] finds no home'). Indeed, the poem is thought to be based on a visit made by Celan to Heidegger's cabin in the Black Forest in 1967; the poet's attempt, as 'an outsider', to 'disrupt the *Heimat* of the philosopher' (Rapaport 1997: 126). Bate focuses on a fragment of the poem concerning orchids ['woodland sward, unlevelled / orchid and orchid, single / course stuff, later, clear in passing'] growing outside Heidegger's cabin:

> when Celan, a Jew and a child of the camps, writes of orchids he invites us to reflect on the sacredness of many diverse forms of life. He permits the comparison which says: without Jews the human race would have been diminished, without orchids the earth would be diminished. ...

[The orchids] which he memorialized in the poem [and] which we imaginatively reanimate when we read the poem, effected for him and may effect for us an unconcealment ... Celan's kind of poetry ... does not admit solution or fixed interpretation. What matters is not the conclusion which we draw about the orchid, but that we are made to attend to the orchid. The poem makes us ask the question concerning the orchid, the question concerning the earth. And that in itself is enough of a beginning. (2000: 272–3)

Semprun's work, like that of Celan, opens itself to many readings. Just as digging into memory does not exhaust it, his mnemonic representations do not pin meanings down. As he listens for bird song and immerses himself in an encounter with the beech, he draws attention to the unique and eternal wind, snow and sunshine of the Ettersburg slopes. These environmental tropes that structure his experience and memory are still part of the Buchenwald landscape today. They are there for us to encounter, just as they were for Goethe, the SS guards, and Semprun himself. What matters in this case is perhaps not the conclusions we may draw about these particular tropes and forms, but the importance of attending to them; of looking at and listening to the world.

I referred earlier in this chapter to Smith's (2005: 219) contention that an immersion in nature is an 'intimate participatory [practice] that draw us closer to others ... giving us a feeling for and an understanding of our relational emplacement within [the] world'. It is with this focus on relational emplacement in mind that I suggest a parallel between such immersion and LaCapra's (2001: 102) discussion about the role of 'empathy in understanding, and its complex relation to objectification and dialogic exchange'. LaCapra's work, as discussed in the introduction, situates this relation specifically in terms of contemplating the past: 'Empathy is bound up with a transferential relation to the past, and is arguably an affective aspect of understanding which both limits objectification and exposes the self to involvement or implication in the past, its actors and its victims.' It is on this foundation that he concludes desirable empathy to involve 'not full identification but what might be termed empathic unsettlement in the face of traumatic events, their perpetrators and their victims' (2001: 102). As such, relational emplacement is fundamental to achieving this balance between full identification and totalizing objectification.

This point draws attention back to the premise with which I began this chapter: that Baer's notion that a survivor's experience is necessarily 'all too much' their own, and that any attempts to inhabit their world – that of the camps – 'through empathic identification and imaginary projection via transferential bonds, [is] illusory at best' requires revision. Semprun's testimony, I have suggested here, does not render his experience 'too much' his own; as he himself questions:

Has one really experienced something that one is unable to describe, something whose minimum truth one is unable to construct in a meaningful way – and so make communicable? Doesn't living, in the full sense of the term, mean transferring one's personal experience into consciousness – that is to say, into memorized experience that is capable at the same time of integration into the future? ... The history – the stories, the narratives, the memories, the eyewitness accounts in which it survives – lives on. The text, the very texture, the tissue of life. (*WBS* 39)

The slopes of the Ettersburg have been the backdrop to a multitude of narratives, both real and imagined. From the dukes of Saxony to the contemporary tourist, the Thuringian forests outside Weimar have continued to attract visitors for hundreds of years. The landscape itself does not 'tell' anything – none of this history is self-evident. Testimonial narratives animate landscapes of atrocity; in the case of Semprun, we are presented with Buchenwald as palimpsest, an example of how 'literary techniques of reading historically, intertextually, constructively and deconstructively at the same time can be woven into our understanding of [memorials] as lived spaces that shape collective imaginaries' (Huyssen 2003: 7). The space is mediated and textualized, as it was for Semprun himself, by German literary and philosophy. Whilst Buchenwald and Weimar, like Semprun's Goethe, may have come to exist in one sense as a *lieu de mémoire,* its meanings are constantly involved in evolutionary processes shaped by a variety of literature and participation.

Notes

1. Hartman refers here to 'Wordsworthian memory places' ("points of connection with another time or place, remembered or imagined" (Whitehead 2003: 288).
2. On 'radical and traumatic displacement' as a result of 'loss and exile' in Semprun's Buchenwald testimonies, see Ursula Tidd (2008); on literary repetition and trauma see Tidd (2005) and Susan Suleiman (2006).
3. The main voice is that of 'Gerard', a young Spanish resistance fighter. Throughout, he remains largely anonymous; however, by the end readers understand 'Gerard' to be Semprun's character's name to his Resistance comrades; he is addressed as 'Manuel' by other Spanish prisoners. This 'doubly displaced' narrator (Jones 2007: 36) switches between different voices – Gerard, Manuel, and an occasional 'I'/'je' – and times – from deportation to arrival at the camp to post-camp experiences.
4. See also Berghahn (2001: 3-15). It is worth noting that in this regard, Goethe's travel writing is radically different from his approach to natural philosophy, which 'rejects by its very definition the hierarchy (ascribed to Plato and Aristotle) of soul over body, Cartesian dualism, and the Kantian emphasis on the subject, because such views deny the interrelatedness and the constant dynamic motion of the phenomena' (Tantillo 2002: 47).

5. At one stage, for example, Semprun notes the German Army's 'revealing military tradition' of using poetic name codes such as *Meerschaum* (Sea Foam) and *Frülingswind* (Spring Wind) for mass deportations of French prisoners in 1944 (*LL* 40).

6. See for example Goethe, Eckermann and Soret DATE 52, 86, 106, 385, and 387.

7. Goethe had himself been responsible for setting up the first government-run weather observations network in 1776 in Sachsen-Weimar (Lamb 1977: 26) and became known late in his lifetime as a keen meteorologist (Magnus and Schmid [1906] 2004: 30).

8. Although it is often assumed that the tree was originally left intact in respect for the memory of this legendary literary figure, as Semprun's Goethe suggests (also see Farmer 1995: 100), the Buchenwald Tour Guide suggests that 'this was due to the fact that the SS had the tendency to see a symbol in the oak rather than any sentimental reminiscences of Goethe' (*BMT* 33). According to Thomas Lekan (2004, 15), throughout the history of German environmental preservation, historic oaks were among the natural features that became 'designated as natural monuments', in line with priorities that 'placed the cultural landscapes of home, not the sublime places of the distant wilderness, at the centre of environmental perception and care'. Indeed, the oak left standing at Buchenwald had been marked on maps of the Ettersburg as the 'Thick Oak' (*BMT* 33), suggesting an existing status as a significant landmark. One contemporary Buchenwald guide book suggests that the tree was significant for the camp prisoners, representing 'unspoilt nature' and 'the positive world' outside the camp (BGE 33). Gorra (2004: 16) speculates that this 'bit of greenery' could, in fact, have sustained or mocked the prisoners, depending on their perspectives.

9. Karyn Ball (2008: 123) has described Lyotard's elevation of the Holocaust's 'moral impact above experience' to 'an "absolute otherness" that transcends imagination'. Given Lyotard's casting of the Holocaust as a postmodern sublime trope, as Ball (2008: 140) points out, it becomes difficult to defend his work from the accusation that he posits 'Auschwitz' as 'a priori* incomprehensible', and that in casting 'Auschwitz' itself as a metonym he encourages us to elide the specificity of the historical/political context in which the Holocaust occurred.

10. Indeed the postmodern sublime arguably constitutes what Rose (1996: 43) calls 'Holocaust piety', casting the Holocaust as both ineffable and beyond representation and resulting in a conflation of 'the search for a decent response to those brutally destroyed ... with the quite different response called for in the face of the "inhuman" capacity for such destruction'. Gross and Hoffman's (2004: 40) work on the reception of Holocaust testimonial literature, as discussed in the introduction, describes the logical outcome of this overextension: 'Since most victims of the Holocaust did not understand what was happening to them or why, contemporary students of the Holocaust should not try to understand either.'

THREE

BUCHENWALD TO NEW ORLEANS

This chapter explores the dynamics of an unlikely discourse of remembrance that brings Buchenwald into a comparative relation with a natural disaster: the Atlantic tropical cyclone, Hurricane Katrina, which struck the Southern American coastline in August 2005. The co-ordinates of this comparative framework stem from journalist Mark Jacobson's investigative travel memoir, *The Lampshade: A Holocaust Detective Story from Buchenwald to New Orleans* (2010). I suggested in the preceding chapter that Semprun's phenomenological engagement with landscape encouraged a form of future-orientated empathic unsettlement. Notable throughout was 'the coincidence in something more than space' that underpinned his critique of Goethean humanism, and his reliance on 'quirks of fate' to bring different times and places together. I argue that Jacobson's book also works towards a future-oriented form of memory work in the wake of suffering and injustice, as he writes towards a redefinition of what constitutes a crime against humanity. In doing so, he seeks the dilution of a binary opposition between human perpetrated atrocity and natural disaster. Like Semprun – whose work Jacobson reads in the course of his research for *The Lampshade* – Jacobson relies on quirks of fate, and interrogates the possible meanings behind geographical co-incidences. He 'was convinced there was a link between the terror of Buchenwald ... and this sad, beaten down New Orleans, where the most recent incarnation of the icon had turned up. But I couldn't quite put it together' (Jacobson 2010: 203). Whilst I suggested that Semprun's work carried an implicitly transcultural insistence on universal ethical engagement, Jacobson's book explicitly engages in a transcultural comparison between Hurricane Katrina and the Holocaust.

Jacobson's initial goal is to return a lost or stolen object – the aforementioned lampshade apparently constructed from human skin – to its proper owner. For Jacobson, the 'proper owner' of the mysterious lampshade is not the person from whose house it was looted in post-Katrina New Orleans, but the person from whom the skin was originally (or might have been) taken.

This goal is fraught with difficulties – the only restitution he can hope to give the dead, he feels, is to find the 'right' thing to do with the lampshade, be it burial, museum display or destruction. He is hampered not only in that his imagined victim is dead, but also by their inevitable anonymity, for whilst an initial forensic analysis suggests that the skin is of human origin, he will never be able to even get close to isolating their ethnicity (which would have consequences for its proper burial). As a result, Jacobson's journey, and his book, turns into an attempt to answer larger and more urgent questions. His desire to provide a form of restitution for one past victim evolves into a broader call for recognition of an intimate relationship between past, present and future forms of violence and the location of structural, institutional evil. It takes in not only the Holocaust and the abandonment of New Orleans's impoverished black citizens during and after Hurricane Katrina, but also the region's roots in African American slavery.

The Holocaust, Hurricane Katrina and African American Slavery

In placing the Nazi Holocaust, U.S. race relations and a natural disaster in dialogue, Jacobson prompts the first of three very different transcultural examinations undertaken in this book. In later chapters, I explore commemorative dynamics which bring events of the Holocaust into comparative relation with 9/11 and the War on Terror (in Part 2), and the Azerbaijan-Armenian conflict (in Part 3). Of all these comparisons, that of the Holocaust with Hurricane Katrina is perhaps the most challenging to navigate, because, unlike all the other events discussed, natural disasters have no human perpetrators. However, if, as Rob Nixon has suggested, we broaden the category of violence to include the impact of climate change, toxic drift and a capitalism that 'writes the land in a bureaucratic, externalising and extraction driven manner' (2011: 17) then a comparative investigation becomes more feasible.

Nixon's primary goal is to find ways of making slow violence visible; fundamentally, a representational challenge. For its disasters are 'slow moving, long in the making … anonymous … and star nobody', unlike those with 'visceral, eye-catching, and page-turning power' (2011: 3), of which 9/11 is perhaps the most paradigmatic example (see 2011: 13). Arguably Hurricane Katrina's arrival in New Orleans falls into the latter category, for it was the subject of immediate and international media attention, and provided viewers with a cast of heroes and villains and visceral, heart-rending evidence of the destructive power of nature. Nonetheless, the slow violence of climate change that foregrounds such extreme weather events remain invisible. Furthermore Nixon's unmooring of what constitutes violence is helpful for attempts to understand the aftermath of Katrina, not least its impact on the lives of New Orleans' poorest communities. Furthermore, examples such as Katrina potentially unsettle Nixon's distinction between slow violence and spectacle, not least because of their contested causal roots in global warming. Tanya Gulliver (2010: 174), in surveying the post-Katrina debate on this issue, reports that '[f]or each person who blames climate change for Katrina's impact, there is another who shouts the opposite'. She posits that, in fact, 'the climate change debate is of little relevance to the people most affected by Katrina', whereas 'environmental degradation and environmental justice are more clearly connected'. It is these elements that have shaped 'the historically-developed vulnerabilities of the communities' most affected by the disaster (2010: 174). The poorest – and often black – communities rendered vulnerable by history, many of whom lived in the areas most affected by the flooding, became Katrina's 'dispensable citizens'. Suffice to say, whether or not one agrees that Katrina was a result of climate change, elements of environmental slow violence contributed to the scale and nature of the devastation caused by Katrina.

The scale and nature of this devastation has been discussed in detail elsewhere, and subjected to interpretation from scholars across a number of disciplines as well as in the media and in cultural texts. This is not the place for a full overview of Katrina's impact or the resulting discourse. Nonetheless, it is worth briefly considering some key points, not least as these underpin Jacobson's text. Rather than dwelling in particular detail on who suffered most, and who was responsible for this suffering, Jacobson relies on his reader's familiarity with related debates, in particular those concerning racial inequality. He does, however, trace the history of racial conflict in New Orleans, including race riots, Homer Plessy's pivotal but failed challenge to 'separate but equal' Jim Crow legislation in 1892, and well-known examples of lynching (Jacobson 2010: 195–99). He then brings his brief history up to date with a description of Bush's clumsy speech at a memorial event on the second anniversary of the disaster: 'One of the things people said about Katrina was that it pulled the covers off the question of race in America. Maybe for out-of-towners it did. But few in the Crescent City needed Kanye West to tell them that George Bush didn't care about black people' (2010: 200). Over the course of these five pages, Jacobson situates racial inequality in Louisiana as historically and politically rooted, an unsurprising thesis commensurate with scholarly discussion. Thadious Davis (2011: 187) comments that, since the time when '[s]lavery structured spheres of production and power', the South continues 'to call up ... a racial dynamic marked by fixity and rigidity, lines and division, boundaries and binaries'; in New Orleans after Katrina this racial division was more pronounced than any time since the civil rights movement. The evidence Davis mentions for this pronouncement – 'stranded black citizens', 'abandoned in untenable public structures' and 'demonized and slandered in the grossest of stereotypical labels' (2011: 187) – are the same instances that surface at intervals throughout Jacobson's book. Whilst contextual specificities forbid the forging of easy comparisons between, for example, German–Jewish and white–African American race relations, 'boundaries and binaries' are shared structural premises.

Perhaps the spaces generated by Katrina's aftermath that resonate most obviously with those of the Holocaust are those of the 'untenable public structures', such as the New Orleans Superdome and the Ernest N. Morial Convention Center, after the breaching of the Seventeenth Street Canal on 30 August. In the following days 38,000 people were relocated to these two sites alone (Barnshaw and Trainor 2007: 100). The overcrowding, shortage of basic resources, and rumoured reports of rape, looting and piles of murdered bodies made such rescue sites microcosms of the chaos of the city as a whole. The report published by the Bipartisan Committee to Investigate the Preparation for and Response to Hurricane Katrina (commissioned by the House of Representatives), stated that the conditions at the convention center and the Superdome 'resembled concentration camps': 'internment without adequate food, water or sanitation, and a growing sense of helplessness' (Davis 2006: 497). Similarly, in the congressional hearing held 100 days after Katrina at which New Orleans residents described their experiences, the activist Leah Hodges (2009: 219) described how she was 'lured' to a 'so-called' evacuation point:

> Soldiers … loaded us onto military trucks after they told us they would take us to shelters where our basic needs would be met.
>   We were dropped off at a site where we were fenced in, and penned in with military vehicles. The armed military personnel brought in dogs. There we were subjected to conditions only parallel to a concentration camp … During the days we were exposed to hot sun … Our skin blistered. My mother's skin is still not fully healed.

She goes on to describe surroundings mired in 'muck and trash', deliberate 'sleep deprivation' caused by low-flying helicopters; 'They set us up so that we would rebel, so they could shoot us. At one point they brought in two truckloads of dogs and let the dogs out' (Hodges 2009). In conjunction with Hodges' claim that 'nearly all the white people had been selected to evacuate first … leaving the population 95 per cent black' (2009), her account overall posits New Orleans' evacuation points as zones of racially motivated persecution, and even murder, rather than mere mismanaged refuges.

Experiential comparisons between victims of the Nazi Holocaust and those that formed the backdrop of African American slavery could also certainly be made, not least according to the way I have conceptualized topographies of suffering in this book. Clearly, both genocides created spaces of forced labour and interrupted pastoral sentimental visions of man's harmonious relationship with landscape. Slavery itself is perhaps the example most frequently mobilized alongside the Holocaust in zero-sum memory debates. It is no coincidence that Rothberg (2009: 1–4) draws on this very debate to introduce his alternative to competitive memory, multidirectionality. Indeed, slavery, like the Holocaust, has been said to challenge scholarly understanding, 'a candidate for uniqueness' (Drescher 2009: 158) that calls the singularity of the Holocaust into question. It is not the desire of this chapter to either summarize or add to this debate. Furthermore, as Naomi Mandel warns, '[p]utting the Holocaust in dialogue with slavery in America neglects the different methods and manners of these genocides, the ideologies under which they were conceived, and the means by which they were carried out'. Such debates, and responses to them, 'raise the complex implications' of comparisons between 'the extent, degree, and clout of … respective victimizations' (2006: 170).

Yet Jacobson's investigation is not, in fact, primarily concerned with comparative suffering, or even with its cross-cultural relatability. Whilst alert to these issues he is more concerned with uncovering particular political, cultural and socioeconomic conditions that create landscapes in which diverse forms of violence occur and new victims are created. It is these structural co-ordinates and their re-casting of landscape that emerge as the primary concerns in the forthcoming analysis. As such, whilst he does explicitly put the Holocaust in *dialogue* with African American slavery, there is a notable attempt to tackle the method, manner and ideology of his respective case studies. In moving from Buchenwald to New Orleans, Jacobson is not attempting equation, but, theoretically and physically, travelling *from* one *to* the other. Nonetheless, in his travels his approach to landscape echoes the experiential immersion found in Semprun's work, certainly in his attention to the ideologies that shape them. Furthermore, like Semprun, his narration is structured according to the paths he travels. I go on to explore how his journey unravelled, and its implications for comparative discourse.

The Forest to the Flood

From the beginning of his book, Jacobson implicitly draws on the connective tissues that bind landscape settings of diverse violations of human rights and bring different forms of violence together. Having grown up with the 'myth' that the Nazis made objects from human skin, for Jacobson the origin of the *story* of the lampshade (although not necessarily the lampshade itself) was unquestionably Buchenwald, and the infamous wife of its one-time commandant, Ilse Koch: 'If you're interested in a lampshade allegedly made out of human skin, Buchenwald is the place' (2010: 12). In an explanation echoing the method of travel and exploration discussed earlier in this book, Jacobson 'thought that seeing these things would provide context, a way to collate the experience of standing in the cold with what can be read in books and movies' and famous images of the camp by photo-journalists such as Margaret Bourke-White. He thus visits Buchenwald, which is '[s]ocked in by fog', on his arrival. 'So many had died here. At any moment I expected them to assemble in their striped pajamas for yet another roll call' (2010: 93). As in Semprun's account, Buchenwald becomes a porous space of encounter.

Also much like Semprun, Jacobson finds Goethe a good starting point for his investigation. His opening chapter begins with an image of Goethe walking through the Ettersburg forest, saying to Eckermann: 'This is a good place ... here we feel great and free... as we always ought to be' (2010: 7). Jacobson then moves on to trace the now familiar story of Goethe's oak – Nazi protection, its possible effects on inmates, its place in the contemporary memorial complex[1] – before narrating his own contemporary journey to Buchenwald, a 'trip appalling mostly in its ease' in comparison to former inmate deportation (2010: 10). He makes this journey to show the lampshade to the curators and ask for their assistance in tracing its history, but also to unravel a less tangible and perhaps more urgent mystery: the meaning of the quirk of fate that led the lampshade to surface in New Orleans; like the geographical proximity of Buchenwald and Weimar, this is his co-incidence in something more than space.

Jacobson interviews a comprehensive range of people in his quest to find out where the lampshade came from, beginning with the medical examiners who had honed their forensic methodologies working on fragments of bodies in the wake of 9/11, New Orleans spiritualists, notable Holocaust scholars and deniers, and curators from Yad Vashem and the USHMM as well as the Buchenwald memorial. Amongst this array of disparate commentators is a historian from El Paso, Texas, named Albert Rosenberg, who he hears had been at the liberation of the camp and been involved in presenting evidence to the press about the atrocities uncovered (including shrunken heads and human skin objects). Rosenberg, it turns out – unbeknownst to Jacobson, who has not yet encountered Semprun's writing – is none other than *Literature or Life*'s Lt. Rosenfeld. He tells Jacobson that Semprun's comments about the Ettersburg birds had prompted a discussion between them about what the essence of an experience of Buchenwald might be. They agreed, he reports, that this came down to an experience of radical evil, an evil which is not 'inhuman' but rather is fundamental to 'humanity'. As Rosenberg explains: 'It's ridiculous to oppose Evil, to distance oneself from it, through a simple reference to what is human ... Evil is ... the freedom from which spring both the humanity and inhumanity of man.' Jacobson decides that, after Nuremberg, 'the innate righteousness of the species was called into question, the argument that one group might be guilty of the crimes *against* humanity [lost] credence to the idea that genocidal incidents were really crimes *of* humanity' (2010: 107). Echoing Adorno and Horkheimer's position on human barbarism in *Dialectics of Enlightenment,* Jacobson's uncertainty about what a crime against humanity constitutes, underpins the comparative framework of his later investigations.

Before leaving, Jacobson asks Rosenfeld how he ended up living in El Paso. Rosenfeld replies that it was 'a place to hide' (although he fails to state what from). But 'eventually, you realise there's no escaping, no matter how far you go' (2010: 169). He goes on to describe the drug wars that had given El Paso a murder rate triple that of Detroit, amongst them the murder of women. 'Women are killed and have their organs removed. They're left hollowed out corpses ... They say its drug cartels, or some cult that uses the body parts ... Over and over the same thing happens. It is so horribly familiar. Evil, radical evil— everywhere you go, there it is' (2010: 170). In mentioning parts removed from bodies, Rosenfeld himself draws an implicit comparison between the El Paso murder victims and Buchenwald's dead, and it seems to be his own past, his role as a witness to the atrocities of the camp, from which he had attempted to escape in his move to Texas. This notion of universal pervasive violence also shapes the questions Jacobson asks from this point on.

A New Orleans musician, when asked for any reason, practical or otherwise, why a lampshade identified with Nazi concentration camps would turn up in New Orleans, suggests the existence of a broad comparative framework, including the Holocaust and Louisiana's past, both as a slave state and, more recently, as the site of Katrina's most deadly phase. The co-ordinates in this comparative framework – the Holocaust, slavery and Hurricane Katrina – stem from 'institutional evil': 'Slavery was an institutional evil. What happened down here in Katrina was like that, the way the wetlands were eaten away, the way the city's run, the way the private armies moved in, what you had with Bush. A whole way of life being swept away. That's the institutional evil. *Nazi evil*' (2010: 204). Probing this notion, Jacobson turns to an article by New Orleans Confederate and newspaper editor Henry Hearsey from 1900, on 'The Negro Problem and the Final Solution', 'more than forty years before the Nazis used the phrase at the Wannsee conference' (2010: 195). The article called for a race war which, although might result in some 'regrettable' white casualties, would solve Louisiana's Negro problem through 'extermination'.

With the lampshade's possible construction in Buchenwald in mind, Jacobson goes on to mention a case of lynching in which portions of the body and pieces of skin were removed by spectators as souvenirs. Jacobson refers here to the lynching of Sam Hose, a black man accused of the murder of his employer and rape of his employer's wife, in 1899. Jacobson (2010: 202) further concretizes this implied connection between the Holocaust and the racial violence of the turn-of-the-century American South in his juxtaposition of two photographs: one an anonymous black man tied by the neck to a tree and surrounded by a mob, and the other of Masha Bruskina, a Byelorussian Jewish Communist Partisan being hung by SS officers. Jacobson is by no means the first to suggest comparisons between images of African American lynchings and unrelated acts of violence; as Edwin T. Arnold (2012: 5) remarks in his examination of cultural memories of Sam Hose, similarities have been noted between these photos and those taken of prisoners being tortured by members of the U.S. Army at Abu Ghraib in Iraq between 2003 and 2004. Arnold suggests that, rather than 'equating these actions unconditionally', such comparisons alert us to the fact 'that anxious times may result in similar responses … the world of 1899 Georgia may not be as foreign to ours as we might wish to think' (2012: 5). Jacobson similarly implies certainly a representational, and perhaps a deeply structural, proximity shared by the violent persecution of the Jews and that of former African American slaves.

This representational proximity is pronounced in a broader comparison of lynching photographs with hangings committed at and surrounding Buchenwald. This pronouncement stems from the similarity of the forested backdrops in several notable cases, including images of the hanging of Buchenwald inmates in the Thuringian woods[2] and a significant number of the most circulated souvenir photographs of lynching attacks (see Allen 2000). Just as lynching became culturally 'acceptable' within 'the same value system that idealized [the] soft breezes, magnolia trees, gallantry, and politeness' (Martin 2007: 95) of the agrarian South, the Buchenwald hangings were rendered justifiable according National Socialist hierarchy of human life despite their continued homage to the majesty of German forests. These visual records present the disruption of pastoral landscapes with figures of extreme violence and suffering, echoing Young's description of the unseemly beauty of concentration camp landscapes; these images, to reiterate Lindenberger's discussion of the pastoral as cited in the introduction, show us 'island[s] in time' which gain 'meaning and intensity through the tensions [they create] with the historical world' (Lindenberger in Peck 1992: 75), in these instances the worlds of the genteel South and Goethe's Thuringian *Heimat*.

Occupied with the causal factor – racial violence – behind these disrupted pastorals, Jacobson next turns to David Duke, 'Louisiana's most famous fascist'; for: 'If you happen to be in possession of a lampshade possibly made in a German concentration camp that turned up in a flooded building in New Orleans after the storm of the century and you want to find someone who best personifies the psychic connection between those two points, David Duke is your man' (2010: 243). Duke, who in his early years had appeared in public wearing a Ku Klux Klan hood and hosted a birthday parties for Hitler at Louisiana State University, entered politics as a Republican candidate in the late 1980s (2010: 244). Despite losing to Democrat Edwin Edwards in his bid to become governor of Louisiana, Jacobson reports that this well-known racist received 55 per cent of the white vote (2010: 245). In reciting Duke's history, Jacobson implies an indictment of Louisiana's white voting community, alerting readers to undercurrents of racial discrimination in the region. Nonetheless, even this 55 per cent eventually abandoned their support for Duke; Jacobson puts this down to the breakdown of the Republican's 'regular-Christian-guy pose' upon the publication of his deeply racist autobiography, which contained fantastical claims concerning the low IQs of African Americans and the nefarious methods of 'Jewish-controlled media' in their attempts to cover up the 'Aryan gene' (2010: 245). It is unsurprising then, that Duke places responsibility for chaos in the aftermath of Katrina in the hands of New Orleans' black citizens. 'Face it,' he tells Jacobson, 'black people were out of control in those streets ... New Orleans was so far gone before Katrina that the disaster was inevitable ... race is the natural order of things' (2010: 249). For those such as Duke, as Jacobson comments elsewhere in the text, it was no mistake that 'Katrina' can be traced to *katheros*, the Greek for 'cleansing' (2010: 39). Whilst the photographic images of lynched African Americans and Jewish prisoners seem to disrupt natural scenery with figures of atrocious violence, Duke's final comment exemplifies the discourses of naturalization that create a world in which such violence can occur; indeed, a world in which violence becomes a 'cleansing' force. These discourses, through which the 'science' of eugenics is filtered into social worlds, are universal precursors to atrocious acts from lynching to genocide.

Confluences such as those discussed above – representations of disrupted pastoral landscapes, institutional 'evil', the bounded binaries of racial inequality and its naturalization – contribute something to explaining the link Jacobson perceives between Buchenwald and New Orleans. Nixon's description of land written 'in a bureaucratic, externalising and extraction driven manner that is often pitilessly instrumental' seems particularly pertinent to this link. Just as at Buchenwald, where the Nazis deforested the Goethean Ettersburg outside Weimar to build the largest concentration camp in Germany, towards the end of his book Jacobson remarks that Hurricane Katrina 'laid a brutal kind of poetry on New Orleans, created a one-of-a kind landscape of desolation in the country's most romanticized city' (2010: 306). In each distinct case, ideological instrumentalism is fundamental to the evolution of the landscapes in question.

Jacobson does not find the answer to his questions about the lampshade during the course of writing his book, and the issue of what to do with it remains unresolved.[3] But some elements of his attempt to unravel connections between Buchenwald and New Orleans are more conclusive. One of the last images Jacobson presents to his readers is based on a story told to him by Holocaust survivor and New Orleans resident Henry Galler. Amongst Galler's list of possessions lost in Katrina was a piece of soap he claimed was made from bodies in the concentration camps; 'kept all these years, dissolved in the flood' (2010: 311). The dissolving soap functions as a symbol of a key recognition Jacobson's book demands: that confluences exist between different forms of naturalized violence. Furthermore, implicit in his book as a whole is the acknowledgement that the term 'crimes against humanity' fails to accommodate the very human nature of genocidal destruction, just as the designation of events like Katrina as 'natural' elides crucial issues of human culpability. Finally, both Semprun and Jacobson prompt us to honour past suffering by attending to others in the present and future: Semprun, in his desire to see Buchenwald as a centre for Democratic reason, and Jacobson in his in dedication to disrupting binary oppositions between past and contemporary violence. Their narratives imply what could be described as a future-oriented awareness of the past that seeks to arrest apparently unending cycles of violence in all its many forms.

That the destruction of the environment exists in intimate relation to man's destruction of man is slowly beginning to emerge in studies of genocide and climate change. Mike Davis, for example, proposes that apparently 'natural' disasters are rarely divorced from cultural activity; Victorian 'imperial policies towards starving subjects' were in fact the 'exact moral equivalents' of the bombs dropped on Hiroshima, Nagasaki and Dresden (2002: 22). Indeed, he echoes Levene's (2004: 440) aforementioned suggestion that '[a] world without genocide can only develop in one in which principles of equity, social justice, *environmental stability* – and one might add genuine human kindness – have become the "norm"' (my emphasis). For Levene, man's behaviour on earth has exacerbated the power relationships between both 'man and nature' and 'man and man' (Levene 2011). To view these disintegrations in isolation is both critically short-sighted and potentially ethically irresponsible. There is a pressing need to contemplate the relationship between ecological destruction and genocide, an issue which implicitly relates to the way in which the Holocaust and other atrocious historical events are assimilated and represented. Semprun and Jacobson's works imply that we should start recognizing the ground that is shared by superficially distinct categories of genocidal and environmental violence, and that one way of doing so is to look to the landscapes left in its wake.

Coda

I first visited Buchenwald in April 2008. My visit was not planned to coincide with the anniversary of the camp's liberation so central in Semprun's work, but was merely a matter of convenience. It was early in April, the wind was biting, and the snow was still clinging to the Ettersburg slopes. But spring was in the wings: crocuses and violets were poking their noses through the snow-covered leaf mulch.

It would be sentimental to trace out every part of that site that resonated with Semprun's narratives. It would also be out of place, because despite the emphasis throughout this chapter on both Semprun's work and the cultural history of Weimar and the Ettersburg landscape, the point of this argument is that everyone takes something with them when they experience a site – that it is, and can be, different for everyone; that is the beauty and capacity of spatial experience. However, I will mention one place where thought about Semprun and his stories of Buchenwald.

There is an avenue of trees that leads up to the main gate of the camp. Today, this avenue is not the first stop on a tour of the camp, as it is now pre-

Figure 3.1. Violas © Charlotte Rea

Figure 3.2. Walking traces © Charlotte Rea

ceded by the museum shop, canteen, information centre and various other necessary tourist amenities. I walked along this avenue and two of Semprun's stories came into my mind.

The first was the story of the beech that he pretended he thought was Goethe's tree in order to avoid a beating from the SS. The other is infinitely less peaceful, one of the few passages in Semprun's Buchenwald texts in which he retells in minute detail the 'suffering and horror' he had always been so reluctant to avoid in his representations. The story involves the arrival of a group of Jewish children from a Polish camp in the last winter of the war. He seems compelled to tell the story for the sake of the children, although it had 'lain buried' in his memory 'like some mortal treasure' until he wrote *The Long Voyage* (*LV* 162). He stands on the road leading to the camp:

> That was the day I saw the Jewish children die … Suddenly, in the snow on the station platform, amid the snow-covered trees, there was a group of Jewish children, about fifteen in all, gazing about with an air of amazement, looking at the corpses piled up as the trees of trunks already stripped of their bark are piled along the side of the roads, waiting to be taken somewhere else, looking

at the trees and the snow on the trees, looking like children do ... the S.S. loosed their dogs and began to hit the children with their clubs, to make them run, so that the hunt along the avenue could get underway ... And the children were running ... their legs were moving awkwardly, slowly and jerkily, as in the old silent films, as in nightmares when you run with all your might and can't move a step and the thing pursuing you is going to overtake you, and does overtake you and you awake in a cold sweat, and that thing, that pack of dogs and S.S., running behind the Jewish children, soon engulfed the weakest among them, the ones who were only eight years old, perhaps the ones who no longer had the strength to move, who were knocked down, trampled on, clubbed to the ground, who lay there on the avenue, their skinny disjointed bodies marking the progress of that hunt, of that pack swarming over them. And soon there were only two left, one big one small, both having lost their caps in their mad race, and their eyes were shining like splinters of glass in their grey faces, and the little one began to fall behind, the S.S. were howling behind them and then the dogs began to howl too, the smell of blood was driving them mad, and then the bigger of the two children slowed his pace to take the hand of the smaller, who was already stumbling, and together they covered a few more yards, the older one's right hand clasping the smaller younger one's left hand, running straight ahead till the blows of the clubs felled them and, together they dropped, their faces to the ground, their hands clasped for all eternity. The S.S. collected their dogs, who were growling, and walked back in the opposite direction, firing a bullet point blank into the head of each child who had fallen on the broad avenue, beneath the empty gaze of the Hitlerian eagles. (*LV* 163–66)

I remembered this part of *The Long Voyage* when I visited Buchenwald and walked down that road whilst keeping one eye out for Semprun's beech. It has remained a piece of testimony that never loses its emotional affectivity through repeated reading. Just as Semprun struggled with the memory of the way the children died on the road, I struggled with the attempt to comprehend his memories. For, as Semprun admitted, to 'tell about all that death' would take 'several lifetimes'. There is no way in which one person can empathize to the extent that they entirely identify with the suffering of another, but on that day I was perhaps standing in the best possible place to try, just as Semprun's writing constitutes his own necessarily never-ending attempts to tell. And as far as this argument is concerned, the ethical significance lies not in the result, but in the fundamental nature of the attempt.

Notes

1. In this account, the idea of Goethe is as powerful as it was for Semprun, although Jacobson (2010: 9) takes a position closer to those such as Rost, citing that 'Goethe's story was so big that everyone in the camp could envision its author on their side'.

2. See for example photographs of the public execution of twenty Polish inmates near Poppenhausen, Thuringia, in 1942, by an anonymous photographer in the Thuringisches Staatsarchiv Meiningen, and artistic representations by inmates such as Karl Schulz's *Tree-Hanging* (1943) in the Gedenkstätte Buchenwald collection.

3. Developments in forensic testing facilitated new tests on the lampshade after the completion of Jacobson's book, and confirmed that the lampshade was made from cow hide, revealing the earlier analysis of human skin to be inaccurate (National Geographic 2012). For the purposes of this chapter, this result is of no particular significance, as the journey pursued by Jacobson its focus rather than the precise origins of object that inspired it.

PART II

BABI YAR

Stop! – for thy tread is on an Empire's dust!
An Earthquake's spoil is sepulchred below!
Is the spot mark'd with no colossal bust?
Nor column trophied for triumphal show?
None; but the moral's truth tells simpler so,
As the ground was before, thus let it be; –
How that red rain hath made the harvest grow!
—George Byron, *The Complete Works of Lord Byron*

The following three chapters examine, in turn, two landscapes 6,000 miles apart, both of which serve as memorials to a Holocaust massacre committed at Babi Yar [tr. *Grandmother's Ravine*] in Kiev, Ukraine: the ravine and the Babi Yar Park in Denver, Colorado. Each of these transcontinental co-ordinates in contemporary Ukrainian Holocaust memory is the result of a dialogue between distinctive cultural groups. Accordingly, these places direct attention to the various transcultural affinities and tensions that have alternately driven or hindered their development as commemorative landscapes. Levy and Sznaider's thesis on Holocaust memory in the global age urges us to 'uncover memoryscapes that correspond to emerging modes of identification' (2006: 2); this chapter takes up this challenge, and in doing so attempts an evaluation of ethical and political implications of the identificatory modes these particular memoryscapes reveal – and also those they refuse.

As in East Germany, political regimes in Ukraine have had a significant impact on the representation of the Holocaust in public space. In both countries, the collapse of European Communism in 1991 has had a decisive and clearly visible impact. Like Buchenwald, Babi Yar lies on the outskirts of a city, on the periphery of everyday activity. However, while Buchenwald became a place of commemoration immediately after the camp's liberation in 1945, Babi Yar remained an unmarked chasm in the earth for many years. Due to the political marginalization of the Holocaust in Ukraine, no official

commemorative monuments appeared at the site until 1976. Whilst Buchenwald has been used to exemplify the multifaceted ways in which a landscape can be seen to remember, in comparison Babi Yar has for decades been
an example of what appears to be its amnesia. Between the end of the war
and the collapse of the Soviet Union, there was little recognition that the
events of the Holocaust had even touched Ukrainian territory. Even after
1991, when the political situation became more conducive to an exploration
of the Ukrainian Holocaust, its memory has been significantly marginalized;
the focus of official commemorative activity has instead been the Great Famine, or *holodomor*, which took place in 1932–3.[1] Millions of Ukrainians died
of starvation and related diseases during this period. Whilst historians argue
over exact figures as well as exact causes (the official status of the *holodomor*
as a genocide is still contested), there is little doubt that the Soviet government under Stalin were partially culpable for the extent of the famine, and
none that they later denied it had ever happened (Ellman 2007: 663–93).

Chapter 4, 'Marginalized Memories', explores Babi Yar itself within the
Kiev landscape, revealing the impact of the faltering history of Ukrainian
Holocaust commemorative activity on the site of the massacre. This activity
is only now beginning to occur at Babi Yar on a scale comparable to Holocaust sites in other European countries. Rather than positing the Holocaust
as a unique event in Ukrainian history, I then deliberately discuss the years
1941–5 within a broader context, with a particular emphasis on the intimate
relationship between the nation's people and their land. The analysis focuses
specifically on the years immediately preceding the Holocaust, during which
this relationship was significantly disrupted by the *holodomor*. In a scrutiny of
testimony from Ukrainian sources I demonstrate a pronounced experiential
parallel between the *holodomor* and the Holocaust. This analysis leads me
to suggest that it may be possible to productively dilute the competitiveness
which has come to characterize the relationship between the Holocaust and
the *holodomor* in Ukrainian memory discourses today by considering the various individual memories involved according to a multidirectional logic; that
is, by acknowledging the 'ongoing negotiation, cross-referencing, and borrowing' to which such memories are subject (Rothberg 2009: 3).

Chapter 5, 'Babi Yar's Literary Journey', discusses the mobilization of testimony in fiction as mediation and remediation (see Erll and Rigney 2009),
a dynamic journey which introduced the story of Babi Yar to a transcultural
audience, and which can be understood to give readers an increased sense
of engagement with the events that took place at Babi Yar in 1942. Thus
literature in this chapter is cast as a form of memorial displacement which
is more often productive than destructive. Through this mediation the site
of the Babi Yar massacre has come to shape related memorial discourses
and commemoration, including the creation of the Babi Yar Park in Den-

ver. The analysis of the park in the final chapter of this section, 'Kiev to Denver', discusses the geographical displacement and de-territorialization of memory which informed its inauguration. Originally landscaped in the 1970s and 1980s, the site of the park bears a topographical similarity to Babi Yar itself, and integrates elements which notably reinforce the tropes identified in related literature in the preceding section, relying heavily on the signification of soil and topography as vessels of memory. The park in Denver fell into relative disuse in the decade after its inauguration (Young 1994: 296). It is now being redeveloped and reorientated. The design proposed for this new landscape retains many existing elements but, as I will argue, also notably engages with contemporary discourses around commemorative politics, focusing particularly on visitor engagement and the contextualization of the original massacre within an international history of genocide. Rhetoric around the redevelopment is particularly rooted in forging links between the Holocaust and the War on Terror, and thus prompts an interrogation of certain ethical issues and implications raised by comparative, transcultural models of remembering and commemoration.

As the new project in Denver gets underway, the status of the original site in Kiev remains controversial. In concluding the chapter, I return to this landscape. As previously noted, the *holodomor* has somewhat dominated Ukrainian memory discourses and commemorative activity since 1991, whilst the Holocaust has been comparatively marginalized. In 2010 tentative council plans to build a hotel on the Babi Yar site to accommodate soccer fans for the 2012 European Championships were leaked to the press, prompting national and international outrage, particularly from Jewish groups (Beaumont 2009). The plans were withdrawn. In April 2011, the council announced a competition for the design of a memorial complex for the Babi Yar site. Although little has been heard since of this competition, the reinvigoration of interest in the site that occurred in Kiev, and throughout Jewish organizations worldwide, on the occasion of the seventieth anniversary of the massacre has resulted in a new announcement: that two Holocaust museums are to be built in Kiev, one at the Babi Yar site (Shefler 2011). These plans, and their implications for the memorial discourse surrounding the Ukrainian Holocaust, will be considered in Chapter 6. I suggest that an increased recognition of the Holocaust within this agenda may not necessarily result in a decreased acknowledgement of the *holodomor* as central to Ukrainian memory; rather, in focusing on certain commonalities of Holocaust and *holodomor* experiences, it may be possible to resist the competitive logic that has characterized recent national memorial discourse, and replace it with something more productive and democratic. Arguably, such a multidirectional approach may be more legitimately employed here than in the Babi Yar park in Denver, where the attempt to integrate the Ukrainian Holocaust within the context

of the War on Terror raises troubling questions about the conflation of comparatively unrelated historical events. In both cases, I will be asking if it
is possible for a form of genuinely 'differentiated solidarity' to emerge from
dialogical commemorative endeavours; that is, whether they enable us 'to
distinguish different histories of violence while still understanding them as
implicated in each other and as making moral demands for recognition that
deserve consideration' (Rothberg in Moses and Rothberg 2014: 33).[2]

Notes

1. The word *holodomor* is based on the Ukrainian words *holod* (starvation) and *moryty*
   (to kill or induce suffering) (Golson, Penuel and Statler 2011: 304); there is no ety-
   mological similarlity between the terms *holodomor* and Holocaust. .
2. Originally employed by Iris Young (2000: 155–178) to describe a democratic form of
   local governance, Rothberg adopts the term 'differentiated solidarity' here to articulate a potentially desirable element of transcultural memory discourse.

MARGINALIZED MEMORIES

From September 1941 to 1943, Babi Yar was used by Nazi *Einsatzgruppen* squads as a place of slaughter and mass burial. In excess of 100,000 people, including Jews, Roma and Soviet prisoners of war were killed here, their bodies burnt and their ashes buried in the ravine. During an initial massacre over two days (29–30 September) in 1941, 33,771 of these people were shot in the largest isolated killing operation of World War II. Today Babi Yar lies on the outskirts of Kiev within a public park which is roughly a kilometre in size. The exact position of the original ravine is no longer discernible, although several ravines shape the landscape woodland, lawns and paths. There are two distinct sections; one contains nearly all the officially inaugurated Babi Yar memorials including a central monument to slain Soviet citizens and a vast bronze sculpture group of oversized figures looming over this half of the park.

Figure 4.1. Soviet-era monument

Eight other memorials to various groups and individuals have since been added there.[1] One might easily assume that the broad, sweeping ravine at the centre of this space is the original site of the massacre. The landscape aesthetic in this area is more formal and manicured in appearance than in the other half, which is partially quite densely wooded, and to casual observation looks much as any other large city park.

Figure 4.2. Preparations for seventieth anniversary events

Figure 4.3. Babi Yar Park, Kiev

A stone menorah is one of the few memorials to be found in this second half of the park, and this is rumoured to be much closer to the original ravine than the Soviet sculpture group (although there is no way one could know this without researching the subject), and indeed there is an overgrown ravine just south of the menorah, which can be reached from the other half of the park by walking along a path named 'the Road of Grief'. As one landscape, the park is a somewhat incoherent space. Each memorial bears little stylistic resemblance to those around it. Signage has recently been added on the northern edge of the park to show visitors where each official memorial is (in Ukrainian only). In September 2011 temporary banners were also positioned at intervals over the roads around the park announcing the seventieth year since the massacre. Otherwise there has been scant evidence of any attempt to provide an overall view of the landscape's history or of how, or exactly where, so many people of diverse cultural groups came to lose their lives here.

The incoherence of Babi Yar's landscape can be related in part to its slow and fractious development as a memoryscape, which corresponds to the larger context of Ukrainian Holocaust memory. Of the approximate 4 million Ukrainians and Jews killed during the Holocaust in Ukraine, up to 150,000 were killed and buried at Babi Yar. As in other locations throughout the country, victims were shot and their bodies thrown in a freshly dug pit. Many elements that characterize the landscape of the Ukraine Holocaust can be observed at Babi Yar; it is in some respects a microcosm of the larger topography of the country as a whole. In Patrick Desbois's account,[2] the full impact of this campaign emerges. 'The landscape of Ukraine, village after village,

Figure 4.4. Menorah

east to west, was transforming itself under my eyes into an ocean of extermi-
nations … The horrors of the Holocaust were not necessarily the same from
one place to another, but they did unfortunately cover the whole country
without exception' (2008: 147). His narrative is not one of isolated atrocities
but of an apparently endless landscape of burnt bodies, offering a powerful
image of nation-space as cemetery: 'I imagine that if we could open all the
mass graves we would have to take aerial photos of the whole of Ukraine.
A mass cemetery of anonymous pits … Not a camp but a country of graves'
(2008: 178).[3]

As elsewhere in Ukraine, commemoration of the Holocaust at Babi Yar
preceding the fall of Communism in 1991 was notable mainly in its absence,
reflecting the pervasive silence about the Holocaust in Ukrainian territory under the Soviet government. Indeed, the concept of the 'Holocaust in Ukraine'
has existed only on the margins of academic perception for many years, and
in some respects this trend persists (see Brandon and Lower 2008: 2–6; Shapiro 2008: viii). The complex and troubling history of Ukrainian anti-Semitism and complicity in Nazi atrocities (see Dean 2003: 20, 101–102), which
for many years has been elided in national discourses, may be in part responsible for the long delays between the events of the Holocaust in Ukraine and
their commemoration in public space. Brandon and Lower (2008: 6) also
note that for a long time, and for understandable reasons, interest in the
Holocaust was characterized by what they dub 'Auschwitz Syndrome': 'many
historians, philosophers, and political scientists as well as the general public
focused on the killing centres and methods used to deport Jews' to the camps;
'country and regional studies had to wait'. Ukraine was very much in the latter category.[4] Paul Shapiro, director of the Center for Advanced Holocaust
Studies at the U.S. Holocaust Memorial Museum, has stated that the spaces
of killing in Ukraine, unlike the concentration and death camps elsewhere,
'offer up none of the architectural design elements that shape the iconic imagery of Holocaust memorial sites worldwide' (2008: viii). This is not to say,
however, that the Ukrainian Holocaust did not result in a landscape replete
with perceived symbolic significance; Ukrainian soil, rather than Ukrainian
architecture, provides an alternative Holocaust memoryscape to many of
those in other European countries. In both rural and urban areas of Ukraine,
the traces of the mass killings that took place here between 1941 and 1943
are faint, but the evidence lies very close to the surface.

The Curse of Babi Yar

Russian writer Victor Nekrasov revealed how low a priority Babi Yar's commemoration was in Kiev immediately after the war when, apart from 'some

suspicious characters who crawled along the ravine's bottom in search of either diamonds or golden dental crowns', people 'faced tasks more important than Babi Yar'; it became 'simply a rubbish heap. A small lopsided post with the laconic inscription 'It is forbidden to pile rubbish here, fine – 300 roubles' did not in the least prevent local residents from getting rid of no longer useful old beds, tin cans, and other rubbish' (in Tumarkin 2010: 280). Nekrasov was among the first to attempt to raise public awareness of Babi Yar's neglect and wrote against plans to build a sports stadium at the site in 1959 (Tumarkin 2010: 280). The stadium was never built, but the local authorities embarked on a comprehensive project to wipe 'the good-for-nothing ravine' from 'the surface of the earth' by constructing a dam to flood it. The dam, which later collapsed, released 'a great billow of liquid mud around ten metres high ... from the mouth of Babi Yar. ... There were thousands of victims ... those who lived at ground level were killed instantly' (Tumarkin 2010: 281). Maria Tumarkin further remarks that the 'idea of the curse or the revenge of Babi Yar became understandably widespread' in Kiev after the flood (Tumarkin 2010: 281). A similar description appears in the testimonial accounts of Anatoli Kuznetsov, a resident in Kiev from his birth in 1929 until his defection from the Soviet Union in 1969. On the subject of the mudslide, he notes that '[t]he phrase "Babi Yar takes its revenge" was much on people's lips' (Kuznetsov 1972: 474). This sense of place as cursed, as will be discussed, can be seen as a reflection of local responses to other mass graves across the rest of Ukraine. Also in 1961, the Russian poet Yevgeny Yevtushenko wrote the poem 'Babi Yar', with its oft-cited opening line: 'Over Babi Yar there are no monuments.' Both a memorial in itself and an explicit condemnation of the Soviet authorities, Yevtushenko's poem was to play an important role in creating international awareness of both Babi Yar itself and continuing anti-Semitism in Ukraine in this period. I return to the question of how Babi Yar's memory came to travel through literary texts in the second half of this chapter.

In 1967, five years after the dam collapsed – and twenty-five years after the massacre – thousands of people attended an apparently spontaneous event at the site (Kuznetsov 1972: 475) in the first significant attempt by a large group to mark its atrocious history. Local authorities installed the first-ever official marker at the site two weeks later: a granite rock which read 'A monument will be erected at this site'. Kuznetsov suggests that this was put in place simply to show any foreign visitors who might have heard about the spontaneous meeting and who would expect Babi Yar to be marked in some way: 'If [they] insist, they can be taken along and shown the stone plaque, which will have some flowers lain around it in advance. Once the visitors have departed the flowers are removed' (1972: 475). In 1977 – ten years after the appearance of the granite marker – an official monument was finally erected, eliding the issue of 'Jewish' persecution by simply 'invoking the theme of slain Soviet citizens' (Tumarkin 2010: 9). As in East Germany, the overall narrative – both at Babi Yar and across Ukraine – was one of a violent, tragic, but ultimately triumphant struggle against fascism, focusing particularly on heroic Communist figures. Again, Jewish victims were missing from the discourse and the landscape. Even when the stone menorah finally appeared at Babi Yar in 1991, historian Stefan Rohdewald argues that it served only to '[symbolize] the marginality of Jewish remembrance of the Shoah in Ukrainian society, rather than its incorporation into the national framework' (2008: 176). This observation is borne out by the striking difference between the simplicity of the menorah and the aforementioned ostentatious memorial to Soviet citizens. Rohdewald suggests that such marginalization also characterizes recent efforts to include Jewish victims of the Holocaust in Ukraine's commemorative landscape as a whole, despite an evolution in research on the subject since 1991 and the mandatory inclusion of the Holocaust in school programmes laid down by the Ukrainian Ministry of Education in 2001.

> [L]inking the murder of Ukraine's Jews with Ukrainian national history remains a taboo in most public debates … Ukrainian history textbooks [confirm] this: the tragedy is linked to German anti-Semitism and extermination camps in Poland, and is 'silent' about the death of Jews in the territory of today's Ukraine. Hence, a strategy to externalise the Holocaust can be observed. (Rohdewald 2008: 17)

In 2008, director of the Ukrainian Centre for Holocaust Studies Anatoly Podol's'kyi condemned the Ukrainian government for their lack of interest in 'promoting a discussion of Jewish life and the Holocaust in Ukraine', practically resulting in a failure to maintain the few memorials that have appeared or to provide any support – 'moral, institutional, or financial' – for the few independent institutions now working to keep Ukraine Holocaust memory alive (Podol's'kyi 2008: 5). Reviewing the peripheral presence of the Holocaust in Ukrainian school and education programmes, Podol's'kyi echoes Rohdewald, perceiving 'the subordination of academia to political interests' (2008: 4).

In 2009 a city council proposal to build a hotel on the Babi Yar site as part of a larger plan for the construction of twenty-eight new hotels to accommodate thousands of visitors expected to visit Kiev for the 2012 European Football Championships was leaked to the press by an opposed council member. It sparked immediate international controversy, unsurprisingly most heated among Jewish groups (BBC News 2009), but was publicly vetoed by the mayor of Kiev on the sixty-eighth anniversary of the massacre (Ellingworth 2009). As noted, the memorial topography at Babi Yar now includes monuments to a number of victimized groups, but the sports proposal of

2009 – echoing that of fifty years before (Tumarkin 2010: 8) – suggests a continued suppression of Holocaust memory in Ukraine despite the lack of direct prohibition.[5]

The Holocaust in Ukraine and 'the Ukrainian Holocaust'

Podol's'kyi notes a recently emerging competitive framework of Ukrainian memory generated by a refusal 'to perceive … national history' as one of 'various cultures':

> The 'other' tends to be excluded and viewed as something alien. Apparently it is more comfortable to talk about 'us' and 'others', for example about 'our Great Famine' and about 'the others' Holocaust'. A certain narrative is taking shape, in which the Holocaust does not appear … in recent times, the Great Famine in Ukraine is increasingly being called 'the Ukrainian Holocaust'. (2008: 4)

Rohdewald, too, argues that the Holocaust is frequently used as 'a rhetorical framework' for the *holodomor* (2008: 178), as the Great Famine became 'the most important new element of Ukrainian collective memory' in post-Soviet historiography (Kappeler 2009: 58–59). A necessarily brief survey of memorial activity instigated by official Ukrainian institutions in the recent past is suggestive of a similar tendency. The Ukrainian Institute of National Memory (UINM), in its first incarnation from 2005 to 2010, has been key in bringing the *holodomor* to public attention and was instrumental in facilitating the legal recognition that it constituted a genocide against the Ukrainian people.[6] There can be little doubt that in recapturing the memory of the Great Famine, the UINM amongst others has performed long overdue work. The Ukrainian government recognized 2008 as '*Holodomor* Victims Remembrance Year' and plans for a substantial memorial to commemorate the tragedy were announced. The UINM administered the competition for designs for the new space and oversaw the project to completion. The result is a monumental 'Candle of Memory' perched on a steep slope overlooking the Dnieper River, in a central and much-visited area of the city alongside UNESCO world heritage site the Peshersk Lavra. The candle itself, an impressive glass, concrete and metal structure, towers over the entrance to a comprehensive memorial museum, and is surrounded by a complex of walls, plaques, walkways and statues. The aims of the memorial, inherent in the designs of the monuments, museum and UINM publications sold in the small museum shop, are twofold: the provision of an appropriate space in which people may remember and pay tribute to the suffering of *holodomor* victims, and the integration of the famine years as a central co-ordinate in the creation of contemporary Ukrainian national identity. The former commemorative agenda is visible in several elements within the museum in particular: a series of memorial books containing the names of victims from each region affected surrounds a pillar of corn kernels, into which visitors may place lighted candles. The associated museum publications also give a voice to the victims by reproducing their testimonies, which are featured in a film projected on the museum's inner walls at timed intervals.

The centrality of the *holodomor* to the construction of a new Ukrainian identity is manifest in the decisive casting of Stalin as a perpetrator of genocide, thus providing ' a convincing argument' for the elimination of 'Communism from the lives of all the world's peoples once and for all' (Yukhnovskiy, then acting head of the Ukrainian Institute of National Memory in Hetnov and Yukhnovskiy 2008: 3); an emotive argument in the context of the *holodomor*, but one which fails to differentiate between different phases and forms of Communism. Ukraine's independence is partly defined, for the institute at least, by anti-Communism. The museum catalogue also states that the principles that 'every nation forms a natural union with its native land' and 'Ukraine's land has consistently and indivertibly given birth to Ukrainians' are central to the exhibit. This is borne out by the many reminders of the traditional Ukrainian relationship with soil and wheat in and around the museum; in the design of the outer complex (which features golden wheat behind black metal cages), film footage of Ukrainian farmers working the land in the aforementioned projection, and in an installation of related farm equipment, also within the museum. This overriding aesthetic implies that a traditionally productive union between man and soil, violently subverted under Stalin, remains central to contemporary Ukrainian national identity.

Figure 4.5. Memory Candle

Figure 4.6. Wheat sculpture outside the Candle of Memory

The 'Candle of Memory' and the other work done by the UINM warrant a more lengthy analysis than I can provide in this context,[7] but the above summary at least gives some weight to the argument that the centrality of the *holodomor* to discourses of Ukrainian national memory is manifest in the landscape of the country's capital city. Such cannot be said of the Holocaust; as the proposal for the 'Candle of Memory' was being put into action, the Kiev city council was discussing the practicalities of building a hotel at Babi Yar. In recapturing vital memories of the *holodomor,* those of the Holocaust have remained peripheral. According to Andreas Kappeler, the very notion of a Ukrainian 'national history' raises questions: 'What should be regarded as Ukrainian history? Is it represented only by the national Ukrainian narrative, focused on the Ukrainian people and their attempts to create a Ukrainian national state? Or does it embrace the territory of Ukraine, with its multiethnic population, from antiquity to the present time?' (2009: 56). Ukrainian historians, he goes on to suggest, have until now adopted a national paradigm; from the brief survey above, it may be suggested that memorial activity has proceeded along much the same lines.

Yet I would suggest that the Holocaust and the *holodomor* share more ground than current memory discourse and landscapes imply, and that any competitiveness that exists could be productively neutralized by an official recognition of this ground. Hence I go on, now, to consider the possibility that embracing Ukrainian territory, and the experience of the multiethnic population on that territory, may be productive for the future of Ukrainian memory; that, rather than promoting a superorganic version of Ukrainian identity, attending to the experience of landscape across a broader period might encourage a more inclusive perception of Ukrainian history as one as one of 'various cultures'. In order to draw connections between these two events, whilst retaining their individual specificity, I consider testimonial accounts written by both Holocaust and *holodomor* victims and witnesses alongside a discussion of the various political and geographical factors that determined and contextualized their experiences across Ukraine from 1930 to 1945. This analysis leads me back to representations of Babi Yar itself in testimony, where the journey undertaken by the second chapter in this section will begin.

Multidirectional Experience?
The Holocaust and the *Holodomor*

In exploring the experiences of Ukraine's population in relation to Ukrainian landscape, it is first necessary to note that I do not mean to replicate the logic of 'blood and soil' and thus construct a mythological, superorganic vision of

Ukrainian identity; I am wary of assuming 'naturalized affiliations between subject and object' (Campbell 2008: 3). I recall too Buell's argument that '[n]ational borders by no means regularly correspond with "natural" borders' (Buell 2005: 81–82). Yet Ukraine is an example of a nation whose borders are almost completely determined by natural elements and topographical forms. The term *ukraïna,* by which the land which now constitutes modern Ukraine was originally known, means 'undefined borderland'. The name *Ukraine* did not come into popular usage until the early nineteenth century (Magocsi 2010: 189–90). This land and the people who lived there have been histori-cally defined according to their relationship with, and between, neighbouring states, rather than to any fixed conception of nationhood; indeed Ukraine did not become a nation in itself until the early twentieth century. The connec-tion between inhabitants and territory was determined far more by the fertil-ity of the rich black *chernozem* soil, ideal for growing wheat (Subtelny 1991: 3; Cooper 2006: 24–25), than by any particular 'national' narrative. The land of the Ukrainian steppe has for centuries been regarded as amongst the rich-est in the Europe, and as the continent's 'breadbasket' Ukraine has been 'valued for its natural resources more than its diverse population' (Lower 2005: 2). Unlike their Russian neighbours to the north, who had to farm col-lectively to be effective, the fertility of Ukraine allowed inhabitants to farm independently, a natural circumstance that came to affect the 'mentalit[y], cultur[e], and socio-economic organization' of Ukraine and its people (Sub-telny 1991: 5).

Ukraine's borderland position and fertile soil have led to repeated coloni-zations; effectively, that is, attempts to territorialize the land. Thus as much as geography has played a part in defining Ukrainian identity, it has led to frequent, violent attempts to destroy the fundamental basis on which this identity exists. According to Lower, the perception that the 'space and its people could be exploited and radically transformed was most extreme in the 1930s and 1940s when Soviet and then Nazi empire-builders unleashed their utopian schemes in Ukraine' (2005: 2). There is, then, a fundamen-tal parallel between the context in which the Holocaust and the *holodomor* occurred. Perhaps the most prominent example of comparative historiogra-phy to recognize this is Timothy Snyder's *Bloodlands* (2010). Snyder follows up Hannah Arendt's argument that 'the Nazi and Stalinist systems must be compared, not so much to understand one or the other but to understand our times and ourselves' (Snyder 2010: 380). Yet the reluctance to embrace the notion of a double Ukrainian genocide – and subsequently, perhaps, to consider any possible confluence between victim and witness experience – is evident in responses to Snyder's text (see Zuroff 2010 and Bartov 2011: 424–28). Furthermore 'identification of the Holocaust with the Holodomor has … been rejected by most non-Ukrainian historians' because it presents an unwanted challenge to 'the singular and exclusive place of the Holocaust and Auschwitz in the collective memory not only of Jews but also of most other Western Europeans and Americans' (Kappeler 2009: 59). Elie Wiesel, in reporting on Soviet Jewry, argued that '[a]n abyss of blood separates Moscow from Berlin. The distance between them is not only one of geography and ideology; it is the distance between life and death' ([1966]2011: 5). Examining the impact of these two totalitarian regimes within one geographic location at least removes one obstacle from this equation. The two regimes had different policies about the Jewish population, but whilst this was the central concern of Wiesel's report it is less so to my own; I pursue instead a focus on the experience of landscape as a co-ordinate shared by people across cultures under both Stalin and Hitler.

Concerns about the conflation of different histories are entirely legitimate. But in some instances such concerns can be contextualized within a broader rejection of recent attempts to open up the field of history to transcultural analysis, a rejection commensurate with the 'phallic logic' of much debate on empire, colony and genocide since 9/11 (Moses 2010: 6). In asking whether historiography needs to 'be a zero-sum game' (2010: 7), Moses also alerts us to the fact that possible alternatives exist as far as the interpretation of the past is concerned, and the most nuanced of comparative work supports this contention. As Craps and Rothberg suggest, some of the most influential work on the Holocaust has drawn attention to the fact that by refusing to consider interconnected histories together '(except in a competitive manner) we deprive ourselves of an opportunity to gain greater insight into each of these different strands of history and to develop a more comprehensive understanding of the dark underside of modernity' (2011: 518). Accordingly, I pursue here the possibility of a multidirectional contiguity between two events which are inevitably drawn together by the Ukrainian experience of territory as a factor that both structures history and mediates memory.

The historical specificity of each event must be first addressed. The *holodomor* was a consequence of Stalin's Five-Year Plan, which, from 1928, violently enforced a programme of collectivized farming on the Ukrainian people (Snyder 2010:28). Under collectivization, which was well under way by 1930, the Ukrainian people were no longer able to live off their own soil. In fact they were alienated from it; although they were in charge of food production, they did not own the results of their labour. Harvests were poor for a number of reasons, but many of these were related to the disruption caused by the major shift to collectivized methods. Much of what had been grown was shipped to other parts of the Soviet Union and elsewhere; in many cases nothing at all was left to feed the Ukrainian people. Furthermore, Stalin's plan involved the destruction of the wealthier independent farmers, the 'kulak' class, many of whom were either executed or deported (Snyder 2010:

26). This evacuation of space had lethal consequences: some of Ukraine's most reliable producers were unable to work their land. The liquidization of the *kulaks* was ideologically commensurate with Stalin's vision for a Communist society, but it was also a pragmatic move; he anticipated that collectivization would lead to a struggle between the peasant class and the Soviet police whose job was to enforce it. In depriving the peasants of their leaders, this clash would be minimized (Snyder 2010: 25). The idea that the annihilation of the *kulak* class would liberate the poorer peasant classes was undermined by the mass starvation that followed.

According to Snyder's account, Hitler mobilized the *holodomor* as an example of the failure of Marxism in practice (2010: 61). In turn, in 1934 Stalin used antifascist rhetoric to marshal the European Left (2010: 66). Yet despite the binary opposition they were constructing, Hitler duplicated several of Stalin's tactics within Germany itself; just as Stalin had forcibly removed the *kulaks* and taken their grain, Hitler organized boycotts of Jewish businesses: 'like collectivisation, the boycotts indicated which sector of society would lose the most in coming social and economic transformations' (2010: 62). Forced deportation was considered a 'territorial solution' to Germany's Jewish 'problem' in the years leading up to the Second World War (2010: 112). Hitler and Stalin's policies thus share some methodological ground. Furthermore, in a display of pragmatism over ideology, Hitler and Stalin were to join forces to invade and conquer Poland in 1939. However, the alliance was short lived and the Nazis invaded the Soviet Union in June 1941 (Snyder 2010: 160–61). As a result the Jewish population suffered most; under Stalin, a high percentage of the dead were non-Jewish Ukrainians.[8] Nonetheless, as will become clear, the landscapes and experiences of the *holodomor* substantially foreshadow those of the Ukrainian Holocaust that would follow.

The Nazi colonization of Ukraine was fundamentally a fight for soil and space, what Hitler called 'the shift to the soil policy of the future' (Lower 2005: 3): the campaign to reclaim Germany's 'garden of Eden' (Lower 2005: 101). Hitler aimed to settle Ukraine with German peasants: 'Sacred German soil, in the Nazi view, had no specific boundaries; Ukraine would effectively become part of Germany' (Kiernan 2007: 432). The campaign was 'naturalised' by colonial rhetoric, which depicted Germany's role in Ukraine as a form of 'manifest destiny' (Snyder 2010: 15). In 1942, children in Hitler's Germany played a board game in which armed forces competed for the 'fertile black earth' of Ukraine (Lower 2005: 187). In order to claim it in reality, Hitler needed to remove as many non-Germans as possible, resulting in a rapid and widespread ethnic cleansing programme. Whilst killing in Ukraine under Hitler was, in the course of time, to occur primarily as organized mass shooting operations, the first strategy planned for the country was the deliberate starvation of the unwanted Soviet population: the Hunger Plan.

Ukrainian food was again a central motivating force for this destruction of life. 'The Soviet Union was the only realistic source of calories for Germany and its West European empire … Like Stalin, Hitler tended to see Ukraine itself as a geopolitical asset, and its people as instruments who tilled the soil, tools that could be exchanged with others or discarded … Food from Ukraine was as important to the Nazi vision of an Eastern empire as it was to Stalin's defence of the integrity of the Soviet Union' (Snyder 2010: 161). Hitler's approach to territorializing the land was pursued via policies of 'starvation and colonization' (Snyder 2010: 163). That shooting, rather than starvation, came to primarily characterize the Ukrainian Holocaust may have been because it soon became clear that the Hunger Plan was impossible to implement in full (Snyder 2010: 167–69). Nonetheless, the German invaders did seize much of the food they came across, and famine again cast a shadow over many parts of Ukraine. As well as reducing the Soviet population as a whole, Hitler was determined to clear his new territory of 'agitators, partisans, saboteurs, and Jews' (Snyder 2010: 182). As had been the case throughout Germany's invasion of Poland, the task of eliminating these groups was given to the *Einsatzgruppen*.

Beyond these methodological similarities, both the *holodomor* and the Holocaust affected Ukraine and its people on two interconnected levels: topographical and experiential. The alienation of many Ukrainian peasants from soil in life, a direct consequence of the Five-Year Plan, very soon led to their internment within it in death; at the height of the famine, Ukrainian villagers were dying at the rate of 25,000 per day, equivalent to seventeen people a minute (League of Canadian Ukrainians website). Historian Robert Conquest introduces an initial parallel to the Holocaust by comparing the landscape of Ukraine in the early 1930s to 'one vast Belsen. A quarter of the rural population, men, women and children, lay dead or dying. At the same time (as at Belsen) well-fed squads of police or party officials supervised the victims' (1986: 3). Conquest's description resonates with Desbois's image of Ukrainian nation space as cemetery; throughout the Holocaust and the *holodomor* the landscape and soil of Ukraine was steeped in recent death. In recalling the difficulty of burying famine victims, *holodomor* survivor Maria Katchmar describes scenes reminiscent of Holocaust testimonies: bodies were thrown 'like mud', into a pit 'big enough for [an] entire village' (2008). Snyder similarly notes the problems faced by those left alive with regards burying the dead; 'healthier peasants … barely had the strength or inclination to dig graves very deeply, so that hands and feet could be seen above the earth … Crews would take the weak along with the dead and bury them alive … In a few cases such victims managed to dig their way out of the shallow mass graves' (2010: 52). A parallel to the Holocaust again emerges; in nearly every account of Nazi mass murder and burial recorded by Desbois, at least one witness recalled how the ground would continue to move for days: 'shot Jews were very often only wounded, not dead. Everywhere, from east to west, north to south, the witnesses always ended their testimonies by muttering: "The pit moved for three days."' (Desbois 2008: 96–97). In both cases, the genocide's impact on topography directly affected those who lived on the land and witnessed these events. Kuznetsov too returns periodically to the transformation of the Ukrainian landscape as a corruption of the soil. In an initial passage on Babi Yar, to which I will return in more detail later, the ground is described as made up of ashes and small pieces of bone; he also tells of a trench in a village field outside the city, a 'local Babi Yar': 'partly filled in and partly washed away by the spring rains ... In one place there was something sticking up out of the ground. It was a blackened, moist human foot in the remains of a boot' (Kuznetsov 1972: 269–70).

The impact of the famine was thus the dual destruction of millions of lives and of 'the essence of a peasant-based, rural Ukrainian culture' (Wanner 1998: 41); 'irreversibly sapped of life', its 'soul destroyed' (Wanner 1998: 43). Whilst the relationship between people and land is couched in somewhat sentimental terms by Wanner, there is little doubt that the experience of many of those who lived on Ukrainian soil was radically altered. The harmony mourned by pastoral logic is often naively formulated, constitutive of a longing for a past which never really existed. In Ukraine post-*holodomor*, however, there is some legitimate cause for mourning. The lives of the Ukrainian peasantry may not have been defined by a truly harmonious relationship between man and nature, but what relationship there had been was subverted throughout the famine years.

That this subversion was to continue throughout the Holocaust is evidenced in Kuznetsov's account. Early in the Nazi occupation, when Nazi activity was centred in Kiev itself and the outlying countryside remained relatively intact, Kuznetsov walked through the Pushcha-Voditsa forest. He could still find peace there, but events in nearby Kiev loomed in his consciousness.

A BEAUTIFUL, SPACIOUS, BLESSED LAND
There was the world itself. So vast and with so much life always surging up. The tall old pine trees of the dense Pushcha-Voditsa forest towered into the sky ... full of peace and wisdom.

I lay face up in the straw ... thinking, I suppose, about everything at once ... Babi Yar, Darnitsa, orders, starvation, Aryans, Volksdeutsche, book-burnings; yet close at hand the fir trees were swaying gently in the breeze as they had done a million years ago, and the earth, vast and blessed, was spread out beneath the sky, neither Aryan, nor Jewish, nor gypsy, but just the earth intended for the benefit of people ... How many thousands of years has the human race been living on the earth, and people still don't know how to share things out. (Kuznetsov 1972: 187)

In this passage, Kuznetsov characterizes the earth as 'intended for the benefit of people', an anthropocentric suggestion but one which, it becomes clear, is firmly rooted in the idea of a productive, rather than destructive, union between man and nature. Leo Marx has discussed two categories of pastoral, 'sentimental' and 'complex' (1964: 25); '[h]is sentimental pastoral is precisely the escapist, simplistic kind attacked by the pejorative use of the term' (in Gifford 1999: 10). Kuznetsov adopts the position of a sentimental commentator only to introduce a pejorative conclusion; man should be able to exist in a harmonious, innocent relation with the natural world as it was 'a million years ago' but has failed to do so in his obsession with eugenic superiority. His own sense of the pleasure to be found in working with soil is evident in his description of digging trenches, one the many jobs he undertook in wartime Kiev: 'Earth has a very pleasant smell. I always enjoyed digging it. ... it can make you quite dizzy, the pleasure of that smell' (Kuznetsov 1972: 398). Passages such as this are suggestive of Kuznetsov's sense of what work characterized by a harmonious man/nature relation could be, a harmony missing from the destruction of the forest:

> It was a beautiful, well-kept pine forest, in which every single tree used to be cared for ... The Germans had starting cutting the forest down. Not the Germans themselves, but workers who were paid a pound of bread a week for doing it ... the saws rang out, the tractors chugged away, and the tops of the fir trees trembled and shed their snow and then came sailing down, to hit the ground with a crash like an explosion. (1972: 232–33)

The next time he walks through the forest – unfortunately for the purposes of dating his experiences accurately, Kuznetsov's narrative appears to follow the whims of his memory rather than a definite chronology – large areas of it have been cleared. He describes the scene in a chapter clearly titled to resonate with the earlier section about Pushcha-Voditska.

NO BLESSED LAND

> Once again I travelled across that beautiful spacious blessed land. But now it looked rather different ... I had none of the feeling of joy and peace I experienced once before. They were still cutting down the pine trees; there were now clearings in the forest, and big lorries and trailers were carrying long, straight tree trunks. ...
>
> The forest along the banks of the Irpen was also being felled ... prisoners were building a bridge across the Irpen. Covered in mud, some of them with their feet wrapped in rags, others simply barefoot, were digging the still-frozen ground and handling the planks of wood, standing up to their chests in water. On both banks there were guards with machine-guns sitting in towers and patrols with dogs standing ready. (1972: 266–67)

As at Buchenwald, a forest is destroyed by the forced labour of prisoners of war. Kuznetsov concludes: 'Everything in the world was terribly mixed up' (1972: 267).

Desbois's account reveals further evidence of the subversion of the Ukrainian landscape experience and topography, and the consequences of this for Ukrainian memories of the Holocaust today. The Nazis' use of the Ukrainian landscape and farming equipment as tools in genocidal processes took 'the beauty from everything. The most luscious green landscapes became extermination fields ... The perpetrators of genocide used everything – cliffs, grain silos, beaches, irrigation wells, ditches' (Desbois 2008: 98); local people were ordered to collect hemp and sunflowers to help burn corpses (2008: 66–67). Aspects of the landscape in Ukraine were central to the planning and co-ordination of Nazi atrocities. Topography determined where and how local people were executed and buried. German soldiers checked each village and town in advance, ascertaining soil type, and searching for existing ditches, forests and any other topographical elements which might prove useful (2008: 106). Repeatedly Desbois encounters a peaceful rural, 'bucolic' (2008: 165) scene only to reveal atrocity just below the earth's surface. Desbois's interviews constantly provide evidence of deliberate avoidance, deep-rooted unease, and, in some cases, superstition about these landscapes from those who inhabit them. A road outside the Rawa-Ruska camp, for example, had been constructed after the war with sand from the nearby Jewish cemetery. A local man reports: 'You know, there are lots of accidents on this road, and people say that the road should not have been built with the bones of the dead' ('Maxim' in Desbois 2008: 33).

In many cases, Desbois found that local people who had witnessed the original massacres would never return to these sites again, despite having lived their whole lives in close proximity to them. '"Did you never come back?" ... "No, for me, this is hell"' ('Adolf' in Desbois 2008: 114). Whilst, understandably, such witnesses seemed to feel the sites of atrocity were cursed, in some villages the burial grounds are simply too central to be avoided and were necessarily reintegrated into everyday life. One man leads Desbois and his team to a group of village houses with gardens.

> He said: 'This is where they were killed ...' The owners of several neighbouring houses came running out ... One of them interrupted the witness: 'My vegetable allotment patch. That's my vegetable patch! Leave our gardens alone.' Without realizing it, with their protestations they were only confirming what everyone else in the area knew: the bodies of shot Jews resting under the tomato plants. (Desbois 2008: 64–65)

Thus the destruction of the relationship between Ukrainian people and Ukrainian land, which began in the *holodomor,* can be seen to have continued throughout the Holocaust, with a lasting impact on the memories of witnesses. A resonance can be seen in Soviet writer Vasily Grossman's novel *Life and Fate*:

> Once … I thought that good was to be found … in the silent kingdom of the trees. Far from it. I saw the treacherous way [the forest] battled against the grass and bushes for each inch of soil … a constant struggle of everything against everything. Only the blind can conceive of the kingdom of trees as a world of good. ([1985] 2006: 391)

In Grossman's work it is not a mourned, if imaginary, harmony between man and nature that has been destroyed, but any sense of good, in any form of life. This statement is made by Ikonnikov, a character introduced early in the novel by a sceptical narrator as a 'dirty, ragged old man'; his 'absurd theory' that 'morality … transcended class' (13) developed in response to witnessing the cannibalism that resulted from 'all-out collectivization' followed in later years by 'the torments undergone by the prisoner-of-war and the execution of Jews' during the Nazi campaign in Belorussia ([1985] 2006: 391). The pains-takingly realistic *Life and Fate* includes many details gathered in Grossman's notebooks from his time as a journalist in World War II, and Ikonnikov's loss of faith in goodness has been called a direct expression of Grossman's own beliefs (Chandler 2006: xxi).

The cannibalism Grossman refers to was a fact of daily life during the *holodomor*, as the state police recorded in 1933: 'families kill their weakest members, usually children, and use the meat for eating';[9] 'Survival was a moral as well as a physical struggle' (Snyder 2010: 50). That the Nazi Hunger Plan resulted in similar experience during the Holocaust is evident in Kuznetsov's testimony. To return to his description of a land which is no longer 'blessed':

> [The fields] had not been dug since the previous year, and there were little rows of humps made by the potatoes which had been left in the ground and had gone bad. The corn had been beaten down and was also rotten. Yet there had been such a famine in the city at the time. (1972: 266–67)

The famine to which Kuznetsov refers was that engineered by the Nazis in their bid to deurbanize Ukraine. The young Kuznetsov finds work assisting a sausage-maker, Degtyaryov. The sausages are made not from pigs, which are unheard of in wartime Kiev, but from horses which are too old to be useful for other purposes. Also at this time, a man in Kiev is hanged for making sausages out of human flesh. 'He would go around the market, pick on some likely man or woman, and offer to sell him or her some cheap salt which he would say he had in his home. He would take them home, let them through the door first, crack them over the head with an axe – and turn them into sausages' (1972: 347). On one occasion, Degtyaryov relates to Kuznetsov the story of the 'graveyard gang' – a group led by a graveyard keeper. They opened new graves after funerals and fed the bodies to pigs to fatten them up: 'Even if a corpse today is pretty skinny, it's meat just the same, and what's the sense of letting good stuff go to waste with such hunger about?' (1972: 348).

For Kuznetsov, burdened by empathic imagination, even the slaughter of the horses is difficult to assimilate (1972: 348). Degtyaryov asks Kuznetsov if it still hurts him to kill them:

'Yes, it hurts.'

'Silly little fool, why bother about them? As you see, that's the way life is – not only horses; even human beings go for sausages...' (1972: 348)

Kuznetsov presents an image of wartime Kiev under the Nazis as a realm in which human life is reduced to units. Explicit in his reference to the production of sausages, units of flesh are evaluated in terms of use value. This paradigm can also be traced throughout the city in the everyday actions to which its inhabitants are reduced. The narrative is suggestive of Agamben's description of the reduction of citizens to bare life within states of exception (1995). The citizens of Ukraine, beyond the Jewish community, fall into the category of 'life unworthy of being lived', the counterpart to German life which deserves to live simply for the fact of birth into a favoured nation-state.

Following this logic, based on the experiential parallels noted throughout this chapter the spaces of the Holocaust and the *holodomor* in Ukraine were those in which life was rendered bare despite differences of racial or ethnic denomination. As Snyder notes, one of the first authors, alongside Arendt, to break the 'taboo of the century' by 'placing the crimes of the Nazi and Soviet regimes on the same pages, in the same scenes' was Grossman, in both the aforementioned *Life and Fate* and *Everything Flows* ([1994] 2011). Grossman juxtaposes the cannibalism under Stalin with the shooting of Jews under Hitler 'in the same breath', and draws attention to the physical similarity between children in concentration camps and those starving in Ukraine during the *holodomor*: 'They looked just the same ... Every single little bone moving under the skin, and the joints between them' (in Snyder 2010: 386). For Grossman, '[h]uman groupings have one main purpose: to assert everyone's right to be different, to be special, to think, feel or live in his or her own way ... The only true or lasting meaning of a struggle for life lies in the individual, in his modest peculiarities and in the right to his peculiarities' (2006: 214). Indeed on the first page of the novel he states, echoing Celan's demand we attend to the orchid, '[e]verything that lives is unique. It is unimaginable that two people, or two briar roses, should be identical ... if you attempt to erase the peculiarities and individuality of life by violence, then life itself must suffocate' (2006: 3). Snyder's conclusion states accordingly, following Arendt and Grossman, that legitimate comparisons between the two regimes must 'begin with life rather than death. Death is not a solution, but only a subject' (2010: 387). My own comparison can be seen as legitimate in this sense. Whilst recognizing the intrinsic uniqueness of each life, I have considered alternative ways to group those who suffered which are based not on 'a race, a God, a party or a state' but on the experience that results from the 'fateful error' that such groupings are the very purpose of life' (Grossman 2006: 214). One result of this error, in both Stalin and Hitler's campaigns in Ukraine, was the reduction of life to bare life within the Ukrainian landscape.

Notes

1. Others in this area include monuments to Soviet citizens, prisoners of war, and officers of the Soviet Army executed by German Fascists at Babi Yar, to a 'Hero of Ukraine', the Kiev underground worker and revolutionary T. Markus, and a separate monument to executed children; and various monument crosses, for priests executed (shot) for praying for the protection of the Motherland from Fascists, and monuments to members of OUN (the Organization of Ukrainian Nationalists) and the Ukrainian poet O. Teliha.

2. The French Catholic priest Patrick Desbois has contributed significantly to an improved understanding of this period, and in the section to come I integrate several of the many testimonies he collected from survivors, as well as certain observations these have allowed him to make about Ukrainian experience of the Holocaust.

3. Desbois's team excavated only one of the graves in full, in order to pre-empt accusations from Holocaust deniers.

4. There were concentration camps in Ukraine territory, but they have not captured the popular imagination of the public or extensive interest by researchers. Janowska, a concentration camp in L'viv (Lwow/Lemberg/Lvov), has been described as 'a death camp by any reasonable understanding of the phrase', although there were no gas chambers built there (Winstone 2010: 382). Regular selections took place at Janowska, and many deportees were shot in a ravine to the north of the camp. Between 100,000 and 200,000 prisoners, many Jewish, were killed at the camp over the course of two years (1941–3). The camp is still a prison today, which may go some way to explaining why there is no official commemoration at Janowska, although a privately funded memorial stands at the northern ravine where shootings took place (Winstone 2010: 383). Various attempts have been made to research other Ukraine concentration camps, but for the most part there is either very little left to see or the sites are still being used as prisons or military bases; see for example Desbois's account of Rawa-Ruska (2008: 27–37).

5. Whilst further investigation, certainly into sources beyond those made available in the media, would be required to determine reliable details about the 2009 hotel

proposal, it is at least suggestive in light of Rohdewald's argument about continuing Ukrainian externalization and marginalization of the Holocaust.

6. The *holodomor* was officially categorized as genocide against the Ukrainian people according to the national parliament (Verkovna Rada) in 2006. Then President Victor Yanukovych has controversially argued that '[t]he Holodomor was in Ukraine, Russia, Belarus and Kazakhstan. It was the result of Stalin's totalitarian regime. But it would be wrong and unfair to recognize the Holodomor as an act of genocide against one nation' (*Kyiv Post* 2010) – the implications of this statement will be considered at a later stage in this argument.

7. The museum further deserves attention as constituting a marked development in Kiev's gradual move towards the provision of Westernized visitor spaces. It has left many of the 'Soviet' museum features behind. Multilingual staff and the availability of museum publications in several European languages are particularly notable in this regard.

8. Snyder (2010: 53) estimates a total number of deaths in Soviet Ukraine during the famine years at 3.3 million, of which approximately 3 million were Ukrainian. The remaining 300,000 were 'Russians, Poles, Germans, Jews, and others'. A further 3 million Ukrainians died in other areas of the Soviet Union during the same period.

9. Snyder reports the recorded number of people sentenced for cannibalism between 1932–3 at 'at least 2,505 … although the actual number of cases was almost certainly greater' (2010: 51).

FIVE

BABI YAR'S LITERARY JOURNEY

This section covers a series of textual representations that have facilitated an awareness of Babi Yar beyond Ukrainian territory. Babi Yar is perhaps the only event of the Ukrainian Holocaust that has been integrated into international discourse on – and commemoration of – the Holocaust overall (certainly until Desbois's work drew attention to the scale of the shootings elsewhere on Ukraine territory). The scale of the massacre, particularly the initial shooting operation on 29–30 September 1941, was in part responsible for this international recognition. But this chapter suggests that the literary remediation of the events at Babi Yar has also played a part. The journey discussed here takes place across three texts, beginning with an oral testimony collected by Kuznetsov as he documented life in Kiev under Nazi occupation: that of Dina Pronicheva, a Kiev puppeteer who had escaped from Babi Yar during the first massacre in September 1941. Kuznetsov's account was published in the West in 1970, and the sections into which Pronicheva's testimony was integrated were instrumental in taking the experience of suffering at Babi Yar beyond Ukrainian territory. These sections were then transposed into D.M. Thomas's fiction, *The White Hotel,* more broadly placing Babi Yar within international public consciousness.

Erll and Rigney call attention to:

> the central paradox of remediation. On the one hand the recycling of existing media is a way of strengthening the new media's claim to immediacy, of offering an 'experience of the real'. On the other hand, remediation is an act of hypermediacy that, by multiplying media, potentially reminds the viewer of the presence of a medium. (2009: 3–4, in summary of Bolter and Grusin)

Their application of these phenomena to the dynamics of cultural memory prompts an increased awareness of the complex possibilities and restrictions inherent in the remediation of narratives of the past. Whilst this chapter presents memory in both literary and spatial terms as being in some sense displaced, this move is seen as a potentially productive, performative journey rather than something which *necessarily* elides or erases original forms and narratives. Crucially, the specificity of certain elements of the experience had by victims at Babi Yar and across Ukraine has been preserved throughout this literary remediation, resulting in the communication of an 'experience of the real' (see Erll and Rigney 2009: 3) with a tangible immediacy. As a result Babi Yar's position in cultural memories away from Ukraine resonates with the experiences of those who lived through the Ukrainian Holocaust; at least to the extent that Ukrainian soil plays a key role. The phenomenological experience of Babi Yar presented in the texts discussed in this section – one of being buried alive within a landscape of dead and dying human flesh – presents readers with images of extreme suffering within a topography transformed by atrocity. This, as discussed in the following chapter, eventually resulted in that soil itself travelling across the world as a perceived vessel of memory. At the same time, the transparent self-conscious intertextuality employed by the authors whose work carries these memories results in a reader's awareness of the hypermediated nature of this memory. This is not necessarily an obstacle to the creation of empathic memory, but rather an effective way of preserving the other's experience in a way we can encounter meaningfully whilst resisting a complete inhabitation of that experience. Thus, whilst Soviet authorities deliberately excluded Babi Yar from national discourses of memory and communal remembrance, and Ukrainian authorities have continued to marginalize the Holocaust overall, the events that occurred there are taken up in textual displacements which carry its memory by facilitating an imaginative engagement beyond Ukraine.

Pronicheva was a Soviet citizen with Jewish parents. When the Nazis launched an operation to empty Kiev of Jews, they issued instructions demanding that all Jewish citizens were to appear at a particular intersection of roads in the north of the city. Pronicheva and her family were amongst those that took their places in the long queue that formed in the streets around the Jewish and Orthodox cemeteries on 29 September 1941. Her parents and sister were killed in the massacre that followed, but Dina was one of the very few to survive, and 'the only person known to have fallen into the ravine unwounded and feigned death' as a means of that survival (Berkhoff 2008: 294). Multiple written records of her testimony, which is detailed, harrowing and graphic, have emerged over the years (see Berkhoff 2008: 295). It was first published in the Ukrainian press in 1946, and was given by Pronicheva herself shortly afterwards at a Soviet military tribunal (Berkhoff 2008: 295–96). In Kuznetsov's text her experience in the ravine is described as follows:

When she struck the bottom she felt neither the blow nor any pain, but she was immediately spattered by warm blood, and blood was streaming down her face, just as if she had fallen into a bath full of blood.

All around her she could hear strange submerged sounds, groaning, choking and sobbing: many of the people were not dead yet. The whole mass of bodies kept moving slightly as they settled down and were pressed tighter by the movements of the ones who were still living. (1972: 110)

Pronicheva creeps over the settling bodies that night to escape from the ravine:

Finally she got herself out from under the earth.

The Ukrainian policemen up above were apparently tired after a hard day's work, too lazy to shovel the earth in properly, and once they had scattered a little in they dropped their shovels and went away. Dina's eyes were full of sand. It was pitch dark and there was a heavy smell of flesh from the mass of fresh corpses. (1972: 111)

It is this experience of Babi Yar, of an immersion in a topography of death, that is taken forward in this discussion of literary remediation. Kuznetsov's text incorporates Pronicheva's testimony alongside his own recollections of Babi Yar, which themselves contribute to an intensely geographically orientated account overall. Initially, for Kuznetsov, Babi Yar is a landscape of childhood. He had played there, and his book opens with his recollection of it:

The ravine was enormous, you might even say majestic: deep and wide, like a mountain gorge. If you stood on one side of it and shouted, you would scarcely be heard on the other.

It is situated between three districts of Kiev ... surrounded by cemeteries, woods, and allotments. Down at the bottom ran a little stream with clear water. The sides of the ravine were steep, even overhanging in places; landslides were frequent in Babi Yar. In fact it was typical of the whole region: the whole of the right bank of the Dnieper is cut into by such ravines. (1970: 15)

One day soon after the end of the war Kuznetsov visits the ravine with a friend. Although he knew that people had been brought to the ravine and shot, and that the bodies had later been burnt, throughout the occupation the area has been fenced off and out of bounds; the two boys were curious.

The river bed was of good, coarse sand, but now for some reason or other the sand was mixed with little white stones.

I bent down and picked one of them up to look at it more closely. It was a small piece of bone, about as big as a fingernail, and it was charred on one side and white on the other. The stream was washing these pieces of bone out of somewhere and carrying them down with it. From this we concluded that the place where the Jews, Russians, Ukrainians and people of other nationalities had been shot was somewhere higher up.

... the ravine became narrower and split into several branches, and in one place we saw that the sand had turned grey. Suddenly we realised that we were walking on human ashes ...

We walked around the place and found many whole bones, a skull, still not dried out, of someone recently buried, and more pieces of black ash amongst the grey sand. I picked up one of the pieces and took it with me to keep. It contains the ashes of many people, all mixed up together – a sort of international mixture.

It was then I decided I must write it all down, from the very beginning. (1972: 17)

It is, then, with the corruptive transformation of landscape that Kuznetsov's text begins. As he makes clear, Babi Yar, like the mass graves across the country discussed in the previous chapter, became synonymous with death and disaster for local people, not only during the war but long after its conclusion. It was a constant threat: 'Do you want to end up in Babi Yar?' his mother asks when he makes an antifascist leaflet. It is a place with 'abhorrent associations' throughout Kiev (1972: 301), and becomes the centre of what sound like urban myths but which, all too often, turn out to be disturbingly accurate. The rumour that Ukrainians refused for years to eat cabbages grown on the farms around Babi Yar because of the human ashes sprinkled on them has somehow lived on in contemporary accounts of the massacre (see for example Frederik Pohl's *Chernobyl: A Novel* 1987: 233). Although it seems impossible to trace the origin of this rumour as far as Ukrainian reactions are concerned, Kuznetsov's account documents in full the practice of distributing the ashes in his description of the 'gardeners' (one of the many groups of prisoners forced to work to obliterate the bodies at Babi Yar): 'their job was to load the ashes onto barrows and distribute them under escort around the environs of Babi Yar and scatter them over the vegetable gardens' (1972: 376). Thus Kuznetsov's own memories, along with those of Pronicheva, offer up an image of Babi Yar grounded in explicitly geographical terms.

This geographical engagement is transposed and extended in *The White Hotel,* an inter-textual documentary fiction. It comprises a formal structure of prologue and six sections which together build a pseudo-Freudian psychoanalytic case study of fictional patient Lisa Erdman. Lisa is the character that 'takes on' Pronicheva's memories. Early sections of the text integrate Freud's own case histories and letters, and present what appear to be Lisa's hysteric symptoms and vivid sexual fantasies. In the penultimate section 'The Sleeping Carriage', these symptoms are revealed to be real injuries, mental and psychological, sustained during the Babi Yar massacre, which is described in detail incorporating lengthy sections of Kuznetsov's text. Lisa has a form of 'second sight' that manifests itself not only in her mind but in her body; a physical, pre-emptive form of memory making. Vice describes *The White Hotel* as a 'narrative satire on backshadowing', as frequently repeated tropes and events build up a 'particular view of time and history' (2000: 38). I will consider these tropes in a somewhat different light throughout this section, arguing that they are important structural devices in the development of contemporary memories of the Holocaust in Ukraine and pursuing the notion that the landscapes which shape *The White Hotel* provide the reader with a displaced topography of the Ukrainian Holocaust. This displacement is dually manifest: in the psychologically constructed world of mountains, lakes and forests in which the white hotel stands, and in the imaginations of Thomas's readers as they follow the narrative from this symbolic landscape to the topography of the ravine in Kiev.

Substantial sections of Thomas's Babi Yar chapter are based on Kuznetsov's documentation of Pronicheva's oral history testimony. Thomas was criticized for this integration. In addition to prompting outrage by bringing sexual fantasy and the Holocaust together in the same literary space, he was accused of plagiarism. He responded with a description of his book as 'a synthesis of visions and voices' and reminded critics that he had formally acknowledged his use of Kuznetsov's work (in Hilton 1982). The controversy surrounding the text proved to have a certain value. There can be little doubt that *The White Hotel* made a considerable global impact. An international bestseller, translated into at least thirty languages since its publication in 1981, the novel has also been awarded a *Los Angeles Times* Fiction Prize and a Cheltenham Prize (for books that receive 'less acclaim' than they deserve in their year of publication), and was shortlisted for the Booker Prize. It is certainly possible to speculate that the book is partly responsible for a reinvigorated popular interest in Kuznetsov's work. Thomas himself pointed out that *Babi Yar* was reissued by publishers in the wake of *The White Hotel's* controversial reception (Vice 2000: 40).

Thus Thomas can be seen to have made an important contribution to the integration of Ukrainian history into the Holocaust master narrative. As I have suggested throughout this book, literature facilitates a different kind of imaginative engagement to other forms of media. Langer has called attention to the centrality of literature in rendering 'the experience of horror' accessible to readers (1993: 12). To Langer, such literary renditions should rightfully be produced by the survivor-writer. Whilst *The White Hotel* is a piece of fiction by a nonsurvivor, the passages about Babi Yar are largely directly transposed from Kuznetsov's text;[1] and Kuznetsov transcribed Pronicheva's testimony as rigorously as he documented the entirety of the data he collected for *Babi Yar*.[2] The original testimony, therefore, is remediated but still explicitly present in these later works. Whilst he was accused of 'appropriating Pronicheva's pain' (Wirth-Nesher in Vice 2000: 39), Thomas argued that 'it would have been "immoral" if he, "a comfortable Briton, fictionalized the Holocaust"' in the production of a new imaginary narrative (in Vice 2000: 39). Both Kuznetsov's and Thomas's texts function as vehicles for introducing Pronicheva's testimony to a broader audience than it would ever otherwise have received. In order to define in more precise terms the details of *The White Hotel*'s imaginary world, I take the intertextual sections as metanarrative guides to the exploration of Babi Yar's atrocious topography.

Testimony to Fiction

The White Hotel, unsurprisingly given its form as a Freudian case study, has frequently prompted psychoanalytic readings. Laura Tanner describes Lisa's symptoms – hysteria, hallucinations, pains in the areas in which she is later injured at Babi Yar – as 'the transformations of real facts into the symbols of memory. Trauma from the past which is not consciously acknowledged is symbolized bodily in the present; the repressed memory is a signified whose signifier is the symptom' (Vice 2000: 45, summarizing Tanner). In Lisa's case, the symptoms are related to an event in the future. Trauma is clearly central to *The White Hotel,* both overtly as pseudo-Freudian case study and implicitly in the physical manifestation of Lisa's experiences at Babi Yar. I here reconsider Tanner's concept of the 'transformations of real facts into symbols of memory' away from the framework of trauma, examining the way in which tangible phenomenological tropes become key signifiers for secondary witnesses of historical suffering, providing a way into an experience which can be encountered but not fully inhabited. Again, the tropes I focus on here reinforce the geographic dimensions of atrocious human experience. The imaginary landscapes that dominate *The White Hotel* are for the most part geographically distant from Ukraine but direct the reader's imagination back to Babi Yar; furthermore, Thomas's landscapes are transformed by disaster, becoming radically altered topographies which correspond to those of the Ukraine Holocaust as a whole as described by Kuznetsov and more recently by Desbois and his interviewees.

Vice's analysis of *The White Hotel* suggests that key tropes in the novel function to trigger a postwar reader's 'knowledge of the vocabulary and geography of genocide' (2000: 61), in many cases specifically related to the events at Babi Yar. Those that relate to geographic elements are of particular interest to this analysis. Central events of the novel, whether described in verse (as in the first section, 'Don Giovanni') or in narrative prose (as in the longer, later section, 'The Gastein Journal'), take place against a mountainous backdrop, with a white hotel at the edge of a lake. Thomas draws attention to the contours and tones of this landscape early in both sections, depicting an initially tranquil alpine idyll, with blue skies, 'snowcapped mountains above the trees' (1981: 19) and a brilliant emerald lake (1981: 40). In these descriptions the only implicit parallel to the Ukrainian landscape can be found in the dark green of the fir trees (1981: 21), ubiquitous in Ukraine and the only trees mentioned in Kuznetsov's descriptions.[3] As the landscape around the hotel is disrupted by extreme weather and surreal natural disasters, more explicit echoes of Babi Yar appear. A violent gale rips the roof off the nearby summerhouse and overturns a boat, killing several people (1981: 41), and a storm causes a flood (1981: 43–44). The 'trail of debris' left behind is lit by flashes of sheet lightning (1981: 46). Almost immediately afterwards the hotel is struck by a fire, apparently caused by the reflection of the sun's rays on the snowy mountain; many more people die. A funeral is held, and as mourners stand on the edge of a mass grave in the shadow of the mountain, thunder arrives. A landslide descends, and mourners 'fall, one by one, into the trench, as if intolerable grief afflicted them … they twitched a little and the earth and rocks began settling on them' (1981: 67–68). Finally, a cable car crashes and more guests fall to their deaths on the mountainside. A notable number of the examples of a genocide 'vocabulary' that Vice identifies as trigger-tropes – the 'mass graves' of the drowned hotel guests (1981: 66) the vast 'trench' in which mourners are buried (1981: 68) – consolidate the argument that Thomas deliberately mobilizes land forms to create a parallel between this imaginary place and Babi Yar.

In both 'Don Giovanni' and 'The Gastein Journal', explicit descriptions of the protagonist's sexual relationship are juxtaposed with the details of the natural disasters that shape this landscape: 'I jerked and jerked until his prick released / its cool soft flood. Charred bodies hung from trees'; 'it was incredible / so much in me, yet still I was not full / they bore the bodies from the flood and fire / on carts, we heard them rumbling through the pines / and fade to silence' (1981: 26). After the cable car crashes, a drunken observer, a German named Vogel, comments that 'it might have been worse – there were a large number of Yids among the victims' (1981: 78), a thinly veiled reference to the SS at Babi Yar who were reported to have remained inebriated throughout the extermination process (Thomas 1981: 222; Kuznetsov 1972: 374). The hotel itself is resonant with the logistical battle for space and resources of which the destruction of Kiev's population at Babi Yar was ineluctably part: '[T]he white hotel was extremely popular and there were … more requests for rooms than they could possibly accommodate. From this point of view alone, the catastrophic deaths of the past few days were a godsend; but even this unusually rapid turnover could not keep pace with the demand' (Thomas 1981: 79). Accounts of the operations at Babi Yar, too, frequently suggest that soldiers were struggling to keep up with the task of shooting, burying and later burning those transported there (see Kuznetsov 1972: 377).

Geographical descriptions are among the lines that Thomas transposes directly from Kuznetsov; not this time from his documentation of Pronicheva's testimony, but from his own memory of Babi Yar as a child as included in the above discussion of *Babi Yar: A Document in the Form of a Novel*. Thomas's version is noticeably transposed (direct examples of words which duplicate Kuznetsov's own in bold):

> There was a steep wall of sand, behind which the firing could be heard. They made the people form up into short lines and led them through the gap which had been hurriedly dug in the sand-stone wall. The wall hid everything from view, but of course the people knew where they were. The **right bank of the Dnieper is cut by** deep **ravines**, and this particular **ravine was enormous, majestic, deep and wide like a mountain gorge. If you stood on one side of it and shouted you would scarcely be heard on the other. The sides were steep, even overhanging in places; at the bottom ran a little stream of clear water. Round about were cemeteries, woods and allotments.** The local people knew the ravine as Babi Yar (1981: 213).

Pronicheva appears in Lisa Erdman's tale as an old friend she knows from the theatre. She survives again in Thomas's hands; Lisa becomes the dead for whom Pronicheva lives to bear witness: 'Yet it had happened thirty thousand times; always in the same way and always differently. Nor can the living ever speak for the dead. / The thirty thousand became a quarter of a million. A quarter of a million white hotels in Babi Yar' (Thomas 1981: 221). Lisa's description of the mass grave is as follows:

> The rustle of cockroaches filled her mind. Then she started to understand that the sound came from the mass of people moving slightly as they settled down and were pressed tighter by the movement of the ones who were still living. / She had fallen into a bath of blood. (Thomas 1981: 218)

Lisa, not yet dead, is discovered, groaning, by a soldier who beats her and rapes her with a bayonet. She dies in the ravine.

> During the night, the bodies settled. A hand would adjust, by a fraction, causing another's head to turn slightly. Features imperceptibly altered. 'The trembling of sleeping night,' Pushkin called it; only he was referring to the settling of a house. (Thomas 1981: 220)

Thomas integrates an accidental fire at the hotel, a natural mudslide and flood into the landscape surrounding it, echoing the burning of bodies, the dynamiting of the ravine walls to fill the mass grave at Babi Yar and the later collapse of the dam in 1960. In a short section at the conclusion of 'The Sleeping Carriage', he provides a brief overview of the landscaping of the ravine, including the construction of the dam, stating that 'the effort to annihilate the dead went on, in other hands' after the war (Thomas 1981: 222).

The life-time of Pronicheva's story in the hands of Kuznetsov and Thomas can be effectively conceptualized as memory's 'mediation' and 'remediation'. The model significantly echoes Confino and Fritzsche's argument as discussed in the introduction, revising the concept of static *lieux de mémoire* to accommodate memory's dynamism. 'As the word itself suggests, "remembering" is best seen as an active engagement with the past, as performative rather than reproductive ... If stories about the past are no longer performed ... they ultimately die out in cultural terms' (Erll and Rigney 2009: 2). Particularly in view of Thomas's appropriation, it is also worth reiterating Erll and Rigney's statement that throughout performative processes, texts 'may be replaced or "over-written" by new stories that speak more directly to latter-day concerns and are more relevant to latter-day identity formation' (Erll and Rigney 2009: 2). The controversial reception of *The White Hotel* is all the more valuable when we keep in mind that 'fighting about memory is one way of keeping it alive' (Erll and Rigney 2009). Throughout the central narrative of *The White Hotel,* Thomas presents a series of imaginary natural events which can be directly related to the real history of Babi Yar. None of the original events were natural; they were, conversely, the results of human-perpetrated violence. Yet by mobilizing them in fiction, Thomas captures both the phenomenological experience of the mass grave and the radical disruption of landscape that characterized both individual and collective suffering at Babi Yar and across Ukraine under Nazi occupation. His remediation thus contributes to the evolution of cultural memories of Babi Yar whilst preserving its fundamental geographical, and to some extent experiential, specificity. Pronicheva, Kuznetsov and Thomas between them present a powerful mediation and remediation of Babi Yar, as an 'experience of the real' (Erll and Rigney 2009: 3) – albeit with the inevitable limitations of hypermediacy – which I propose has structured contemporary imaginations of the Ukraine Holocaust. I now move on to consider one result of this awareness of the massacre beyond Ukraine: the creation of the Babi Yar Memorial Park, Denver.

Notes

1. Whilst criticism has been directed at Thomas for altering and adding to Kuznetsov's transcript, as Vice (2000: 42) has remarked, 'Thomas's version is remarkable for what it keeps as much as for what it adds', and ultimately the result is that 'we can still learn what happened to [Pronicheva]' (2000: 41).

2. Kuznetsov (1972: 13) repeatedly reaffirms the veracity of his account from the first page of the text; 'This book contains nothing but the truth'; 'I am writing it as though I were giving evidence under oath in the highest court and I am ready to answer for every single word. This book records only the truth - AS IT REALLY HAPPENED' (1972: 14). Immediately before embarking on Pronicheva's story, he claims: 'I am now going to tell her story, as I wrote it down from her own words, without adding anything of my own' (1972: 98).

3. See for example 'pines' (1972: 448) ('fir' is a synonym).

SIX

KIEV TO DENVER

As noted in the introduction of this chapter, the Babi Yar Park in Denver was inaugurated in the 1980s. This was a result of a series of discussions held in the 1960s by a group of American Jews who were motivated by the marginalization of Holocaust memory in Ukrainian territory, and who perceived a continued persecution of minority groups in the Soviet Union as a whole. To draw further attention to these issues in their local community and beyond, they decided to create a memorial space for the victims of Babi Yar on American soil. They aimed to give Ukrainian Holocaust memory the place it was being denied in Ukraine. The lack of commemoration in Kiev at the time was central to the park's stated agenda. This is mentioned frequently in early speeches and press releases made by the Babi Yar Park Foundation, and further suggested by the choice of the following lines from Yevtushenko's poem as a header on Foundation stationary: 'There are no memorials over Babi Yar / Only an abrupt bank like a crude epitaph rears'. The early stated aim of the park was to 'commemorate the tragic events which occurred in 1941 at Babi Yar' (Babi Yar Park Foundation n.d.). Initially, then, its premise can be seen as both ethical and political. The nucleus of the idea came from the Colorado Committee of Concern for Soviet Jewry (CCCSJ); an organization formed to educate people about the plight of Soviet Jews, particularly those who wished to immigrate to Israel but were prevented from doing so by the Soviet government (known as 'refuseniks'). The first plans for a memorial were comparatively modest; organizers thought to name a street after Babi Yar. Whilst no streets were then nameless, an area of Denver parkland was available and subsequently earmarked for a memorial project in September 1969. Both Yevtushenko and Kuznetsov wrote to support the endeavour, in an extension of their existing role in promoting awareness of Babi Yar on an international level. A separate committee, the Babi Yar Park Foundation, was formed in 1970 to run the project. A series of disagreements about the appropriate use of the space led to a rift between the CCCSJ and the newly formed Foundation,[1] and from this date architect Alan Gass and local activist Helen Ginsburg became the key 'memorial entrepreneurs'.

Landscapes in Dialogue

There are certain characteristics of the park as it was originally landscaped which significantly illuminate its relationship with its Ukrainian counterpart and demonstrate the way in which soil and topography have become central in remembering and commemorating Babi Yar. I am not suggesting that the texts discussed in the previous section all played a part in the way the park was developed; rather that, in both this literature and the commemorative endeavour in Denver, natural forms and the way we experience them are central co-ordinates. From its earliest incarnation, certain resonances between the park landscape and that of Ukraine have been essential to its design. The park bears a topographical similarity to Babi Yar itself; the land includes a small ravine, which, according to Babi Yar survivor Batya Barg, who visited the park in 1971, is reminiscent of the one in Kiev. This resemblance is frequently referred to in speeches and planning documents relating to the park and associated fundraising campaigns, and such documents make clear that this geographical correspondence became a guiding principle in its curatorship and design. Ginsburg argued that a 'topographical and climatic comparison of Denver and Kiev, as well as typical flora are concerned' was 'astounding' (Ginsburg, n.d. ca. early 1970s, speech draft); and furthermore

Figure 6.1. Ravine, Babi Yar Park, Denver

that a 'study has revealed that the flora and topography of Denver's Babi Yar Park [are] similar to, and bears a haunting resemblance to, the original ravine in Kiev, as it was in 1941' (Ginsburg n.d. ca. early 1970s, voiceover transcript).

The extent to which the ravine in Kiev as it was in 1941 really resonates with the one in Denver can only be judged according to photographic evidence, due to the extensive re-landscaping of this site and the mudslide of 1961 as discussed in Chapter 4. Certainly a difference in scale must be taken into account, for the ravine in Denver is too small to have functioned as a substantial mass grave. Other resonances are easier to establish. Whilst there is no evidence of the mentioned 'study' into the flora and topography of Denver and Kiev in the Mizel Museum's archive, the claim is verified by a brief examination of the physical geography of these two areas. Both the prairie land of the American West and Eurasian steppe are classified as natural temperate grasslands.[2] Whilst they are often supported by different types of soil, grasslands, with their flat, rolling form and limited arboreal features, they are visually 'remarkably' similar (Chiras 2004: 94). Specifically, '[i]n many respects, Ukraine's natural vegetation landscapes are very similar to those of North America's interior' (Cooper 2006: 17). Unsurprisingly given the similar climatic and topographic features that support them, plants native to the steppe and the prairie are also of notable similarity. Their appearance is determined by their need to function in dry climates: bunch forms and narrow leaves which help to retain moisture, and light colours which reflect the sun. (Cushman and Jones 2004: 18–20). Thus Gass and Ginsburg's claims for the topographical similarity of their location in 2011 to the Ukraine in 1941 are geologically sound. Beyond this resonance, Gass also states that it has become important to preserve the prairie land that still covers much of the Babi Yar Park, because there is very little left elsewhere in Denver. He recalls the landscape surrounding the park from his own childhood, before the prairie had been destroyed to make room for the encroaching sprawl of the city.[3] Thus conservation, as well as symbolism, has played a role in determining the appearance of the park. However, in embracing this opportunity for conservation and avoiding the typical 'lawn', the park overall does not correspond to the Babi Yar site in Kiev *today*; certainly in the eastern half, lawns rather than prairie grasslands are the aesthetic of choice. In commemorative terms, this perhaps allows the Babi Yar Park a claim to apparent 'authenticity' that its counterpart in Kiev cannot share.

There are, however, other resonances between the two sites today which emerged long after the design for the park was conceived; these are in no way deliberate and, in fact, even the current curators of the Denver memorial are unaware of them.[4] Both sites are surrounded by busy, multilane roads, creating juxtapositions between the parks and the larger landscapes within which they exist; both are peaceful green spaces within larger urban areas, with the result that both are used by local communities for everyday, noncommemorative activities: jogging, dog-walking, and sunbathing, for example. Rather than normalizing the memory of atrocity, there is a sense, for the Mizel Museum's executive director Ellen Premack and Ginsburg at least, that this is an appropriate way for the park to be used; the memory of Babi Yar is integrated into the lives of those who visit it, a constant reminder to consider the lives of others.

All planting was to reflect the aforementioned similarity between the two landscapes. The haunting resemblance is mentioned in a speech dated 1974, author unknown, which is noted as written for the occasion of the unveiling of the first sign at the site:

> General landscape construction would be harmonious with the site. The plantings and planting areas will be designed using plant materials which are native to, or compatible with, the rigorous climate of both Denver and the Babi Yar of Kiev. (Babi Yar Park Foundation n.d.)

The aforementioned manually activated voice-over at the entrance to the park – which is formed from two block of stone with a space between them to echo a ravine – tells visitors the history of Babi Yar and the park, informing them that the place they stand bears a 'haunting resemblance to the original ravine in Kiev as it was during 1941' (transcript of narrative recorded 2011; this extract was also included in the earliest version of the transcript in the archives). The idea that the park's landscape, in its resemblance to Babi Yar, could bring visitors somehow 'closer' to the tragic history of the original ravine, was implicit in the Park Foundation's rhetoric. Plans for landscaped features also included a 'Forest that Remembers' and a 'People Place', an amphitheatre with a cylinder of earth from the original ravine at Babi Yar at its centre. The earth was transported by Denver State Senator John Bermingham when he visited Kiev, according to Ginsburg's recollection, at some point early in the 1970s. Apparently, Bermingham had, upon visiting Babi Yar, felt a sudden compulsion to scoop some soil into his bag to take back to Denver with him. He presented it to the Park Foundation on his return, and its burial at the centre of the park in Denver serves to highlight the notion that the earth itself constitutes a carrier or vessel of memory. Having travelled across the international cultural imaginary, prompted in part by literary remediation, Ukrainian soil itself now took a transcontinental journey.[5] The soil 'mixture', to use Kuznetsov's description, was now operating within an international context, as well as being internationally constituted.

For Gass and Ginsburg, however, along with other members of the Babi Yar Park Foundation, the symbolic resonance of the park's natural features goes beyond its similarity to Babi Yar. From its earliest inception, the space

Figure 6.2. Seal over buried cylinder of earth

was designed to be a 'living monument'. It was meant not only to present visitors with a 'Ukrainian' topography but to restore and perhaps even redeem that topography in Denver. Coincidentally, in doing so, they reinscribe a faith in nature that Kuznetsov and Grossman, albeit in different ways, imply was lost throughout their exposure to atrocity in Ukraine. This is evident in the park's design, for example the 'Forest that Remembers'. A draft inscription for a sign planned to stand next to it reads:

> In this grove … one hundred trees stand tall. Each a living memorial to men, women, children … In every leaf, their lives; in every branch, their families; in every rooted trunk, their past. / Life courses even when leaves have fallen. Memory persists even after presence parts. / Can we not learn from the trees? Each stands alone – yet, flourishes in the benevolent shade of the others. / Seasons change, so must we. Winter's madness must not dry the sap of loving life again. (Babi Yar Park Foundation n.d.)

As a way of fundraising for the planting of the grove, the Park Foundation ran a scheme in which participants could sponsor an individual tree. They received cards on which the following legend was printed: 'Why a Tree? It is a 'being' and a 'becoming' – symbolizing the promise of a continued circle of life.'[6] The memorial potential of the forest as presented diverges notably from the 'treacherous' realm described by Grossman, in which the relationship between natural forms is instead defined by constant battles and struggles (Grossman 2006: 391).

The rhetoric surrounding the forest fits into the larger discourse of the foundation, positing the park as a 'place of life' in opposition to Babi Yar as 'a place of death' (Ginsburg n.d., ca. early 1970s, speaker system narrative). Such is notable throughout their promotional and fundraising endeavours, for example in the juxtaposition of the seeds 'of human agony' sown at Babi Yar with 'seeds of conscience and concern' from which the park in Denver was to grow (Ginsburg 1974). These statements also prompt us to consider another element of the park's remit: its transcultural slant. 'The concept of Babi Yar reflects a spirit of humanitarianism that transcends all boundaries' (Ginsburg, *n.d.,* ca. early 1970s, speaker system narrative).

> Because Judaism's love of its own, and love for all mankind are inextricably interwoven, the Babi Yar Park concept has evolved beyond commemorating solely the tragic history of the Jew ... With the aid of people throughout our country, this park will grow in beauty and viability, thriving on its message of freedom and dignity for all men, regardless of religion, race, ethnicity or national citizenship. It will speak out against anti-humanism anywhere in this world of ours... for wherever a man is harmed, we are all hurt. (Ginsburg 1974)

By this stage, then, it becomes clear that the specific political thrust of the CCCSJ had been replaced by a more general message promoting international solidarity beyond national and cultural boundaries. From 1971 to 1983 the park was developed in phases as a result of the Park Foundation's persistent dedication to raising awareness and funds (see Gass 2010 and Park Foundation correspondence and minutes throughout this period). Significantly, Gass recalls, '[t]he support of the Jewish community was astonishingly meagre' (2010). For twenty-three years, the Park Foundation continued to develop the site. Although they do not corroborate Young's description of a park fallen into disuse, Gass certainly acknowledges both himself and Ginsburg, recognizing '[their] own mortality' (2010), were aware that their ultimate goals for the park would require new collaborative partners in order to be fulfilled. With this in mind, the Park Foundation was eventually disbanded in 2005 and the stewardship of the park passed to Denver's Mizel Museum, although members of the original foundation continued to play a key role in the park's development in an advisory capacity.

From the Holocaust to the War on Terror

From 2005 the aims to 'improve the public visibility of the park and adapt it to the museum's program' became central to its development (Gass 2010). With regards the former point, conversations with Gass, Ginsburg and Premack reveal that 'visibility' was and continues to be both a local and a global is-sue: the way the park has been landscaped to date meant that there was little view over it from the surrounding area, thus casual passers-by were unlikely to realize its presence and significance; Premack also believes that the park potentially has relevance to the national and international community and that its profile should be raised accordingly, as do both Gass and Ginsburg. In order to say a little more about the latter point that the park should be able to enhance the Mizel Museum's program, it is necessary to briefly foreground its main aims and remit as an institution, that is, to function as a 'portal to the contemporary Jewish experience. Its exhibits, events and educational pro-grams inspire people of all ages and backgrounds to celebrate diversity' and 'offer interactive experiences that promote community, understanding and multiculturalism' (Mizel Museum 2012a). The permanent exhibit is focused on a 'Jewish journey across time and space from a contemporary perspec-tive', with an essential goal 'for each visitor, in examining the experience of the Jewish people, to think about and feel proud of his or her own personal journey, and to feel inspired by the fact that journeys don't end but rather continue to unfold' (Mizel Museum 2012a). Thus whilst it centres on Jewish culture specifically, it is used as a platform for engagement *across* cultures; Premack sees the museum's exhibits and education programmes as ways 'to open minds, change attitudes, and discover paths that tie our world together through respect for our common humanity' (Mizel Museum 2012b). These are what we might call transcultural priorities.

In 2006 the Mizel announced an international competition for a design to develop Babi Yar Park, and in 2009 confirmed that a design by the artist-ar-chitect team Julian Bonder and Krzysztof Wodiczko had been selected to take the project forward. The development, as previously, is currently taking place in stages by necessity, for substantial – and as yet to be found – fi-nances are required to carry out the design as a whole. However, it is possible to assess the nature of what it is hoped will unfold via the publicity brochure produced by the Mizel Museum to showcase Wodiczko and Bonder's design. Notably, elements such as the 'People Place' and the 'Forest that Remem-bers' (referred to in the new design as the 'Grove of Remembrance') are to be maintained and integrated into what Wodiczko and Bonder describe as 'an active site of memory' which will facilitate 'three kinds of memories': the first focused 'on maintaining the memory of the Holocaust and of Babi Yar', the second 'on present and historic events and their immediate emotional aftermath', and the third 'on active emotional and thinking responses to new, unfolding world events that contain and bring back the memory of past terror and genocide which elicit a call for action towards a better future' (Bonder and Wodiczko 2009). In order to achieve this the team propose the addition of four new elements to the original design: an Empty Volume (an empty space surrounded by 'monumental' walls with square holes running through them containing memorial flames; the empty space is to be a 'forum for conversations, … contemplation and solitude'); the transformation of the ravine into a 'reflective and active path' with a stream of 'continuous running water' to 'represent on going life'; and a Monitoring and Information Center where 'the world situation indicating all points of emerging terror activities' will be displayed to visitors. Throughout, the new design functions in accordance with recently emerging scholarship in acknowledging and further encouraging the dialogical nature of the memorial experience in landscape. Given that Bonder's published work (2009) on commemoration has been part of this discourse, this is unsurprising. The team suggest that their Working Memorial 'will significantly transform Babi Yar Park into a unique and new kind of public landscape: a participatory public place and an active agent for culture and dialogue' that 'encourages visitors of all ages to be conscious and productive' (Bonder and Wodiczko 2009). The new park is to be as much about the visitor as the victim.

It is thus obvious that the new design echoes the Mizel Museum's transcultural priorities. However, a more specific narrative arguably emerges prominently in the brochure, in sections authored by both the design teams and the museum respectively: the integration of Babi Yar within a discourse on acts of terror. In this respect, the new design can also be seen to complement the aims of the Mizel Museum's partner museum, another Denver institution also founded by Larry Mizel, the Counterterrorism Education Learning Lab (CELL). Inevitably, this is another project that deserves a more thorough analysis than can be offered here. For the purposes of this argument, it is sufficient to note the main stated purposes of CELL and its permanent exhibition, *Anyone, Anytime, Anywhere: Understanding the Threat of Terrorism*: to 'educate and empower citizens and organisations with the tools to become more informed, prepared and involved with their own communities in order to help combat the threat of terrorism'; the exhibit 'provides visitors with an in-depth understanding of the history of terrorism, the methods terrorists employ and the extent to which terrorism impacts societies around the world' (CELL 2011). CELL, the Mizel Museum and the Babi Yar Park now form a triangle of sites in Denver with intimately related concerns.

In the first phase of Babi Yar Park's redevelopment, a significant addition is being made to the site which is not referred to in the brochure but certainly fits its rubric; the aforementioned sculpture made from World Trade Center steel. The steel, which arrived in Denver in July 2011, is being used to construct two sculptures, one for CELL and one for the Babi Yar Park. The latter 'will feature a so-called "earth sculpture" … a vertical surface with a marble and glass reflective wall leading to a plaza' containing the steel (Marcus 2011). Both Ginsburg and Premack reject firmly the notion that inauguration of the sculpture is in any way intended as a political gesture. As far as Gass and Ginsburg are concerned, their aims have not changed since they became part of the Babi Yar Park Foundation in 1970–1; they see the new developments, including the inauguration of the steel, as commensurate with their original agenda to encourage 'freedom and equality for all men'.

The questions raised by the park are thus: what are the real similarities and differences between two events such as 9/11 and the massacres at Babi Yar in 1941, and do their differences matter if by focusing on their similarities a genuine feeling of differentiated solidarity can be produced? Furthermore, is it possible, as Ginsburg and Premack suggest, to create an apolitical commemorative space?

Shared Ground?

Across this section of the book, the dynamics of two memoryscapes have been uncovered. In pursuing this exploration, I have taken a necessarily brief glance at certain other museums and memorials within the larger landscapes inhabited by these sites (the *holodomor* 'Memory Candle' in Kiev and the Mizel Museum and CELL in Denver). I have suggested that designers and curators at the Babi Yar Park, Denver, have embraced a transcultural approach to Holocaust representation of the type that, to date, has been refused in Ukrainian memory discourses. The 'Anyone, anytime, anywhere' narrative in Denver finds its opposite at the site of the original Babi Yar atrocity, where memorials to a number of cultural groups jostle for space in the shadow of the monumental Soviet sculpture group. The 'memory competition' between the Holocaust and the *holodomor* as discussed in Chapter 4 serves to accentuate this lack of cohesion within the Kiev site as a whole. In this final section I evaluate some of the questions raised by these two memoryscapes.

To take first the examples from Ukrainian territory, the Holocaust and the *holodomor* arguably share more ground than current memory discourse and landscapes suggest. Current competitiveness could perhaps be productively neutralized by an official recognition of this ground. Both the Holocaust and the *holodomor* can be seen as the result of attempts to colonize Ukrainian land. Snyder's research draws attention to the forces that shaped Ukraine under Stalin and Hitler, revealing many parallels – both political and experiential – in the process; furthermore, such parallels become even more pronounced when taken alongside the accounts given by Desbois of his field work across Ukraine and other available testimonial accounts from both periods, particularly those of Kuznetsov. In both the *holodomor* and the Holocaust, people who occupied this territory were forced to fight against each other for survival, experienced or witnessed fatal starvation, were driven to murder and cannibalism. Victims of both regimes were buried chaotically, in mass graves full to overflowing which have come to characterize Ukrainian memories of landscape in these periods. The traditional relationship between those who lived in Ukraine and the nation's soil was also subverted by both regimes. This subversion was a reality for a number of cultural and ethnic groups; more Ukrainians may have died in the famine, and more Jews may have been killed in the Holocaust, but the two atrocities both affected each of these groups and a number of others besides. Only ten years apart, many people from these groups suffered under both regimes, and the commonality of this suffering is explicit in their testimonies, and in the case of Grossman, in his integration of testimony into fiction.

Yet recognition of these similarities is frequently refused both within and beyond the Ukraine. Within Ukraine itself, Kappeler suggests that whilst 'the revived Ukrainian national history ... fulfils the important task of legitimizing and strengthening the new Ukrainian state and the fragile Ukrainian nation', on the other hand, a 'historical narrative that excludes non-Ukrainians' fails to articulate much that is central to the country's development; it is on this basis that Kappeler pleads for 'the opening up of the narrow mono-ethnonational approach and for a multiethnic history of Ukraine' (2009: 61). It is unclear in Kappeler's argument exactly who is being excluded – whether 'non-Ukrainians' is a reference to Jews, which confuses the issue as some Ukrainians are also Jewish – but his argument that instead of engaging in an ethnocentric competition centring on the questions 'Who has suffered most?' and 'Who had the greatest number of victims?' one should 'tell what is known about all the atrocities of the past, their victims and perpetrators, regardless of ethnic origin' (2009: 62) is worth pursuing.

Based on the noted parallels between victim and witness experiences of atrocity throughout the *holodomor* and the Holocaust in Ukraine, recognition of this commonality potentially presents an opportunity to move beyond competitive memory and focus on what those who have lived on Ukrainian soil have shared. Whether the new museums to be built at Babi Yar and elsewhere in Kiev will take up this opportunity and engage with the longer history of atrocity, suffering and perseverance that has characterized the experiences of all cultures on Ukrainian territory remains to be seen. Based on activity up to 2010, it seems fair to suggest that the political concerns which have dominated the Kiev memoryscape have not resulted in any commemorative practices at the original Babi Yar site that attempt to harness its potential to facilitate transcultural identification.

Such an attempt has clearly been central to the redesign of the Babi Yar Park in Denver. The park curators' decision to link the events at Babi Yar to those at the World Trade Center in 2001 is made explicit with the installation of the aforementioned steel sculpture. However, the connection between the Holocaust and the War on Terror which grounds this attempt is rather different to that I have suggested as existing between the *holodomor* and the Holocaust. On both 29–30 September 1931 and 11 September 2001, lives were unjustly cut short by regimes which used terror as a weapon against particular cultural or national groups. However, the disparities between the two events are arguably more notable. The attack on the twin towers was a challenge to the hegemony of the United States, but it cannot be regarded as an attempt to erase that nation and its citizens from the face of the earth. The Babi Yar massacre took place during the occupation of the Ukrainian capital by German troops, and it was one of many similar mass shootings then taking place throughout the country. The attack on the World Trade Center was an isolated, unexpected event for those whose lives it took and for those who witnessed it.

Some feel that such divergences are of little note: 'As the Holocaust has been for many Jews, 9/11 is now for many Americans; though of course radically different in scale, timing and circumstance, both events are emotionally devastating and morally clear cut since the murder of innocents is always, utterly wrong' (Findling and Schweber 2007: 1). Such arguments resonate with the approach adopted by the Babi Yar Park's curators. They do not state that the two events were the *same*; their concern is directing positive and active responses to the persecution of others, whoever they are. That both Babi Yar and 9/11 are 'emotionally devastating' and 'morally clear cut' to their respective constituencies is central to their integration. Yet without attending to the specificity of the two events and their larger contexts – to their 'radical difference' – sameness is implied. As Peter Novick has argued, 'collective memory simplifies: sees events from a single, committed perspective', and may be 'in crucial senses ahistorical, even anti-historical' (2000: 3–4). Whilst curators of the park in Denver laudably integrate the Holocaust into what they hope to be an ethically productive multidirectional narrative – one which acknowledges the extent to which memory is subject to 'borrowing' – the collective memory they promote risks overlooking the specificities of the events it brings together. The co-ordinates upon which parallels between the Holocaust and 9/11 have been based – whether in the museum environment, the media, or in academic discourse, both within and beyond America itself – are not always, I would argue, justified or desirable. Laub's suggestion of a resemblance based on their 'equally unimaginable' nature as events (2003: 204), for example, repeats the fundamental assumption that some experiences are completely ineffable. Furthermore whilst the specific motivations that have prompted the curators of the Babi Yar Park should be given due attention in any attempt to evaluate the project overall, it must also be acknowledged that it takes place within a particular national context, one in which, as Novick (2000: 12) argues, the Holocaust had 'become a moral and ideological Rorschach test' even before the attack on the World Trade Center had taken place. In some instances since, for example at a *Day of Reflection and Remembrance* at the U.S. Holocaust Memorial Museum a year after 9/11 during which Holocaust survivors read out the names of those killed in the attack, this use of the Holocaust as a template effectively 'emptied each [event] of their historical particularity' (Bernard-Donals 2005: 79). This is the existing national backdrop against which the reorientation of the Babi Yar Park is taking place, and, regardless of the particular aims of those who conceived this reorientation, in contributing to this discourse a subscription to its main tenets is implied.

Thus the potential of the site to develop a sense of differentiated solidarity may be somewhat undermined if the new design fails to adequately 'distinguish' two very 'different histories of violence' from one another. Nonetheless, the curators have not gone as far as to imply that any particular trauma is 'bigger' than another; it would be more accurate to say that they are in some sense equating two 'traumas' that perhaps do not share enough, particularly in terms of victim experience, to warrant that equation.

The Future of Memory in Ukraine and Beyond

By considering these two memorial environments alongside other co-ordinates in the respective surrounding cityscapes – the Memory Candle *holodomor* memorial and museum in Kiev, and the Mizel Museum and CELL in Denver – I have drawn attention to the dialogical networks of memory discourse in which they exist. I have suggested that the landscape of Babi Yar, Kiev, and the surrounding cityscape has been largely shaped by political and national concerns: initially those of the Soviet Union, and since 1991, those of Ukrainian nationalism. Conversely, the designers and curators of the Babi Yar Park in Denver, in spite of its political origins in the 1970s, are primarily driven today by a desire to promote ethical engagement beyond national boundaries. Both landscapes are seen, to some extent, as a means to a particular end; as is always the case, memoryscapes reveal as much about present concerns as they do about the pasts they commemorate. In comparing the two, the question of whether it is ever possible to create memorial space that combines an ethical politics of memory with a politically responsible ethics remains unanswered. The Holocaust in Ukraine, in both territorialized and reterritorialized spaces, is yet to find such expression.

Whilst these two memorial spaces say so much about their respective present contexts, it is also worth drawing attention to the varying degrees to which they have retained specificity with regards to the Ukrainian Holocaust and the way it was experienced. The discussion of literature and testimony in Chapter 5 – from Pronicheva's testimony to Thomas's fiction – suggested that this experience was one of a disrupted landscape, embedded in the soil of the Ukrainian topography. Babi Yar, I have suggested, is a microcosm of this larger national landscape. Whilst the ravine itself has been radically altered, transformed into an incoherent memorial space which bears little resemblance to the place experienced by victims in 1941, the Babi Yar Park in Denver, to some extent, takes that original landscape as a starting point for developing memories of Babi Yar for those who did not witness it. Furthermore, its curators attempt to transform the atrocious experience of that landscape into something more positive for the future; whilst the rhetoric is at times arguably redemptive, the 'living memorial' functions as a way of keeping memories of Babi Yar alive in a way that responds to and recognizes memory's dynamism and metamorphosis.

It should be no surprise, given this dynamism, that the Ukraine's competitive memory terrain continues to shift. On 10 December 2010 then Ukrainian President Viktor Yanukovych's website announced transfer of the running of the Ukrainian Institute of National Memory (UINM) to ministers in the Ukrainian cabinet, giving the government direct control of its budget. Whilst Prime Minister Mykola Azarov insisted that the related museum will not be closed as a result, as various media sources have suggested (see Kabachiy 2010), the transfer of the budget is suggestive. The former director of the UINM has been replaced by Valery Soldatenko, a member of the Communist Party who outraged a number of Ukrainian historians and political opponents by arguing that the *holodomor* was the 'the result of difficult circumstances,' and had not been artificially produced (Radio Free Liberty 2010). This was a direct counter to the law of 2006 that pronounced the *holodomor* to be an act of genocide, and entirely opposed to the rhetoric employed in the Candle of Memory. Meanwhile, the seventieth anniversary of events at Babi Yar seemed to prompt a resurgence of interest in the Holocaust in Ukraine in late 2011. Delegations to the site itself were frequent; a touring exhibition showcasing Desbois's project visited Kiev for the first time to coincide with the anniversary; and in October the aforementioned plan to build two new Jewish museums in Kiev, one at Babi Yar itself, was announced. The memory of Babi Yar was also politicized anew in January 2012, when a new international Jewish organization, the World Forum for Russian Jewry, was inaugurated at the United Nations Holocaust Memorial Day service and conference, with images of Babi Yar on screens in the background (Alperin 2012). Alexander L. Levin, president of the Greater Kiev Jewish Community, announced the forum's purpose: 'to bring together the Russian-speaking Jews of the world and save us and others from the next catastrophe and to protect our national land and the State of Israel. We stand ready to unite against the nuclear program of Iran ... We will not let another Holocaust engulf us' (in Alperin 2012). The Holocaust is here mobilized in a way that conflates the historical and political specificity of both the Nazi genocide and the Israel-Palestine conflict, much as Michael Bernard-Donals argues has been the case in American memorial practices that take the Holocaust as a framework for the commemoration of 9/11. In the case of the World Forum for Russian Jewry, the mobilization is simply more transparent in using the Holocaust to justify continuing military conflict.

Meanwhile in Denver, commenting on their inclusion of 9/11 steel in the park landscape, Premack and Larry Mizel argue that '[i]f you want a site to be relevant and meaningful and bring it to life, you have to go forward ... This is Babi Yar Park. We're bringing additional elements to it, but we're not taking anything away' (in Jacobs 2012). Furthermore, in relation to educating visitors about the War on Terror, Mizel argues that 'Jews, who have a tie to Israel, had a better awareness of terrorism before the US woke up to it on 9/11 ... I felt we were uniquely situated to provide the proper background and support to educate the public on the nature of terrorism' (Jacobs 2012). Whether or not one agrees with the notion of a specifically Jewish appreciation of the threat of terrorism, it is clear that Mizel and Premack do not envision that the historical or political specificity of either the Holocaust or 9/11 will be elided at the new Babi Yar Park. Yet there is no way of ensuring a confluence between their own ethical intentions and the collective memories produced, shaped or mobilized as a result. Whilst on one hand the comparative memorial frameworks mentioned here – both at the Babi Yar Park and as set up by the Soviet Forum for Russian Jewry – urge an increased understanding and recognition of the way in which 'different histories of violence' may be 'implicated in each other', the way in which they do this does not necessarily imply or promote due attention to the factors that differentiate them (see Rothberg in Moses and Rothberg 2014: 33).

I have implied here that the inauguration of two Holocaust museums in Kiev would do much to redress an enduring imbalance, yet this clearly should not happen at the expense of understanding the *holodomor*'s place in Ukrainian history. The danger is that one zero-sum competition will simply evolve into another; as Rothberg notes, '[t]he struggle for recognition is fundamentally unstable and subject to ongoing reversal ... today's "losers" may turn out to be tomorrow's "winners"' (2009: 5–6). For a never-ending reversal to be avoided, cultural memories of Ukraine – be it at the centre of the nation or 6,000 miles away – must aim to combine the ethics of remembering with a reflexive awareness of political context. If this can be achieved, between the diverse cultures of present-day Ukraine and the United States there exists a potential platform for ethically oriented transcultural memory work: the creation of a genuine differentiated solidarity. Whether such a platform can be achieved is a question for the future.

This chapter has primarily examined the discourse of Ukrainian cultural memories of the Holocaust and *holodomor* in the years preceding the seventieth anniversary of Babi Yar in 2012. Since November 2013, Ukraine has entered a new political phase. Yanukovych's decision to reject allegiance with the European Union to align Ukraine further with Russia prompted protest across the country. Kiev's Independence Square protest camp, in particular, became a site of increased interest in the international media. In February 2014, when riot police moved in to clear the camp, clashes resulted in the deaths of seventy-seven people, a toll which has since risen to 102 during subsequent violence. Yanukovytch finally fled office, and an interim government now controls the country. The complexities of these developments cannot be explored here, but from the rhetoric that has surrounded them one point emerges clearly: Ukraine is once again subject to explicit political mobilizations of memory. Following Yanukovytch's branding of the protestors as 'fascists' in an attempt to discredit their motivations and tactics, the Kremlin declared the uprising to be 'an illegitimate fascist coup' (Harding 2014). The fact that many protestors were variously liberals, socialists and libertarians rather than nationalists was elided in favour of an easier and more familiar narrative. As *Atlantic* journalist Matt Ford commented in April 2014, international discourse on the situation in Ukraine selectively invokes Nazism to legitimate perspectives, as 'the West invokes the Hitler of 1936 and 1938, Putin and his allies claim they're fighting the Hitler of 1933 and 1934' (Ford 2014). For Putin's government, this became a key justification for the use of Russian military force on Ukrainian soil since early 2014, as Russian troops moved in to occupy the Crimea. In March 2015, the United States assistant secretary of state for European and Eurasian affairs Victoria Nuland argued that military action in Eastern Ukraine constituted an invasion of that nation's territory (Yuhas 2015).

Both nationally and globally, the rhetoric that surrounds recent developments in Ukraine constitutes a repeated phase in an ongoing cycle in which the past is made to work for the exigencies of the present; as a result the experiences, memories and motivations of individuals are all too often ignored. In Ukraine today, new memorials are emerging, but, rather than the aforementioned Holocaust museums, these take the form of spontaneous tributes to those who lost their lives in the Kiev streets in February 2014. These unofficial memorials, photographed and circulated in the international media alongside official statements that ignore such individual specificity, remind us that commemoration continues to play a crucial role in mediating our understanding of history, and, more crucially, our present world.

Coda

I visited Babi Yar, Kiev, in late September 2011, around the occasion of the seventieth anniversary of the massacre. The day before many official delegations were due to visit, the area around the Soviet era memorial was being re-gravelled and the monument itself was being intensively cleaned. Amidst this activity, groups of Ukrainian school children lined up in front of the sculpture group to have their photo taken by their teachers. Many held carnations to leave at the foot of the monument; others talked on their mobile phones. A visit to Babi Yar is part of normal school life in Ukraine today, which, after years of amnesia, is no small achievement. Yet something about the memorial complex makes it difficult to imagine what happened here in 1941, a feeling perhaps down to, or at least exacerbated by, the knowledge that the original ravine does not exist anymore. You cannot be sure, as a result, whether you're standing in the 'right' place.

At the bottom of the small ravine south of the menorah, an A4 paper sign in a plastic cover reads (in Ukrainian; tr. Olga Yelchenko):

RIBBON ALLEY
This is our memory of the victims of Babyn Yar and the Kurenivka tragedy of 1961
TIE YOUR OWN RIBBON!

A collection of ribbons are tied to surrounding tree branches. This area, unlike the memorial complex, has not been cleared up for the anniversary; empty bottles, plastic bags, and the remains of a small bonfire litter the ravine's floor. Nonetheless, somehow it is easier to think about Babi Yar's past – about man's capacity for destruction beyond the limits of the human imagination – here, amongst the ribbons and the rubbish, than it is anywhere else in the park.

It seems to me that Kiev today is no longer silent about its history. Before leaving the city, I make a stop at the Museum of Microminiature in the Perschershk Lavra; one room in which the miniature works of Ukrainian artist Nikolay Syadristy are displayed behind a row of microscopes: a caravan of golden camels set inside the eye of a needle; a model of a windmill perched on half of a poppy seed; a chess set, poised ready for a game, sits atop a pin head. It is hard to comprehend how Syadristy makes these tiny objects. He has to 'catch the moment of absolute silence between two heartbeats' to create them (*HH Journal* 2008). They force the viewer to marvel at man's capacity for creation beyond the limits of the human imagination. The last of his sculptures I see before leaving is an engraved human hair. Faintly visible, under the microscope, are the words 'Long Live Peace' in Ukrainian. The

Figure 6.3. Ribbon Alley

city's co-ordinates speak to one another, today, in unexpected ways, and in voices which have perhaps yet to be heard. But the ribbons in 'Ribbon Alley', like the unofficial memorials in Independence Square, attest to the presence of these voices, and the individuals who have given their lives in the ongoing struggle for Ukrainian land, identity and, perhaps, future peace.

Notes

Sections of this chapter are reprinted by permission of the publishers from 'Babi Yar: Transcultural Memories of Atrocity from Kiev to Denver' in Lucy Bond and Jessica Rapson (eds), *The Transcultural Turn: Interrogating Memory Between and Beyond Borders*. Berlin: de Gruyter, pp. 139–61. Copyright © 2014.

1. The rift was twofold: the Ukrainian community in Denver wanted to be involved in the development of the park, because 'the Jews killed at Babi Yar were Ukrainian Jews' (Morrison 1994: 6), but the CCCSJ argued that the collaboration of Ukrainian nationals with the Nazi perpetrators rendered their involvement inappropriate. Furthermore, the CCCSJ were concerned that their plan for a park which was 'beautiful and meaningful in a simple and unadorned manner' was being replaced with a much more expensive project: 'To think of the expenditure of dollars when our brothers in Israel and the Soviet Union are in such need is contrary to the very core of our Jewish religion' (Morrison 1994: 6). From Gass's later overview of the park's history, it becomes clear that the Park Foundation themselves only agreed to input from the Ukrainian community after they had made a financial contribution to the park's development.

2. Such environments are typically located in the interior of large continents, in the rain shadow of mountain ranges, with continental climates characterized by cold winters and dry, hot summers (Chape et al. 2008: 58). Denver lies on a high plain, in the foothills of the Rocky Mountains. Much of Ukraine too is flat, but the plains are surrounded by the Carpathian mountains to the west and the Crimean mountains to the southeast.

3. The loss of this prairie land is commensurate with the fate of much temperate grassland worldwide; Chape et al. (2008: 59) state that 'little … is now in anything like its natural or undisturbed state'. Whilst Chiras notes that in many cases this is due to the exploitation of the land in agricultural practice (grassland soils 'are probably the richest in the world as a result of thousands of years of plant growth and decay', 2004: 92), in Denver and the surrounding area the gradual eradication of prairie lands is due to modern urban landscaping (Nelson 2008: 47).

4. Premack, Gass and Ginsburg have never visited the site in Kiev; for Ginsburg in particular, her awareness of Ukrainian anti-Semitism had for many years resulted in a reluctance to visit the country.

5. In another recollection of this soil, Gass intriguingly recalls that at one stage the park was vandalized, and the seal that covered the hole where the cylinder was buried was stolen. The culprit was never discovered, and a new seal was commissioned from the original design. Gass was present when the new seal was fitted. He remarked, casually, that as far as he could see the cylinder was no longer there. It had been buried a

few feet underground, but apparently the workers fitting the seal had to dig quite far down to insert the anchors that held it in place. Whether Gass simply did not catch sight of the cylinder or it was truly missing is impossible to say without again removing the seal and excavating the ground. Yet this raises intriguing questions about the symbolism of the soil itself; if it is no longer there, is it right to mislead visitors by signposting its presence? Or is the very idea of the soil enough to facilitate some kind of engagement regardless? These questions deserve further attention.

6. A mock-up of the original card design can be found in the Penrose archive.

PART III

LIDICE

Through the brilliance of an image, the distant past resounds with echoes, and it is hard to know at what depth these echoes will reverberate and die away.

—Gaston Bachelard, *The Poetics of Space*

This final section examines the village of Lidice in the Czech Republic, which was razed by Nazi soldiers in 1942 as an act of retaliation for the assassination of *SS-Obergruppenführer* Reinhardt Heydrich.[1] Today, rebuilt, it has become a symbol of memory's resilience in the face of destruction. Originally home to 483 people, the population of Lidice was decimated by the attack: 173 male inhabitants, mainly miners and factory workers, were shot in the head, and the remaining women and children were forcibly deported, many to concentration camps. Eighty-two of the children and 60 of the women died before the war ended.[2] A total of 340 people were killed. The destruction of the village itself was undertaken with extraordinary attention to detail; it took over a year to complete ordered alterations to the topography of the land, which was to be covered with soil imported from Germany (Stehlik 2004: 96–97). Disproportionately, the Nazis took this opportunity to display the extent of their power in occupied Europe. That they chose to do this via a topographical territorialization is consistent with the argument pursued throughout this book: that the Nazis were significantly centred, both practically and ideologically, on landscape as both means and ends. Landscape was as much a representative, symbolic medium as it was a platform for warfare. The Germans renamed the place where Lidice had stood *Vorwerk* [tr. 'outlying estate'] (Stehlik 2004: 96–97). Its destruction, conceived by the Nazis as a warning to partisans and agitators, was publicized internationally as a demonstration of German domination. Following a fundraising campaign in the United Kingdom, which will be considered in more detail in the final chapter, a new Lidice was built overlooking the site of the old village almost immediately after the war ended, allowing the few survivors of the original settlement to return and build new lives. To date there is relatively little scholarly work about Lidice, yet the memory of events there exists today in a number of communities around the world which have, at first glance, no connection to it.

Echoing the trajectory of previous sections, this examination of Lidice begins at the site itself as a landscape of memory before moving on to consider how memories of the events that took place there have travelled across the world. Lidice became notorious almost immediately after it was razed, as a symbol of complete destruction. As a result of the attention to detail with which this destruction was pursued, there was little left to memorial entrepreneurs; occasional foundations are perceptible in Lidice's landscape, but the almost complete lack of physical remnants differentiates the original village site from many other site-based commemorative spaces. Whilst the Nazi endeavour to eliminate Lidice from history was frustrated by the international response to its destruction, extensive topographical alterations permanently altered the geography of the area. Beyond the few foundations, the original village has disappeared from view. This section demonstrates the way in which Lidice has become a co-ordinate at the centre of a transcultural nexus of memory work which itself operates across local, national and global levels of engagement. Looking firstly at site-based memorial endeavours, before progressing to an analysis of the ways in which the village (and the memory of what occurred there) interacts with a broader Holocaust memoryscape, I finally consider the effects of mobilizing the Lidice massacre; of constructing it as an analogical parable for a contemporary culture of cosmopolitan memory.

Chapter 7, 'Between the Past and the Future', pays particular attention to the outdoor landscape of the memorial, which is today rigorously curated and maintained, the planting in particular designed to function symbolically within the memorial space. Via Lidice's rose garden, in particular, I consider both the affective and ethical potential and limitations of natural 'curation' in the Holocaust context. The approach to managing Lidice's landscape, I suggest, is notably divergent from that found at other prominent Holocaust memorial sites. At Lidice, with few architectural remnants to 'stand in' for history, designers have had to find alternatives. Whilst landscape scholar Joachim Wolschke-Bulmahn (2001: 298) has concluded a discussion of similar issues with regards to the development of Bergen-Belsen with the statement that '[e]cological ideas are of no importance for [its design] … they are not relevant to its history or to its meaning for the future', I argue that ecology is as central to Holocaust commemorative landscaping as any other element of curatorial strategy. This argument is pursued via an examination of ideological and practical strategies of 'fencing in' and 'weeding out', both during the Holocaust itself and at Lidice today, based in part on Bauman's contention that the logic of gardening was central to the creation of a world in which the Holocaust could happen.

Chapter 8, 'Lidice Travels', begins with an exploration of the Nazis' original attempt to territorialize Lidice with German soil, the mediatization of which prompted the creation of memorial texts away from the site itself. Almost immediately after the massacre works of literature, music and film appeared. Notably, I suggest, beyond demonstrating a sense of differentiated transnational solidarity with the Czech people, these representations of Lidice utilize imagery of disrupted seasonal and pastoral landscape to frame the destruction of the village and its population. I continue to consider mobilizations of Lidice since 1990, when many European archives became accessible to historians for the first time since World War II. As a result memories of Lidice have been connected with those of two other villages which had been subject to similar violent destruction by Nazi forces: Oradour-sur-Glane (France) and Putten (Netherlands). The result is an emerging network of local-global memories of resistance and suffering particular to continental Europe (see de Keizer 2012: 120–35). Whilst the relationship between Lidice, Oradour, and Putten is firmly rooted in related historical events, my own discussion examines a recent activity which connects the site at Lidice to international locations which appear disconnected from the Czech village itself: the recently reported town twinning of Lidice with Khojaly, Azerbaijan (February 2011)[3] and proposed twinning of Lidice with Stoke-on-Trent, England (the planning for which has been underway since September 2010). Twinnings such as these, which are the subject of the final chapter in this section, continue the collective effort to keep the Lidice name alive in popular consciousness.[4]

Together, Lidice, Stoke-on-Trent, and Khojaly form a network of mobilized memories, a close examination of which facilitates not only a new understanding of Lidice as a symbol of the Holocaust in a global age, but also, and perhaps more crucially, an interrogation of the emerging critical frameworks which ground the very notion of memory's mobilization. Of particular interest is the model of cosmopolitanism – a 'process of "internal globalization" through which global concerns [increasingly] become part of local experiences' (Levy and Sznaider 2006: 2, after Beck 2004). For Levy and Sznaider (2006: 161) cosmopolitanism leads to positive institutional change, opening the way for 'ethically driven politics in the global arena'; the cosmopolitan memories formed against the Holocaust 'backdrop' have led the international community to establish 'global human rights conventions as [guiding principles] in international peace- and wartime politics' (2006: 183). In examining transcultural mobilizations of Lidice, an opportunity arises to assess the extent to which theoretical models of memory, in particular the move towards cosmopolitanism exemplified in Levy and Sznaider's work, can be seen to coalesce with actual, instrumental memory practices taking place in the world around us. The two Lidice twinning campaigns came about as a result of different motivations, and are characterized accordingly, yet they both emerge throughout this analysis as mobilizations of memory which suggest a disjuncture between the theorization and practice of cosmopolitanism.

Notes

1. Two airmen from Lidice, Josef Horák and Josef St íbrný, were accused of complicity in the assassination; despite lack of evidence for their involvement Hitler announced that Lidice was to be destroyed to 'make up for [Heydrich's] death on 9 June 1942' (Stehlik 2004: 71).

2. The majority of the children were sent to the Chelmno extermination camp, where it is suspected they were killed on the day of their arrival (2 July 1942) (Stehlik 2004: 100). Seven others who had been selected for 'Germanization' were sent to an orphanage run by Lebensborn, an SS organization established to 'reinforce the German population' (Stehlik 2004: 101). The women were initially sent to the Ravensbrück Concentration Camp; some were subsequently moved to Majdanek or Auschwitz (Stehlik 2004: 104–5). 143 women and 17 children survived and returned to Lidice after the war.

3. It should be noted that whilst the Khojaly twinning has been reported repeatedly in the press, in April 2012 Lidice Mayor Kellerova told the Czech magazine *Orer* that Lidice and Khojaly were not 'sister' cities (*Panorama.am* 2012). These contradictory reports demand further investigation, but in this chapter I consider the motivations of those who advocate the project rather than its official outcome.

4. It should be noted that the two projects have respectively been referred to by the press as 'twinnings'; in the case of Khojaly, Azerbaijan, the actual link was formalized by the signing of a 'protocol of cooperation' document by local authority figures from both areas.

SEVEN

BETWEEN THE PAST
AND THE FUTURE

That Lidice's landscape was radically altered by German soldiers was nothing new in itself, for, as discussed previously, the Nazis transformed landscapes all over continental Europe; what differentiates the razing of Lidice from most other examples is that topographical restructuring was the primary aim, not merely an incidental result. This section provides an overview of commemoration at Lidice itself, with a view to revealing how history and memory interact within its memorial landscape. In delineating the way this landscape functions at a local level, I establish a foundation for the broader analysis of national and global activity to come.

Lidice lies approximately 20km from Prague, and is easily reached from the city by an hourly bus. It is one of two prominent site-specific Holocaust memorial spaces in the Czech Republic, along with the former concentration camp and ghetto Theresienstadt (Czech: Terezín). Czech land was being taken over by the German government in two stages after the Munich Pact of 1938 was signed by representatives from the United Kingdom, France and Italy, allowing Hitler to incorporate first the Sudetenland and, within six months, the remainder of Czechoslovakia, into the Reich. Hitler announced the creation of the Protectorate of Bohemia and Moravia in March 1939. Officially it was an independent state within the Third Reich, but in actuality a 'puppet government' (Crowe 1994: 48) put in place by the Germans to ensure them of ultimate control over the land and its people. The central concern for this government was to Aryanize the Protectorate, and Jews were initially the primary victims of the German campaign in what is today the Czech Republic.[1] This is not to say that the Nazis cherished the Slavic races; indeed according to National Socialist ideology they were an inferior people,[2] but in 1942 the 'Jewish problem' was foremost in Hitler's mind. Lidice was thus a special case, in the sense that non-Jewish Czechs were targeted, primarily as a result of the aforementioned assassination of *Reichsprotek-*

tor Heydrich. Beyond the examples of Lidice and Terezín, the main impact made by the Nazis on Czech territory was the removal of Czech Jews from all over the Protectorate of Bohemia and Moravia: of 118, 310 people listed as Jewish, 78,154 were to die at the hands of the Nazis by the end of the war (Burton 2003: 73). Because the Germans needed Czech armaments and agriculture, much of the country, including its capital Prague, was left intact. This was also in part due to the fact that the Nazis were able to occupy it without the need for a military defeat (Cravens 1965: 15). Thus whilst the Jewish population was decimated in this period, and is still far smaller in the city today than in the years before the war, 'the contrast between the richness of the city's preserved Jewish culture and the relative absence of modern Jewish life [is] greater than almost anywhere else in Europe' (Winstone 2010: 160). This, then, is the larger landscape in which Lidice exists today.

As was found to be the case at Buchenwald, different areas of the memorial landscape can be seen to reflect different political moments. Accordingly Lidice's curation and maintenance – again like both Buchenwald and Babi Yar – changed quite radically in 1990. In the years between 1948 and 1989, when the Communist government was in place, the site was primarily used for 'political gatherings which the power-wielders of that time abused to present their own ideological clichés' (Stehlik 2007: 142). This approach to some extent explains the monumental architectural style of the museum and memorial complex, which was completed in 1962 and was the primary site of the aforementioned political gatherings. That the Communists had utilized the site throughout these years radically affected the way Lidice developed after 1989; the memorial's website asserts that 'state representatives wrongfully connected' the village with Communism, and thus 'did not provide any financial support to the village so that the museum and the rose garden could be sustained. They requested for all control over the memorial and the pious area including the rose garden to be taken over by the village' (Lidice Memorial 2012). The village could not finance the continued management of the space, and it was largely neglected until 2000, when the responsibility for its care was transferred to the Czech Ministry of Culture. The rose garden was restored almost immediately; in 2005–6 the museum was overhauled and fitted with a new permanent exhibition; and a separate education centre particularly designed for use by Czech schools now sits alongside it (inaugurated in 2008). The art gallery is home to an International Children's Exhibition, showcasing the results of an annual art competition ongoing since 1967[3] which functions as an active memorial to the children who died in Lidice; the 2011 competition received 25,400 entries by children from 65 countries (Kasalicka 2011), testifying to a considerable global interest in the village.

Both the village and Terezín are frequently associated with the fate of child victims of the Nazi regime.[4] As noted above, the Lidice children were deported and either exterminated or sent for 'Germanization', and their absence from the village is today made present in Lidice's landscape with a bronze sculpture group.[5] The creation of the art gallery, with its International Children's Competition, further provides an active way in which Lidice's lost youth can be remembered. They are also represented in the permanent exhibition in the site's museum, where postcards and letters written to family members at the last stage of their deportation are displayed. The murdered men also have their own memorial in the landscape, at the site of the mass grave in which they were buried, which is today marked by a bed of rose bushes. An image of the mass grave filled with men's bodies is projected on the floor in the museum, allowing the visitor to contemplate it as it was on 10 June 1942. The bed of roses now over the grave aesthetically mirrors the much larger aforementioned rose garden planted on another area of the site in 1955. This larger garden is dedicated to all the deceased inhabitants of Lidice: women are represented by pink roses, children with yellow and men with dark red. Elsewhere at the site the Lidice women are also represented by three separate statues of female forms: one holding a rose which, according to the Lidice Memorial guide pamphlet, is a 'symbol of new life in Lidice' (Vlk 2006), one with a child representing the plight of Lidice's mothers, and one crying with her face buried in her arms, expressing 'deep sorrow' (Vlk 2006).[6] I will discuss the curation of this part of the site in more detail in the next section. Elsewhere, three sets of foundations remain in the grassed

Figure 7.1. Foundations

Figure 7.2. Projections in the Lidice museum

expanse between the rose garden and the memorial complex and museum: those of the farm owned by Lidice residents Stanislav and Anastazia Horák, which warrant preservation particularly because the farm's garden was the location of the mass shooting of the Lidice men. They waited for execution in the cellar; thus the farm's foundations are granted a particular significance in the landscape and marked accordingly with a memorial tablet. The other foundations still visible are those of Lidice's St Martin's church and former local school.

The memorial complex overlooking this landscape comprises a monumental hexagonal plaza with a fountain at the centre, flanked by colonnades, the walls of which are decorated with three reliefs depicting the events of June 1942, and a pillared *gloriet* containing an eternal flame. The education centre, 'memorial hall' (a room used for temporary exhibitions), and museum open onto this space. The museum contains, alongside artefacts such as the aforementioned postcards and letter, a number of spaces for projected images. Beginning with photographs of villagers working the land around the peaceful prewar Lidice, the images trace its destruction, culminating, in the main exhibition space, in an image of the mass grave filled with bodies projected across the gallery floor. From outside visitors can view the gentle sloping valley where the original village once stood, which is divided from the new village by the rose garden.

Other than the marking of the mass grave with a monument built by the Red Army in 1945, the first area to be transformed in the wake of the initial destruction was the site of the new village, which was ready for habitation by 1949 (Stehlik 2007: 137). The rose garden, named the 'Friendship and

Figure 7.3. Hexagonal plaza

Peace Park' was added in 1955 (Stehlik 2007: 137). These initiatives were primarily the result of the English campaign, which will be discussed further in the following chapter.

Thus the topographical diversity of Lidice as it exists today can be seen to reflect the different stages of its historical development. It is notable, too, that Lidice now has its own 'life' beyond its function as a commemorative space, and the rose garden is both commemorative space and wedding venue (it is hired out to couples for ceremonies throughout the summer months).

Figure 7.4. The new Lidice village

Figure 7.5. The Lidice rose garden

The new village, whilst still home to the last living survivors of the original massacre, is popular with commuters to nearby Prague; so much so, in fact, that a new development of thirty-nine houses began in April 2011, offering 'comfortable living' in 'modern and energy-efficient' surroundings (Prague Real Estate 2012); furthermore, plans for another development of forty-five houses are also in place, by M&A Property Investors, 'a private equity real estate investment company focused on opportunistic mid-size deals throughout Europe' (Businesswire.com 2011). Thus memories of the past cohabit with present concerns and future hopes in Lidice's diverse landscape.

Curating Nature: Fencing In and Weeding Out

Lidice today resembles neither the original village nor the topographically reconstructed space left behind by the Nazis. The foundations visible today were excavated from their covering of German soil in the years after the war. The excavation restored something of the shape of the original landscape, but it would have been impossible to put things back exactly as they had been. The decision to leave the foundations and restrict the addition of commemorative features to limited areas affects the way the landscape is perceived; the foundations seem to provide an element of that authenticity so commonly attached to ruins. As Edouard Stehlik (2007: 149) comments: 'Nowadays, the place where old Lidice was looks more like a well-manicured park than a place of bestial crime. However, the foundations of Horàk Farm make sure that everybody knows this was the place where people stopped being people.' If the foundations remind visitors of the past, the roses in the 'Friendship and Peace Park' symbolize 'new Lidice' (Stehlik 2007: 148; Vlk 2006). When couples are married in the park they plant a new rose bush to honour 'the memory of the shot dead Lidice inhabitants in 1942 and also the remembrance of this significant day for the married couple' (Lidice Memorial 2012); the planting is as much about two people embarking on a new life together as it is about remembering past lives cut short. I discuss the symbolism used to achieve this effect in further detail in this section as a way to consider the ethics and impact of various horticultural and landscaping techniques in the context of Holocaust commemoration.

This discussion picks up on two connected yet distinct questions which have been the subject of particularly passionate scholarly debate: firstly, whether gardening practice can conceivably be linked to the way of thinking that led to the Holocaust; and secondly, the connected issue of whether particular horticultural or landscaping practices are fundamentally tainted by the National Socialists' embrace and development of them. I referenced these debates in the introduction, citing Bauman's view that the logic of gardening was implicit in ethnic cleansing, and argued accordingly that debates on museum practice concerning 'unwitting' parallels with National Socialist perpetration should be expanded to consider the realm of the outdoor memorial environment. Thus I now move on to consider Lidice within the broader landscape of contemporary Holocaust commemoration. In doing so, I reference the design and management of two other prominent sites, Auschwitz Birkenau and Bergen-Belsen, which serve to further illuminate the elements of the practices employed at Lidice.

The idea for a rose garden at Lidice came from the leader of the same English group that had campaigned for the reconstruction of the village, Sir Barnett Stross, and the choice is arguably consonant with a specifically British landscaping culture. The design is notably influenced by the formal planting strategies popular in England during the Victorian era, particularly the presentation of vividly coloured blooms in geometric beds, statues and fountains within Italianate terraces (Lancaster and Scott-James 2004: 70). The beds in the Lidice garden are laid out to form a larger image of a rose which is only discernible from above. Appropriately for the commemorative context of Lidice, in the Victorian period roses – either fresh or engraved – were a favourite choice for the adornment of gravestones (Rich 1998: 57). Their perceived meaning was twofold, encompassing both love and death (Rich 1998: 57), each colour carrying a particular resonance: the red rose, for example, signified passion, but was also symbolic of 'the blood of [Christian] martyrs' (Bruce-Mitford 2008: 84).[7] The rose is thus arguably a fitting symbol, given the rose garden's dual functions as memorial and wedding venue.

The Victorians also set a precedent for integrating imported plant varieties into their landscaping projects, a strategy embraced in Lidice's rose garden. Seven thousand of the original bushes were donated by a propagating company from Nottinghamshire, the other 23,000 from 35 countries around the world. Thus the roses are almost entirely nonnative exotics in the Czech context. Far from forgetting Lidice, many national communities contributed towards de-territorializing the Nazis' claim to their 'outlying estate'.

The exotic planting of the traditional formal garden rejects, intentionally or not, landscaping practices which became popular in Nazi Germany; practices which clearly reflect eugenic policies of 'weeding out' unwanted non-Aryan or unfit elements. Prominent German landscape gardener and official 'Reich landscape advocate' (*Reichslandschaftsanwalt*) Alwin Seifert 'rejected the use of foreign plants in landscape design' (Wolschke-Bulmahn 2001: 3) and was 'radical in his attacks on non-native species' (Uekötter 2006: 79). Seifert's passion was for nature in its 'natural' place, and, freed from the shadow cast on his work by his association with the Nazi Party, his approach is fundamentally a holistic one which calls attention to the 'interconnectedness of nature' (Ueköter 2006: 79). A more openly hostile approach is suggested by a comment made by the head of the forestry policy unit of the Nazi Party, Willi Parchmann. Assuming an ideological compatibility between racial superiority and the protection of the German trees, he stressed the need to 'cast out the unwanted foreigners and bastards that have as little right to be in the German forest as they have to be in the German *Volk*' (Imort 2006: 44). Thus it is possible to see Lidice's curators' inclusive donations policy as constituting, whether consciously or not, a laudable rejection of Seifert's purist nativism and Parchmann's vitriolic aversion to foreign species.

Formal gardens, however, necessitate a high level of maintenance and control, another form of 'weeding out'. In Lidice substantial alterations had to be made to the landscape to accommodate the rose garden, including a new series of significant topographical engineering. Chemical soil enhancement was also essential. Without regular pruning and weeding, rose gardens go wild, as did the Lidice garden between 1989 and 2000 when funding was in short supply for political reasons, as noted previously. The plight of the weed, the 'wild plant growing where it is not wanted' (OED), highlights certain contradictions inherent in human responses to nature; the instinctual longing to encounter nature at its most 'natural' is frequently complicated by a desire, indeed a necessity, to control and manipulate. Similarly, pruning aims to cut away any areas that appear diseased or damaged, a form of selective destruction undertaken to protect the overall health of the plant. Gardeners are motivated to remove weeds, not simply because they may appear unsightly – indeed, many 'weeds' are attractive plants and are featured in more 'natural' designs – but because they will inevitably take up space and resources such as water, light and nourishment that might be saved for more desirable plants. There are unsettling precedents; Bauman's (2000: 70) argument explicitly ties weeding to Nazi eugenics, suggesting that '[g]ardening and medicine are functionally distinct forms of the same activity of *separating and setting apart useful elements destined to live and thrive, from harmful and morbid ones, which ought to be exterminated*'. The Nazis infamously put in place a series of programmes and laws to effectively destroy any element perceived as physically diseased within a larger move towards a biopolitical state (Agamben 1995). The 'Euthanasia Program for the Incurably Ill' (*Euthanasie-programm für unheilbaren Kranke*), for example, was designed to eradicate all 'life unworthy of being lived' (Agamben 1995: 138). Having decided which lives were of value and which were not, the government was able to isolate, detain and destroy any people who were making use of resources and space which could otherwise contribute to the health and wealth of Germany's native population. It is possible, then, to draw parallels between the gardening methods used to maintain a rose garden and those employed by National Socialism to transform the racial landscape of Europe.

The effect of the careful management of the Lidice site overall, and the rose garden in particular, is one of formality and precision very different to that apparent at many concentration and death camp memorials. Auschwitz-Birkenau, so central to international Holocaust collective memory, serves as a useful point of comparison. The memorial at Auschwitz I, housed predominantly in brick barracks, requires relatively little in the way of outdoor landscaping beyond the maintenance of a few neat lawns here and there. It is with the far larger Auschwitz II Birkenau site that a notable comparison with Lidice can be made. The size of several football fields, Birkenau is a grassed expanse scattered with intermittent fences and ruins. The ruins are frequently overgrown and appear to be gradually disintegrating; 'the flat expanse of desolation is interrupted only by signs of absence' (Keil 2005: 489). In this way they diverge considerably from the Lidice site, both at the rose garden in particular and the larger landscape, which is kept in good order throughout the year; whilst both Lidice and Birkenau rely on architectural remnants, nothing is allowed to even partially obscure them at the site of old Lidice.

As discussed in the introduction to this book via the example of Dalton, the atmosphere of Birkenau has a considerable impact on visitor behaviour and experience. Bohdan Rymaszewski (2003: 32), from the Conservation Department at the Auschwitz-Birkenau Memorial and Museum, has suggested that '[l]ush vegetation ... lends peace to what was once a malevolent landscape ... The idea is not to reconstruct the look of the camp from half a century ago, but to maintain a historical landscape marked with the presence of nature.' The curatorial role, as Rymaszewski argues, is to maintain the vegetation so that original architectural elements are not eventually destroyed;

this is carefully balanced with a desire to retain an impression of nature in its most 'natural' form (2003: 32). According to Rymaszewski's colleague Barbara Zajac (2003: 62), vegetation control at Auschwitz gives visitors better access to the camp and at the same time 'shapes their emotions'. This aspect of the site's management, initially taken up by Addis and Charlesworth, is further scrutinized in Keil's (2005: 12) discussion of Birkenau. He notes that visitors are in fact 'presented with a series of simulacra' at the site; what appear to be 'unmediated fragments' are in fact installations in which 'natural' elements are controlled as much as manmade structures. The nature/architecture balance is maintained at considerable effort and expense (Zajac 2003: 62–75). The processes and resulting aesthetic at Birkenau are thus similar to those of the nature-garden, in that practices of cultivation produce a deliberate appearance of noncultivated 'wildness'. The affectivity of nature's own 'work' – the perceived capacity of natural forms to lend peace as they overtake malevolent ruins – is not something on which the landscape design at Lidice attempts to rely. Peter Herbstreuth (2000: 151) describes the rediscovery of the mass grave in the Lidice area by local farmers, who noticed discoloured crops above it several years after the war. Herbstreuth argues that this discoloration was 'impossible to improve on as an image of the massacre' for 'the ground preserves an image that can be read like an archive on the surface ... an image of the human imagination that strains the limits of language' (2000: 151). Whatever its commemorative qualities, the rose bed that now stands in place of the discoloured crops does not make use of this 'archive on the surface'; in fact, it effectively erases this imprint.

The ethics of manipulating emotional responses by 'faking' nature raises as many questions as the landscaping of Lidice; both the formal and the 'wild' approach provoke resonances of National Socialist ideology. The nature-garden is an umbrella term for various models of garden design advocated particularly by early-twentieth-century landscape architects (Wolschke-Bulmahn 1997: 1–4). Whilst some proponents agreed that exotic plant species were suitable for use in nature-gardens if they had a physiognomic fit with the larger environment, others, such as Seifert, rejected any nonnative varieties. The terms employed by many nature-garden proponents in this latter category are markedly similar to those of fascist rhetoric; exotics were 'Barbarians' and 'aggressive interlopers' that gardeners feared would bring 'great destruction' (Wolschke-Bulmahn 1997: 2–3). For Wolschke-Bulmahn, the consonance between politics and landscaping goes beyond the metaphorical: '[n]ationalism and racism have been ... factors in the rise of natural garden design' (1997: 3). Certainly, ideas that fuelled the nature-garden fit with the Nazi Party's original sentiments about preserving and propagating their own traditional forests and landscapes, as was discussed in Chapter 1 in relation to the Buchenwald landscape on the Ettersburg.

Despite these onerous origins, the sense that the nature-garden aesthetic is appropriate for commemorative purposes can be seen in the reactions of Jewish survivors of Bergen-Belsen to the Allies' plans for a formal garden at the site. Arguments appeared in a local Jewish magazine insisting that a formal garden at this site would elide the reality of the original events, for 'the tree of forgetfulness would be planted'. In leaving the site as a field, on the other hand, they might achieve a 'field of memory':

> the earth bedizened by nature with plants and wild herbs sustained by the blood and bones, the wild flowers dancing in the wind, glad to be alive and each plant embedded in a human soul. The wild flowers are a sacred carpet and we approach the field filled with a sense of awe. (Wolschke-Bulmahn 1997: 280)

Despite his concluding argument that ecological ideas are irrelevant to this space, even Wolschke-Bulmahn is compelled to question whether victims could 'be honoured properly' by a 'design forged in harmony with nature ... that so strongly echoes the landscape ideals of their persecutors' (1997: 298); landscape ideals which were themselves partially predicated on ecological sensibilities. Perhaps, however, those most suited to approve a commemorative strategy were the survivors mourning their loss; if they are not concerned with parallelisms, perhaps curators should follow their example. At Lidice, where a formal garden now replaces what might otherwise have been left to become a 'field of memory' or, in Herbstreuth's phrasing, 'an image that can be read like an archive on the surface', parallelisms which might echo the landscape ideals of the Nazis as persecutors are avoided, but an 'image of the massacre' which 'could not be improved on' is perhaps lost.

However, just as the meadow at Belsen could never be made to last, neither could the image Herbstreuth finds so exemplary at Lidice be maintained for perpetuity; the sentiments of the Jewish survivors as described above raise practical issues aside from any echoes of Nazi aesthetics, issues inherent to the ongoing management of apparently 'wild' gardens. In order to be maintained over time, the meadow – like the nature-garden – must be deliberately curated, organized and, ultimately, constructed. The wild flowers that were so appealing at Belsen, and which arguably encompassed a sense of natural authenticity, would not have appeared each year had the space been left alone, just as the discoloured crops could only ever have had a fleeting presence at Lidice. What was comforting for survivors to see in the immediate aftermath of the war is an effect that could only be temporarily authentic. Such a programme is untenable at memorial sites as their curators look to the long-term future, as is so apparent from Rymaszewski's comments about the need to protect original structures from nature's encroachment at Birkenau. As a result, any aesthetic suggestive of authenticity created by the juxtaposition of ruins and natural growth will always be, as Keil suggests, a simulacrum. At Birkenau, in order to create the impression that nature is taking over and lending peace to the landscape, it must be carefully cultivated and contained; fencing in becomes essential, although it occurs in a very different way at Birkenau than in the Lidice rose garden, where boundaries explicitly mark out sections of the overall design. The staff employed to limit the potentially destructive spread of natural materials at Birkenau use significant quantities of weed-killing herbicides on plant roots (Zajac 2003: 58). Forestry firms and schools in the local area aid the museum in curbing the growth of vegetation (Rymazewski 2003: 32). The predicted emotional response of visitors to their 'natural' surroundings is deliberately calculated.[8] This simulacrum of authenticity introduces yet another politicized precedent to the approach to nature at Birkenau. Nazi propaganda integrated a calculated appropriation of traditional *Heimat* ideals, as '[s]entimental love of the soil was ... combined with its practical political appropriation' (Glaser 1978: 155). Close scrutiny of Nazi environmental policy reveals that, although the attachment to traditional *Heimat* landscapes was crucial to engaging the public support that brought the party to power, 'racism and the expansion of *Lebensraum,* rather than homeland sentiment, lay at the heart of Hitler's naturalistic conception of history and national fate' (Lekan 2004: 158). Bearing the above legacy in mind, the calculated manipulation of nature in order to achieve a particular emotional connection is rendered somewhat problematic. Given an awareness of this legacy, the statement that 'lush vegetation lends peace' to Birkenau has certain complex connotations which are not raised by the memorial landscape at Lidice, where the formal strategy results in a clear demarcation between remnants of the past and contemporary planting.

That compelling parallels *can* be drawn between past and present has been highlighted by a focus on processes of weeding out and fencing in. However, it is also evident that multiple interpretations of such practices can exist simultaneously, undermining and frustrating any attempt to impose a deterministic reading of spatial aesthetics.; as discussed in the introduction, to treat landscapes only as representative mediums is delimiting. Recalling the debate also referred to in the introduction over curatorship at the U.S. Holocaust Memorial Museum, whilst noting the unfortunate replication of perpetrator objectification, Crownshaw (2010: 210) argues that exhibition space can be read 'against the grain'; 'the meaning of an artefact is determined not only by its placement or emplotment in a narrative matrix [a curatorial construct], but also by the museum visitor'. As I have argued, if the logic of representational decoding is problematic in the museum, it is arguably more so in the 'natural' memorial environment, where space evolves according to both curatorial endeavour and the inexorable dictates of nature.

Perhaps the way to overcome this problem in considering sites such as Lidice would be to embrace a more holistic approach to landscape interpretation, much as the discipline of cultural geography in recent years has embraced a 'more-than-representational' method focusing on a range of experiential expression from 'fleeting encounters' to 'affective intensities' (Lorimer 2005: 84). As Martin Jay's (2007: 58) discussion of Bauman's argument suggests, his 'stress on the link between weeding and pruning and the sinister selection and breeding of humans, however exaggerated it may seem, alerts us to the importance of the non-visual component in any analysis of the gardening impulse'. This urges us to embrace a 'more-then-representational' analysis, which may involve closer study of the behaviour and impressions of those who visit the spaces.

Nonetheless, I would suggest that even this more nuanced and inclusive approach does not necessarily preclude a discussion of nature and associated processes and ideologies, which are in themselves affectively intense. I return, then, to Wolschke-Bulmahn's thesis that ecological ideas are irrelevant to the Holocaust memorial environment. It seems clear that, in focusing on resonances between genocidal practices and commemorative processes without taking into account the motivations that lie behind each example, we risk a lack of specificity which potentially undermines the reality of the suffering that characterized the Holocaust and the intentions of those who design and manage contemporary memorial spaces. As Frank Uekötter (2006: 206–7) argues, 'the need for nuance in moral judgement is imperative … a uniform indictment ends up putting very different types of behaviour on a par'.

Whilst, as Uekötter points out, the recognition of parallelisms may only constitute a first step, it may still contribute something to a broader analysis. This approach does not necessarily abandon representation; in looking beyond parallelisms we do not necessarily either leave them behind or cast them as the end point of discussion. Criticism and practice do not exist in isolation, and new ways of analysing space inform new methods of management and mediation. As Jay (2007: 58) suggests, 'however imprecise the fit between [Bauman's] broad generalizations and the actual practices of Nazi landscape design, his argument helps to undermine the assumption that gardens are best understood as absolutely distinct refuges from the rest of the world, as Edenic places of a grace that is lost outside their boundaries'.

Furthermore, an awareness of the ecological ideologies of perpetrators, and how they may be echoed in current process, may act as a prompt to the curatorial imagination – and consequently the imaginations of those who visit these sites – to engage with particular histories in new ways; these parallels could be starting points for the invention of new practices, as well as for critical scrutiny of how that practice 'works'. The destruction of the planet and its species – including human beings – is an issue for the curators

of Holocaust landscapes today as much as it was for Schrader in his laboratory in 1939 when he accidentally discovered the lethal properties of organic
phosphates (see Carson 1962: 42). I recall again the intimate connections
between natural destruction and human-perpetrated atrocity implicit in the
aforementioned works of Carson, Levene and Nixon. Perhaps as commemorative landscapes continue to evolve, and as awareness of this polemic inter-
connection increases, ecological ideas will come to be seen as relevant and
indeed instrumental to their future curation; not simply because the sensibilities of the past remain visible at these sites, but because the very existence
of such landscapes becomes a reminder of the deeply interconnected nature
of destruction in all its many guises, a phenomenon of which the Holocaust
provides such a compelling paradigm.

Notes

Sections of this chapter are reprinted by permission of the publishers from 'Fencing In
and Weeding Out: Curating Nature at Former Nazi Concentration Camp Sites and Mass
Graves in Europe', in Davide Deriu, Krystallia Kamvasinou and Eugenie Shinkle (eds),
Emerging Landscapes. Farnham: Ashgate, 2014, pp. 161–72. Copyright © 2014.
   1. Winstone (2010: 157) records the first stage in the campaign against the Jews in the
       Protectorate as a decree for the aryanization of the economy in June 1939. When
       Reinhardt Heydrich took over the role of *Reichsprotektor* in October of the same year,
       Theresienstadt was transformed from a garrison town to a holding camp from which
       Jews were deported, most to Auschwitz.
   2. 'Hitler was convinced that the Slavic race was incapable of forming its own state and
       hence had to be ruled by others'; rather than being eliminated, like the Jews, 'Slavs
       were to play the role of slave labour and serve the master race' (Schneider and Wette
       2006: 15). It is worth noting further that Czech Slavs were also differentiated from
       other Slavic races in the National Socialist hierarchy, and some argue that they fared
       somewhat better overall as a result (Berkley 1993: 19). Czechoslovak Gypsies were
       certainly an exception in this regard, and many thousands lost their lives to the Nazi
       campaign (Bugajski 1995: 296).
   3. Initially a national event, the annual art competition has been international since
       1973 (International Children's Exhibition of Fine Arts Lidice 2011).
   4. Terezín was used by the Nazis as a model to show the international community that
       their camps were well-organized and humane internment spaces, an impression suc-
       cessfully corroborated by the Red Cross after a prearranged inspection there in 1944,
       preceded by a "beautification action' … in which buildings were cleaned up, new
       facilities created and entertainments organized' (Winstone 2010: 168). Unknown to
       the Red Cross, the order they saw when they arrived was achieved only by frequent
       deportations of internees to Birkenau, thus limiting numbers and preventing over-
       crowding. That Terezín was in part run as the public face of the concentration camp
       system meant that those children who were not deported fared better than those in
       other camps. The Germans allowed the camp Jewish Council of Elders to institute

special homes for children to 'protect [them] as much as possible from the rigours of adult existence whilst also engendering a communal spirit [...] Within each home, children were organized into groups which were encouraged to develop a collective identity through activities such as sport and entertainment' (Winstone 2010: 171).

5. Named the 'Memorial to the Children Victims of the War', the sculpture group was created by artist Marie Uchytilová as a 'symbol for [the] 13 million children who died in the Second World War' (Stehlik 2007: 144).

6. The woman with the rose and the Lidice mother were created by the sculptor Bedřich Stefan in the late 1950s and early 1960s; the crying woman was a later addition designed by sculptor Karel Lidický to 'counterbalance' the woman with the rose (Vlk 2006).

7. Whether or not this is a deliberate inference, it resonates with a description of the execution by Harald Wiesmann, the chief of the Kladno Gestapo: 'The men of Lidice walked free, straight and brave. There were no unmanly scenes' (in Stehlik 2007: 46).

8. Certain trees at Birkenau constitute a notable exception to the overall approach. Older trees known to have been alive at the site during its years as a concentration and extermination camp are designated mute witnesses to Nazi atrocities, and are protected as such.

EIGHT

LIDICE TRAVELS

This chapter traces ways in which the publicized ideological destruction of Lidice sparked an endeavour to rebuild the village after the war, beginning a global trajectory of Lidice's memory to new localities in literature and beyond. Hitler's desire to completely erase the original village was almost completely achieved during the course of the year 1942–3. A visitor to the area shortly after the war ended recorded the landscape as follows:

> Lidice was a typical Czech village, with low, cream-coloured houses clustered around a six-hundred-year-old church that had a baroque cupola. Nobody in Lidice had much money and nobody was very poor. Automobiles, radios, moving pictures, and newspapers were practically non-existent. There was a school, a firehouse, a sports club, and a reading circle. The men worked in the coal mines and foundries of the nearby town of Kladno, and the women tended the fields and gardens on the slopes behind their houses … As I gazed down on the site of Lidice from a hilltop overlooking the green valley, it was not difficult to imagine the village as it once was. It was harder to visualize the details of what happened to it … From my hilltop, I could see that, topographically, the erasure of Lidice has been complete (Wechsberg 2003: 272–3).

Although whatever long-term intentions Hitler may have had for 'Vorwerk' never came to pass, the destruction of the village in itself was an extraordinary project, revealing much about the Nazis' approach to both the mechanics and ideology of their campaign to extend the German empire.

Having dynamited and burned all buildings, the topographical re-landscaping process ran as follows:

> Stupendous volumes of rubble from the torn-down houses were deployed at various places so that the relief of the landscape around Lidice was changed as much as possible. Some of the hillocks disappeared completely, others were created artificially. The entire area was subsequently covered with imported soil … The piles of rubble coming from the demolished houses in Lidice were also used to level out Podhora Pond, around which most of the tall-grown trees

were felled down. So as to make the identification of the exact place where
Lidice once stood impossible in the future, even the course of the brook was
altered in a few places, which had once flown down the middle of the village.
(Stehlik 2007: 66–67)

John Bradley's (1972: 111) description of the destruction of the village further stresses the technical difficulties faced by those responsible for divert-
ing the brook, removing trees and moving 84,000 square metres of soil to
level the land and prepare it for the sowing of grain. The southern area of
the former village was to be turned into grazing ground for sheep (Bradley
1972: 114). Stehlik (2007: 66) also notes that '[i]n spite of hundreds of RAD
[Reich Working Service/*Reichsarbeitsdienst*] men being employed, the works
did not proceed as fast as presumed, and had to go on all through the year
1943.' That Lidice's destruction was planned as a symbol of German domination is borne out in associated correspondence, for example in this letter
from Karl Hermann Frank (SS police leader and Secretary of State of the
Protectorate, in Stehlik 2007: 62) to the Reich Labour Director in July 1942:

> The elimination of the village is a political measure of the first order, as it
> makes the Czech population see very clearly that the Reich is not going to
> allow any centres of resistance under any circumstances, not even in the re-
> motest corners of the Protectorate. This measure has made a corresponding
> impression on the Czech population. The duration of this effect requires that
> the village be literally levelled to the ground ... it is planned to be converted
> to arable land, which will be allotted to the adjacent state farm, already under
> German management.

All the cattle from Lidice were driven to a German farm in nearby
Buštěhrad on the same day the inhabitants were executed (Stehlik 2004:
81). There was also an educational element to the destruction, as revealed in
the following excerpt from a letter from RAD head Alexander Commichau to
the Reich RAD Commander in August 1942:

> The young man in the Reich Working Service sees that the German sword
> will fall hard and destroy entirely the sources of disturbance not only at the
> front, but also in the hinterland; ... The deepening of the emotions of the men
> deployed in this place will certainly co-work on the consolidation of German
> power; but it will only be achieved after his work results in the complete dis-
> appearance of the village and after the earth is ploughed where the enemy of
> Germanhood had once resided. (Stehlik 2007: 63–64)

The destruction of Lidice was to be used as a training exercise: 'The Nazis
filmed every step of this destruction as a training film – the shootings, the
burnings of bodies and homes, all evidence of a town burned into oblivion,

plowed under. A training film. To help others learn to leave no traces behind'
(Walders 2006: 282).[1]

Ideologically, to plough the earth inhabited by enemies of the Nazi regime was the ultimate triumph; when the German soldiers' work was done,
the German ploughs could begin theirs. This, as discussed previously, was
crucial to Nazi aims in Ukraine, and such was Himmler's vision for Poland
in 1939. Standing with him overlooking the land, 'Himmler's amanuensis'
Hanns Johst (Kiernan 2007: 428) recalls: 'And so we stood there like pre-
historic farmers and laughed... All of this was once more German soil! Here
the German plough will soon change the picture.' The traditional notion of
blut und boden had to be slightly refabricated to accommodate this rhetoric.
As noted in relation to the Nazi colonization of Ukraine, '[s]acred German
soil, in the Nazi view, had no specific boundaries' (Kiernan 2007: 432), yet
blut und boden logic also relied on the premise that generations of Germans
had lived and died on their native soil, their blood a unique, territorializing fertilizer. Accordingly, following this logic, many generations of German
peasants would have to farm the colonized land in order to endow it with
the 'unique' properties of true German soil. Nonetheless the arrival of the
German plough symbolized the beginning of the transformation. Thus it is
slightly anomalous that what the Nazis planned to be the last Czech inhabitants of Lidice were buried in this same soil. As one prisoner from Terezín,
Rudolf Mautner, who had been ordered to assist with the burial of the men
after the mass shooting, later recalled: 'I piled up all the bodily remains of all
the poor souls ... brains, bones, entrails, intestines scattered about. I put the
blood – the blood of our Czech people – into the pit carefully. Czech blood
went into Czech earth' (Stehlik 2007: 52). As another Terezín survivor and
witness stressed, 'the ground was saturated with blood' (Bradley 1972: 111).

Perhaps the transportation of German soil to the area was supposed to
counteract the presence of the Czech bone, brain and blood. The RAD were
also ordered to destroy Lidice's graveyard, and '60 vaults, 140 large family
tombs and about 200 single graves' were plundered in the process (Stehlik
2007: 63); the land was no longer to be the final resting place of previous
generations of Czech citizens. One of the soldiers who took part in the exercise, a boy of sixteen, recalled: 'The greatest fun was when we loaded the
cemetery with explosives. You should have seen the cadavers fly in the air!
Heads, legs, arms; some of the heads had long hair, that was the women...
When we're finished there, it'll all be smoothed out and sown with grain.
Then all the land of Lidice and around will be given to Mrs Heydrich as a
present' (Stehlik 2007: 65).

Given that Lidice's destruction was mainly symbolic, the labour expended
on the project was remarkable. Stehlik (2007: 61) reports that around 100
RAD men spent around 20,000 hours on this work, in addition to support

from the Waffen-SS and a Wehrmacht unit (Stehlik 2007: 60). In June 1942 Hitler was experiencing his 'last high moments' as a military leader: as German troops were driving back the British in Egypt, and his previously faltering campaign against Russia at last appeared to be making headway (Bendersky 2007: 183). Perhaps, at such a time, he felt some resources could be spared to make this symbolic gesture. Taking a broader historical view, the razing of Lidice resonates with other apparently pointless acts of violence, such as took place on Kristallnacht in 1939; in Württemberg, for example, locals criticized the destruction of valuable assets when 'an official campaign against waste and encouragement to recycle' was otherwise in place (Stephenson 2006: 144). These issues aside, the complete topographical elimination of Lidice was very nearly achieved. The landscape left behind by the RAD when the work was finally completed was radically altered.

'Lidice Shall Live'

If the destruction of Lidice was conceived as a warning to the world, an exhibition of German power, its publicization achieved a very different impact. The reaction began in an unlikely location. The aforementioned English fundraising campaign to facilitate rebuilding – named 'Lidice Shall Live' – was organized by a group of coal miners in Stoke-on-Trent. They heard about the village's destruction when it became international news immediately after the massacre; they appear to have felt a sense of identification with Lidice's inhabitants, a group of miners like themselves, who lived in a relatively poor rural location.[2] Indeed, in 1942, Lidice's population largely comprised farmers and miners who worked at the Poldi Smelting Works in nearby Kladno. Many had been skilled craftsmen in preceding years, but were forced to find alternative labour as a result in the worldwide economic crisis during the 1930s (Stehlik 2007: 22). Mining provided a comparatively stable source of income, despite the fact that industry across the country had been adversely affected by the Great Depression across Czechoslovakia (Agnew 2010: 191). That a new Lidice exists today overlooking the old is partly the result of the fact that its men had turned to mining during this economic downturn. For the Stoke miners voted to have part of their monthly pay deducted from their wage packets; they collected a total of £32,375, the equivalent of approximately £1000,000 today, 'not a bad feat for an impoverished community in north Staffordshire' (Flellow in Francis 2012). Employees at the potteries and various trade unions followed their example, and together they raised enough to build the new Lidice (Wheeler 1957: 18).

The leader of the initial fundraising movement, Dr (later Sir) Barnett Stross, proclaimed that 'the miner's lamp' of Lidice could 'send a ray of light across the sea to those who struggle in darkness' (1942).[3] The 'Lidice Shall Live' campaign is now the foundation of the aforementioned twinning campaign between Lidice and Stoke, to which I will return in the final chapter. The original achievement of the campaign was the complete reversal of the Nazis' aims for Lidice. Just as Lidice has survived, albeit in a different form, at the site of the original village, its fate lives on in international consciousness, further refusing the Nazis' desire to erase it from memory. Whilst the Stoke campaign was perhaps the most prominent example of the activism that kept this memory alive, there were other key co-ordinates in a broader network of commemoration surrounding Lidice. In the introduction to this section, I mentioned the production of various memorial texts and the naming and renaming processes, for example, which were also central to the creation of this network. In this section I consider its dynamics in a little more detail, setting up the context in which the recent twinnings – discussed in Chapter 9 – have taken place. I take first the texts initially created when news of what happened at Lidice was broadcast to the world. As noted previously, these texts constitute early examples of cosmopolitan, 'glocal' memory work, and furthermore they present the events at Lidice against a deteriorating pastoral landscape which resonates with that of the Ukraine as discussed in Chapter 2.

As was the case with Babi Yar, literature played a role in preventing the memory of Lidice from being completely erased, and has mediated the cultural memories that circulate around its history as a result. Amongst the most prominent of these to appear in the immediate aftermath was a book-length verse play, *The Murder of Lidice,* written by the American poet and playwright Edna St Vincent Millay in response to a request from the Writer's War Board. First published as a straight poem in *Life* magazine in October 1942, set somewhat oddly alongside advertisements for corsetry, Scotch whiskey, and after-dinner mints, the play version was broadcast on the radio the following month. The poem starts with the construction of Lidice, painting an image of a rural idyll:

It was all of six hundred years ago,
It was seven and if a day,
That a village was built which you may know
By the name of 'Lidice.'
They built them a church and they built them a mill,
All on the fair Bohemian plain,
For to shrive their souls and grind their grain,
And each man helped his neighbor to lay
The stones of his house, and to lift its beams;
Till strong in its timbers and tight in its seams
A village arose called Lidice.

How did the year turn, how did it run,
In a village like Lidice?
First came Spring, with planting and sowing;
Then came Summer, with haying and hoeing;
Then came Autumn, and the Harvest Home
And always in Winter, with its brief bright day,
Toward the end of the quiet afternoon.
(Children at school, but coming home soon.
With crisp young voices loud and gay;
Husband at Kladno, miles away.
But home for supper, expected soon)
Toward the end of the Winter afternoon...
The wise, kind hands and contented face
Of a woman at the window, making lace...
A peaceful place ... a happy place...

Proceeding to describe events of 10 June, the poem tells of the deaths of the men and deportation of the women and children as the bucolic landscape is engulfed in 'terrible flame' from the sky to the earth. The seasons, presented as a harmonious and productive cycle in the second stanza, are then disrupted by the arrival of Heydrich 'the hangman, the Hun'. In this way, the poem resonates notably with an earlier work by Millay, 'Justice Denied in Massachusetts' (1927), concerning the execution of Ferdinando Nicola Sacco and Bartolomeo Vanzetti, two Italian immigrants convicted of murder in South Braintree, MA; speculation at the time of their execution was rife as to whether the two men were really innocent of the charges and were purely convicted due to prejudice against them as immigrants. The poem follows a similar course to 'The Murder of Lidice'; As Michael Thurston (2001: 15) has suggested, 'Justice Denied in Massachusetts', '[w]ith stock images of death and a deadly change in the natural cycles of growth, [registered] the despair many writers and intellectuals felt over the case's outcome; the very earth is, literally, appalled'. Whilst Thurston's insistence on literality here ignores the way in which '[t]he naturally existing external world ... is wholly ignorant of the "urtability" of human beings' (see Scarry 1985: 288), his statement reflects how much the structure of landscape – in this case Lidice's landscape – 'is the *structure of a perception*' (Scarry 1985: 289).

The last stanza asks Americans to take Lidice as a warning of what Hitler might do on their own territory:

Careless America, crooning a tune:
Catch him! Catch him and stop him soon!
Never let him come here!
Think a moment: are *we* immune?
Oh, my country, so foolish and dear,

Careless America crooning a tune,
Please think! – are *we* immune?
Catch him! Catch him and stop him soon
Never let him come here!
Ask yourself, honestly: what have we done? –
Who, after all are we? –
That we should sit at peace in the sun,
The only country, the only one
Unmolested and free?
Catch him! Catch him! Do not wait!
Or will you wait, and share the fate
Of the village of Lidice?
Or will you wait, and let him destroy
The village of Lidice, Illinois?
Oh, catch him! Catch him, and stop him soon!
Never let him come here!

The Lidice, Illinois, Millay refers to here was the first neighbourhood to be renamed to commemorate the events at the original village. I discuss this within the broader context of international renaming shortly. By invoking the Illinois Lidice in this way, Millay was warning Americans against a complacency that could ultimately result in the destruction of their own neighbourhoods. She later referred to the work as 'hot-headed' and said it has been a '"mistake" to write bad wartime poems even to buck up morale' (Fussell 1989: 175). Nonetheless, as Guy Stern (2000: 161) argues, '[w]hilst it is anything but good poetry, it has the virtue of being good propaganda and a moral response to utter immorality'. Thurston's (2001: 15) suggestion that the poem was Millay's call for 'American entry to the war on the Allied side' seem justified by the last stanza, although if she was attempting to mobilize events at Lidice to this end she must have been encouraging the country to take further action, since America had officially joined the war in December 1941. Certainly, by evoking the same disruption of the seasons in 'The Murder of Lidice' she had used in 'Justice Denied in Massachusetts', Millay was presenting a parallel between an instance of the failure of humanity in the United States and that which resulted in the Nazis' brutal act in the Czech Republic; in both cases, the earth itself was presented as 'appalled' by this failure.

Lidice in Wales

Another poetic response to the events at Lidice, written by exiled Czech government official and poet Victor Fischel, prompted the emergence of a more complex and multifaceted transnational parallelism. Fischel decided that the poem would be effective as the basis for a filmic recreation of the tragedy at Lidice in a Welsh village:

> The way from the film to the poem was not so long. My philosophy in life was that if you can think yourself into somebody, if you can feel yourself into somebody, if you can try to live the life of somebody else, if we could do that in the world, then our life would be easier and much better. So I had the idea of trying to replace what happened in Lidice to a village in Wales, and I knew of course that there were many differences between a Czech village and a Welsh village, but there were also many similarities. (Logan 2011: 223)

Fischel's suggestion that to focus on the similarities rather than the differences between two contexts could potentially be a rewarding enterprise could be considered an example of truly cosmopolitan Holocaust memory work long before Levy and Sznaider theorized it as a phenomenon of the contemporary global world. The project was taken forward by British documentary maker, Humphrey Jennings. He decided the film was to focus on the idea of what had happened rather than recreating step by step the events themselves; according to Philip Logan's discussion of the process, this was partly pragmatic, as there was little detailed information of what had actually taken place at Lidice available to the British public at this stage (July 1942) (Logan 2011: 223–24). He cites Jennings: 'We decided to focus on the *ideas* that must have led to the final solution; the *idea* of a mining community in no matter what part of the world, the *idea* of fascism, the *idea* of struggle between the two, the *idea* of the obliteration of a community' (Logan 2011: 224). Whilst this approach might have risked an elision of what actually happened at Lidice, potentially replacing the actual experiences of victims with a fiction primarily designed to express such ideas, Jennings maintained the specificity of the original events by using as source material certain documents which recorded exactly what had been said by Germans about the massacre, before, during, and after it took place. These words were to run through the film, read by a German speaker, either emanating from a radio or loud speaker, or simply as a voiceover; Jennings insisted: 'These documents are perfectly accurately monitored and they do say the most astonishing and hair-raising things: we have not invented any of them' (Logan 2011: 224).

Logan's discussion makes two further points about the Jennings film which are notable in light of the trajectory of commemoration traced throughout this chapter: that the production was undertaken with a particular focus on ensuring enthusiastic involvement and transnational sensibility from the Welsh local community of the village selected; and that the village itself, which was chosen in part for its topographical resemblance to Lidice, was presented as a pastoral idyll disrupted by the Nazis. A sense of 'international solidarity' was central for Jennings (Logan 2011: 226). He worked closely with the inhabitants of Cwmgiedd, the mining village chosen; they were to be his actors, and many were also involved in the filming process. He wanted to ensure that the life of the village, in 'Social, Cultural, Religious, Trade Union, and Political' terms, would be presented in the film, and Jennings and his film crew spent around two and a half months living in the village (Logan 2011: 227). It seems that Jennings felt he would only be able to make the film say anything meaningful about Lidice if it could capture something of the essence of the place he selected to be its counterpart. Thus, by using the transcripts of words spoken at Lidice itself in combination with his determination to present the real life of Cwmgiedd, Jennings's project was notable in its attempt to maintain the respective specificity of both these local contexts even as it brought them together.

The resulting film, *The Silent Village,* shows a 'series of vignettes' constructing 'a day in the life' of Cwmgiedd, encompassing church, school, domestic and working life, showing the village inhabitants of all ages going about their usual activities (Logan 2011: 233). Each vignette is followed by a shot of the broader landscape in which each activity takes place, which, set against the orchestral strains provided by a harp and trumpet and birdsong, provide a typified image of rural harmony. The 'fascists' arrive – peace is shattered with the arrival of gunfire, as a group of miners taking part in a secret meeting to organize resistance against the invaders are discovered and shot. Showing a miner, close to death amongst his family, and a funeral in the chapel, the film implies that 'the cost of physical resistance is absorbed by the community' (Logan 2011: 233). The following day sees the culmination of this absorption – without showing a single German soldier (the invaders are represented, as Jennings had planned, only by the voiceover and various symbols such as boots and machine guns), the women and children are herded together and deported and the men lined up against a wall. The film cuts to a view of the chapel graveyard as the order to fire is given, thus there are no graphic images of slaughter, but the village itself is shown in flames. The final oration at the end of the film explicitly tied the two communities together via the mining profession:

> The Nazis are wrong. The name [Lidice] has not been obliterated. The name of the community has been immortalised, it lives in the hearts of miners the world over. The Nazis only want slave labour and the miners refuse to become slave labour. That is why they murdered our comrades at Lidice. That is why we stand in the forefront of resistance today, because we have the power, the knowledge, the understanding to hasten the coming of victory. To liberate oppressed humanity and make certain that there shall be no more Lidices and then the men of Lidice will not have died in vain. (Jennings 1942)

In this respect, the film echoes the motivations behind the Stoke-on-Trent fundraising campaign; Jennings, like Barnett Stross, wanted to keep Lidice alive, and in order to do so he mobilized the solidarity of miners with other miners. One of the members of the Stoke campaign, Arthur Baddeley, was part of the delegation that travelled to Lidice in 1947 to see the laying of the first bricks of the new village. His daughter, Murial Stoddard, explains his motivation as follows: 'I suppose it was because it was to do with the mining community [to] which all his life he belonged ... He was very concerned about anything to do with mining' (Truswell 2010b). The movement itself, 'Lidice Shall Live', is suggestive of a transnational identification of one mining community with another; the fabric of localized, daily life in this case provided a platform for memory practice. The campaign promotes the notion, in fact, that people employed in particular industries are in some ways bound to one another; that factors such as a person's economic status and professional lives potentially transcend national or ethnically rooted notions of personal and collective identity. In fact, the members of this group enrolled themselves, along with the survivors of Lidice, in what could be described as a memory community; individuals brought together by a shared desire to remember something, or more specifically to Lidice, not to let something be forgotten. In the case of Lidice, this shared desire led to an extremely successful campaign; 'Lidice Shall Live' raised enough funds to facilitate the construction of a new Lidice overlooking the site of the old in 1947. The small number of women and children who survived the war subsequently had a place to which they could return. The Stoke fundraisers, led by Sir Stross, were apparently substantially motivated by humanitarian aims, which were borne from a form of transnational identification projected from one community to another.

This identification, so fruitful in terms of results, may be considered surprising given the official British attitude towards the Republic of Czechoslovakia at the start of the war; anxious to avoid entering into conflict with Germany, Chamberlain, along with representatives from France and Italy, played a key role in permitting Hitler to annex Czech land. The strategy was one of appeasement. In a radio address to the British nation defending the Munich Agreement, he announced: 'How horrible, fantastic, incredible it is that we should be digging trenches and trying on gas masks because of a quarrel in a faraway country between people of whom we know nothing' (Cravens 2006: 13). For the miners of Stoke-on-Trent, the people of Lidice were more than strangers of whom they knew nothing, solely on the basis of their shared profession and the way of life that went with it. Their empathic response to the plight of these strangers seems to have been completely unaffected by the political line of the British government. *The Silent Village* relies on the same transnational affinity. In stating that the inhabitants of Lidice were targeted because of their profession, it does present a distortion; the inhabitants of Lidice were targeted for the spurious connection perceived by the Nazis between them and the assassination of Heydrich, rather than for their identity as miners. However, this was perhaps an understandable distortion at the time, for the link between the village and the assassination remained unproven and to have directly referred to it may have implied otherwise. As Logan (2011: 237) notes, this last statement also served the purpose of 'highlighting the necessity of the miners to the war effort' whilst 'indirectly [providing] echoes of the historic pre-war struggles and the contemporary problems surrounding the industry'; it gave a voice to the miners of Cwmgiedd, who were struggling with their own problems (see Logan 2011: 226), as well as uniting miners all over the world in a transnational alliance.

Logan (2011: 229) summarizes the way in which Jennings's handling of sound and imagery 'draws associations between aspects of the natural world – the land, forest and water for example – and the qualities of the community, while using extreme conditions – the river in spate, the wind and cold – to frame the qualities of fascism', and comments that in doing so the director was using a technique he had practiced in previous films: drawing 'on a range of pastoral themes to embellish his story'. The various juxtapositions – the harp and birdsong replaced by the sound of marching and exerpts from Wagner's *Twilight of the Gods,* a sunny sky clouding over, the formerly peaceful village engulfed in flame – explicitly signpost the destruction of rural harmony in a similar way to the projections in the Lidice museum, framing the transformation of the community of friends and family into victims of fascism within a landscape that is sympathetic to their plight. Thus the poem echoes Millay's suggestion of a witnessing earth appalled by inhumanity, a trope which in both cases is mobilized to resonate across cultural and national differences.

Amongst many positive reviews, the film was criticized by one reporter for a 'strangely oblique approach' which '[robbed] the film of any direct impact because it has been translated into '[i]t might have been like this' not '[i]t was like this' (Logan 2011: 240). As Logan notes, however, Jennings was reassured by the fact that the miners involved in the project were pleased with the outcome, again demonstrating his dedication to producing something meaningful by harnessing genuine solidarity (Logan 2011: 240). A similar sense of transnational engagement is suggested by the renaming of places and the naming of children as Lidice – acts which introduced the name of the village into new communities and lives – all of which took place in locations far from the Czech Republic and which have, certainly at a superficial glance, little to do with the village or its people. These initiatives can be seen as an example of what Avishai Margalit (2002: 20) argues to be an ethical imperative: remembering a name is a 'special obligation' to be honoured in the face of loss. Some of the many places now named Lidice include a street in Leipzig, Germany, a road in Humberside, UK, and towns and villages in Rio de Janeiro, Panama and Caracas. The extent to which engagement went beyond the act of renaming varies in each instance. Wheeler (1957: 17) reports that one inhabitant of a new Lidice in San Jerónimo, Mexico, 'a village so poor that most of the children had to go barefoot' sent a message to the women of the original Lidice which ran: 'Widows in a concentration camp who do not know where your children are, our home is your home.' After the war the bond became reciprocal when 'the Czech Lidice women heard of the poverty in the sister village [and] sent the children a large shipment of shoes' (Wheeler 1957). A somewhat disproportionate number of the renamings occured in South America, phenomenon which requires further scrutiny if it is to be fully understood. By way of explanation, Wheeler (1957: 18) argued that the South American people's response stemmed from the fact that they 'had known for centuries the contempt that colonialists feel for other races', suggesting a transcultural sense of differentiated solidarity.

North Americans also wanted to show their support. The first place to be renamed, as noted, was the Illinois neighbourhood housing development in Joliot, Crest Hill, formerly known as Stern Park. *Time* magazine reported the renaming of the area a little over a month after the original massacre, 20 July 1942. Indeed, exactly one month after the destruction of Lidice, a granite and sandstone monument to Lidice was inaugurated in a Stern Park field, bearing the inscription: 'In memory of the people of Lidice Czechoslovakia, destroyed by barbarism, but living forever in the hearts of all who love freedom, this monument is erected by the free people of America at Lidice Illinois. Lidice Lives' (Meneker 1992). As a resident of the town, 83-year-old Jim Krakora, recalled in 1992 on the fiftieth anniversary of the tragedy at Lidice, '[t]here was no time to waste … Hitler announced that Lidice had been destroyed and that it would never rise again. We wanted this to be the American response, that Lidice, indeed, does live again, even if it happened to be in this empty field'(Meneker 1992).

Yet in 1950, the *Nevada Mail* had printed an article suggesting that there had been little genuine concern about Lidice's fate in the renaming of Stern Park, and that, in fact, officially, it had not really happened: 'Lidice [Illinois] is not even a village, it never has been. It never had a post office … Lidice was just a promotion scheme to sell lots' (*Nevada Mail* 1950). This statement, from the secretary of the Mayor of Joliot, was made in reference to the sale of many new houses that had been built in the area around the memorial over the intervening years. The article also states that the memorial itself had been moved to make way for new housing within a year of its inauguration; it then stood elsewhere, chipped, muddy, and used as little more than apparatus by playing children (*Nevada Mail* 1950). As Rothberg (2009: 310) reminds us, 'if the contest of memories cannot be reduced to a battle over real estate, that does not mean that real estate and all it implies ... do not matter'. Nonetheless, the memory of the original tragedy at Lidice had been preserved by some members of the Stern Park community up until 1992, such as Krakora, who organized the fifty-year anniversary ceremony:

> We have to face reality ... It's pretty damned hard to get people interested ... A lot of the older people who were around when it happened are gone or have drifted away; the younger ones just don't have the sentimental attachment ... But we want the monument to remain. Even though we might not be able to get people excited about it, we still want it to be a symbol of what America stands for and for how it denounces brutality and oppression. (Meneker 1992)

Despite the fact that much of the town had seemed to have lost interest by this time, an annual event still occurs every June in the area (Czechoslovak American Congress 2012). That Krakora's explanation of why he and the other organizers of the fiftieth anniversary events wished the original monument to remain was to symbolize America's intervention – its denunciation of 'brutality and oppression' – rather than to memorialize the victims, demonstrates a particular facet of cosmopolitan memory practices that will be explored further in the following section, alongside the various other elements that have so far come to light in this brief discussion of transcultural commemorations of Lidice.

Notes

1. The order to film the proceedings was given by Frank. Whether this was because, as Walders (2006: 59) suggests, it was to be used as training purposes, or because, as Stehlik proposes, it was to be used as part of the campaign to spread awareness of German domination throughout the international community ('The Germans ... were going to have it included in the official newsreel', is not clear. Ultimately sections of the material filmed were discovered after war and shown during the Nuremburg trials as evidence of Nazi crimes (Walders 2006: 59).
2. Stoke-on-Trent, or Stoke, a city in England's West Midlands, has been historically dominated by industry, foremost as a producer of earthenware and china in its well-known potteries, but also as a significant centre for coal and iron mining (Fogarty 1945: 824).
3. Stross was a family doctor and Member of Parliament for the Stoke district of Hanley.

NINE

TWINNING LIDICE

This chapter interrogates the orthodoxies of cosmopolitanism via the example of the emerging commemorative network surrounding Lidice, drawing attention to a disjunction between idealised theories of memory and actual, instrumental memory practice. The cosmopolitan emphasis, as noted, initially filtered into cultural memory studies in Levy and Sznaider's project. Their application of Ulrich Beck's (2004) model of globalization to memory practice takes Holocaust remembrance as a contemporary paradigm of cosmopolitanism. Following Levy and Sznaider's logic, potential does exist for places such as Lidice to become more accessible to people from diverse cultural backgrounds, as new global geographic links, such as those I will consider here, consolidate their position at the centre of a dynamic creation of 'new connections that situate ... political, economic, and social experiences in a new type of supranational context' (Levy and Sznaider 2006: 10). This process, like an effective transport system, may do more than connect one place with another; a network of pathways may emerge, allowing memory to travel between a series of locations. Memory travels in different ways and for different reasons. The journeys I consider here are discussed as *mobilizations* because they are guided by particular polemics which dictate their constitutive forms and processes. In other words, the 'travel' in which I am interested could also be described as a harnessing of memory for particular purposes, be they cultural, political, ethical or otherwise. I will interrogate the extent to which the particular new pathways currently emerging around Lidice can be seen to represent a form of globalized 'supranationality'.

For Levy and Sznaider, as noted in the introduction, cosmopolitanism foregrounds the way in which site-specific atrocities become de- and reterritorialized from their original locations via related mediatory, commemorative and social processes, generating new global trajectories. The various texts and renamings discussed earlier in this chapter could be considered co-ordinates within this framework. Cosmopolitanism is facilitated by 'universal values that are emotionally engaging, that descend from the level of pure abstract philosophy, and in to the emotions of people's everyday lives' (Levy and Sznaider 2006: 3). In the related process of 'glocalization', in 'which the global becomes internalized', Levy and Sznaider (2006: 10) argue that no 'convergence [or] homogenization' of Holocaust memory necessarily occurs, a theory which the following analysis interrogates. If we consider, in line with Erll's aforementioned argument, that Levy and Sznaider's project is of 'fundamental importance' to the larger movement of transcultural studies, it should also involve a turn towards 'the other'. Indeed, whilst acknowledging that 'the global individual is not completely self-sacrificing', Levy and Sznaider (2006: 28) highlight the global potentiality of rendering comprehensible the current suffering of others via memory discourses. In looking at the distinctly polemic harnessing of Lidice's memory in the twenty-first century, I also question to what extent the motivations involved in twinning projects may interfere with this possibility of cosmopolitan memory's 'supranational' transcendence, and the potential for a turn to the other implied within it.

The mobilization of memory and history implicit in twinning as a form of mobilization is characterized by distinctly 'glocal' values. It emerged as a major European trend in the years following the Second World War, primarily to encourage peaceful relations between disparate communities. According to An Verlinden (2008: 208), town twinning can be defined as follows:

> a formal partnership between municipalities, aimed at encouraging cooperation and mutual understanding between their citizens in order to foster human contacts and cultural exchange, to exchange experience, to promote peaceful co-existence and to raise awareness about the daily lives and concerns of people living in other countries. It relies upon the voluntary commitment and participation of citizens, in collaboration with their local authorities and local associations. The cornerstone of town twinning is real, mutual interaction and concrete problem solving.

Such sentiments are resonant of the descent of 'abstract philosophy' to the 'emotions of people's everyday lives' (Levy and Sznaider 2006: 3). Furthermore, Verlinden (2008: 208) argues, the process of twinning has now evolved to offer 'a possibility to implement trans-national dialogical spaces ... as a means to shared dialogical spaces at grass roots level, [town twinning] succeeds in making concrete the adagio [sic] "think local, act global"'. Thus it potentially presents a network of places, which harbour the possibility for 'cosmopolitanism as a process of "internalized globalization" ... a non-linear, dialectical process in which the global and the local exist not as cultural opposites but, rather, as mutually binding and interdependent principles' (Verlinden 2008: 9–10).

Twinning, then, potentially opens up the 'intercultural delimitation' implicit in container culture as conceived by Welsch, thus combating the 'thinking that generates racism and other forms of tension between local, ethnic, and religious groups' (Erll 2011: 8). As a process, it certainly serves to exemplify the way in which site-specific memory is inscribed into new local contexts via processes of de- and reterritorialization (Levy and Sznaider 2006: 26–28); whether memories of Lidice are homogenized in these processes, contrary to Levy and Sznaider's assertion, will be considered here. Furthermore, whilst the advent of cosmopolitanism seems to mark the end of a spatially fixed understanding of culture (Levy and Sznaider 2004: 6), this analysis asks to what extent this can be seen as a reality in the examples of Stoke-on-Trent, Lidice and Khojaly.

The two sections that follow consider to what extent cosmopolitanism's potentiality comes into being in processes of memory mobilization, at least in the specific contexts of Stoke and Khojaly. Notably, Levy and Sznaider (2006: 28) argue that 'place ... loses its meaning' as an effect of 'glocalization'. I will argue that the transcultural turn need not necessarily preclude discussion of place and territory; as the examples considered here will demonstrate, the transcultural lens facilitates a focus on the de- and reterritorializations of site-specific memory as process, in which sites in themselves are not dismissed but maintained as essential coordinates in new dynamic movements.

Lidice/Stoke-on-Trent: 'A Ray of Light Across the Sea'

The campaign to twin Lidice and Stoke-on-Trent, England, is currently underway, largely under the auspices of local couple Alan and Cheryl Gerrard.[1] Their motivation is based on the shared history of their hometown with Lidice, which, as discussed earlier in this chapter, dates almost as far back as the village's destruction in 1942. The renewing of this bond in the present day is the result of different motivations to those which shaped original fundraising campaign. Whereas this was primarily an act of solidarity, Stoke twinning campaigners in 2010–11 aimed to do more than 'formally restore' the town's 'emotional bond' with Lidice and permanently celebrate the humanitarian work of Sir Stross (Gerrard and Gerrard 2011). The campaign's website stated:

> For Stoke-on-Trent there are aspirational issues involved, but across the country the story of Barnett Stross and Lidice can be used to stamp out racism and bigotry in all its forms ... support the campaign in order to:
> 1) Inspire our young people and raise their aspirations;
> 2) Celebrate the legacy of the achievements of Sir Barnett Stross and the working people of Stoke-on-Trent in helping to rebuild Lidice;
> 3) Actively pursue the future regeneration of Stoke-on-Trent;
> 4) Stamp out racism in Stoke-on-Trent. (Gerrard and Gerrard 2011)

Alan Gerrard also elaborates on the potential of the twinning project as a strong message of antiracism at a time when 'much latent racism exists – particularly among disaffected working class people', perhaps a reference to Stoke citizens (Gerrard 2011a). He hopes that, beyond paying tribute to Sir Stross, the project may be an important inspirational tool, combating the generally low aspirations of the working class of Stoke-on-Trent (Gerrard 2011a). His own statement about his personal inspiration is clearly central to the formulation of the campaign's official message:

> I'm native to Stoke-on-Trent and am disappointed in its perceptions and pro-file. But though appearing drab and unremarkable, Stoke-on-Trent and its peo-ple are responsible for some wonderful feats. This is a fine example. Lidice is promotionally powerful to this city as the 'Lidice Shall Live' campaign's home is Stoke-on-Trent.... That is why I started the campaign – because I believe this uniqueness can be exploited to change perceptions for the better, raise the city's profile. (Gerrard 2011a)

Further statements from Gerrard in a Staffordshire newspaper also illuminate the aims of the twinning: 'Stoke-on-Trent could become the hub for a commemorative place for Lidice. We could see a lot of visitors to Stoke-on-Trent each year' (Truswell 2010a).

Thus there are (at least) three factors to be taken into consideration in an interpretation of the Stoke-Lidice twinning campaign as cosmopolitan memory work. In commemorative terms, Gerrard is primarily concerned, and quite legitimately, with the creation of a platform for the remembrance of Sir Stross and those who gave up part of their small incomes to help rebuild Lidice in the 1940s. The reference to contemporary latent racism is also significant, and aligns Gerrard's motivations with those of major institutions, particularly museums, who take examples from the Holocaust as starting point to engage people in discussions about tolerance and human rights. Thirdly, though, Gerrard aims to provide his city and its residents with a shared history; a source of pride, to change the way a regional group sees their own identity as well as how that identity is perceived by others.

This drive to boost the local economy and to change public perceptions of Stoke should be seen in the context of the West Midlands' recent history. The economic security that the pottery and mining industries lent to Stoke-on-Trent and the West Midlands in the first part of the twentieth century aligned it with the historically prosperous cities of the South until the 1980s, when economic recession had an extremely negative impact on the region, according to the *Financial Times* in 1989: 'If there is a north-south divide in Britain ... the recession of the early 1980s placed the West Midlands firmly to the North of it' (Casey 2002: 157). The area still depends on manufac-turing as a source of employment beyond the national average (Casey 2002:

145). The shared history of Lidice and Stoke-on-Trent is expected to improve tourism to the region, generating revenue, thus there is some economic motivation at stake. Beyond this, a main aim of the campaign is to set up an arts centre to become the UK home of Lidice's annual children's fine art competition. In 2010, there were only nine entries from the United Kingdom, none of which were from Stoke-on-Trent; Gerrard's work is perhaps rendered most visible by the fact that thirty-eight prizes were made to children from Stoke-on-Trent in the 2011 competition (Gerrard 2011b). Campaigners also hope to set up a museum of heritage based on Lidice and its connection with Sir Barnett Stross and Stoke-on-Trent; an exhibition has already been held on this history at the museum at the commemorative complex in Lidice itself. Yet the economic goals that partially ground the project potentially dilute its cosmopolitanism; the Holocaust is arguably appropriated in order to pursue a goal that is unrelated to the memory of its victims and has little to do with the development of human rights directives.

These activities in Stoke, guided by the multifaceted motivations discussed, simultaneously reinvent and reinvigorate the memory community of 'Lidice Shall Live'. Yet the original community was predominantly concerned with rebuilding Lidice for the few survivors who would be able to return to it after the war. The extent to which this present-day community involves the people of Lidice – beyond being a symbol of successful humanitarianism in which the residents of Stoke-on-Trent can take retrospective pride – remains to be seen as the campaign's future unfolds. It is worth noting, however, that the bond is largely reciprocal; in addition to hosting the exhibition about Stoke-on-Trent's role in rebuilding the village, the authorities in Lidice have named a street there after Sir Barnett Stross, who was himself made an honorary citizen of the village in 1957. When Alan and Cheryl visited Lidice, together with other campaigners from Stoke, in 2010, their efforts were reciprocated by a delegation from the village, who toured the Staffordshire potteries in November 2010. According to the Mayor of Lidice, Veronika Kellerova, who had relatives killed in the 1942 tragedy: 'For us Barnett Stross was an inspirational man. We'd be very glad to make a friendship between Lidice and Stoke-on-Trent because that's where Barnett Stross was from' (*The Sentinel* 2010).

Thus the proposed twinning of Lidice with Stoke-on-Trent bears many hallmarks of model town twinning as described by Verlinden; the Gerrards' 'voluntary commitment and participation' as local citizens 'in collaboration with their local authorities' is firmly geared towards a future of 'mutual interaction' (see Verlinden 2008: 208) with Lidice. The twinning, even before any protocols have been signed, promises to involve Lidice and Stoke in a process of cultural exchange, at least as far as the International Art Competition is concerned. Furthermore the campaign brought attention the original fundraising movement, which in its own time resonated distinctly with the notion of a cosmopolitan recognition and investment in the everyday lives of others. However, as noted, the current campaign's focus on attracting tourism to Stoke-on-Trent and improving the city's profile and economic prosperity cannot be so smoothly integrated into a transcultural, cosmopolitan model; whilst the relationship between Lidice and Stoke-on-Trent is fundamentally an example of 'glocal' connectivity, this particular element of the contemporary campaign's direction constituted more of a turning inwards to regionalism than a move towards cultural 'others'.

Lidice/Khojaly: 'Different Places, Same Brutality'

The twinning of Lidice with the town of Khojaly represents a divergent form of transcultural identification from that seen in the example of Lidice and Stoke-on-Trent.[2] In the Khojaly massacre of 1992, part of the Nagorno-Karabakh conflict between ethnic Armenians and the Republic of Azerbaijan (1988–1994),[3] 613 civilians were killed by Armenian troops in a 48-hour period (Heydarov and Bagiyev 2007: 10). Whilst many Armenians insisted that deaths were sustained in the course of legitimate military operations, international human rights organizations asserted that the event was unjustifiable and significantly contravened human rights conventions.[4] Given this history, the twinning of Khojaly with Lidice arguably constitutes a polemic harnessing of the Holocaust paradigm, officially aligning the Nagorno-Karabakh conflict with the most internationally recognized genocide of the twentieth century. In this respect, because the twinning aims to draw attention to a recent violation of human rights, the mobilization of Holocaust memory initially seems to resonate with Levy and Sznaider's assessment of cosmopolitan memory's global potential.

The link between Khojaly and Lidice, as with Stoke-on-Trent, is apparently a reciprocal one. Reports suggest that a street in Lidice is also to be named after Khojaly; an act that mirrors rumours of an earlier naming of a street after Lidice in Khojaly. A memorial event for victims of the massacre was held in Lidice in 2010. The link has not been without controversy, however; according to press reports, the Armenian ambassador to Vienna, Ashot Ovakiman, sent unsuccessful protests to Lidice authorities about the 'twinning' in an attempt to block the initiative (*News.Az* 2010). Whilst the proposal is reported to have gone ahead nonetheless, as noted previously the Mayor of Lidice has refuted any official twinning; she also denies the naming of any street in Lidice after Khojaly. Nonetheless, it is worth considering the dynamics of the project. The destruction of Lidice and Khojaly do share certain characteristics. In both cases unarmed and peaceful civilians were attacked and killed and their bodies stripped of valuables (Stehlik 2004: 79;

Heydarov and Bagiyev 2007: 78). Structures in both settlements were also destroyed (Stehlik 2004: 92–7; Denber and Goldman 1992: 20). However, there are also some substantial differences. More children, men and women died in Khojaly in 1992 than had been killed at Lidice fifty years earlier. The nature of the attacks themselves was also somewhat different. Whilst both cases were undeniably brutal, the Nazi slaughter of Lidice's men was a regimented, highly methodological exercise in which groups of between five and ten were lined up and shot, and their bodies laid out in neat rows. Prisoners from Terezín concentration camp buried the bodies over the course of the following two days. The massacre at Khojaly was a comparatively chaotic and disordered event. The killings were characterized not by cold uniformity but by extreme and uncontrolled violence; fifty-six of the bodies, according to autopsy reports were killed with 'especial cruelty: they were burnt alive, scalped, beheaded or had their eyes gouged out, and pregnant women were bayoneted in the abdomen' (Heydarov and Bagiyev 2007: 10). The corpses were left scattered over the surrounding countryside (*The Times* 1992). The extremity of the violence at Khojaly and the transparently civilian status of the victims garnered immediate attention from the international press (see Heydarov and Bagiyev 2007: 13–33). Far from aligning what had happened with any other genocide, Agdam militia commander Rashid Mamedov stated upon seeing the scattered bodies in the wake of the massacre: 'The bodies are lying there like flocks of sheep. Even the fascists did nothing like this' (Killen 1992).[5] Similarly, French journalist Jean-Yves Junet, a witness to the massacre, reported: 'I had heard a lot about wars, about the cruelty of German fascists, but the Armenians outdid them, killing five- or six-year-old children, innocent people'[6] (Heydarov and Bagiyev 2007: 77).

The twinning campaign aligns the events at Khojaly with those at Lidice in public consciousness, but a close examination of what happened in the two communities reveals many specific differences. Arguably, linking Lidice and Khojaly isolates these two events from their larger respective contexts. At stake, potentially, is a conflation of events, something with which Levy and Sznaider (2006: 18) are apparently unconcerned in their discussion of cosmopolitanism's facilitation of 'new sensibilities and solidarities'. It remains in question, I suggest, whether the alignment of the Khojaly massacre with the destruction of Lidice and its people is justified in casting aside the fundamental historical differences between their respective contexts, to which I now draw attention.

The massacre at Khojaly, not unlike many of those that took place during the Holocaust, was part of a longer struggle for land. Conflict between the Armenians and the Azerbaijani people dates back to at least 1905, and escalated considerably following the establishment of Soviet rule in Armenia in 1920 (Heydarov and Bagiyev 2007: 7–8). Since the conflict began, many

Azerbaijani settlements and national cultural monuments have been destroyed (Heydarov and Bagiyev 2007: 7–8). The destruction of Lidice, as discussed, was deliberately publicized by the perpetrators as a warning to the international community, in particular to resistance groups. In fact, the nature of the massacre was quite unlike the majority of such acts during the Holocaust, which were often more directly connected to the Nazis' colonization of land (as discussed in Part 2), and which the Nazis often went to quite considerable lengths to mask (Lang 2005: 14). Whilst the events at Khojaly in 1992, too, were made public almost immediately by the global media, Armenian officials continue to this day 'to deny responsibility for the crimes committed during the [Nagorn-Karabakh] conflict, including against the population of Khojaly' (Heydarov and Bagiyev 2007: 10).

Furthermore, whilst the massacre at Kholjaly allows a fairly straightforward categorization of victims and perpetrators, the larger Nagorno-Karabakh conflict suggests a more complex oscillation of collective innocence and guilt. According to Human Rights Watch (then Helsinki Watch), both sides have committed acts that violate the laws of armed conflict:

> while legitimate military targets were apparently interspersed within these locales, neither party had unlimited licence in attacking these targets. Armenians and Azerbaijani forces had a duty to observe the law of proportionality and to take the necessary precautions in launching attacks in order to avoid, and, in any event, to minimize civilian casualties and damage to civilian objects incidental to such attacks. Both sides appear to have flagrantly disregarded these obligatory legal restraints on attacks in these particular military operations. (Denber and Goldman 1992: 31)

The Holocaust, to which the Lidice-Khojaly twinning inevitably aligns the Nagorno-Karabakh dispute, allows a less problematic division; if not between Germans as perpetrators and other national groups as victims then certainly between the Nazi Party and the cultural and ethnic minorities they proposed to enslave or annihilate. Bearing this in mind, the extent to which the Armenians can be decisively designated perpetrators within the Nagorno-Karabakh conflict overall is somewhat less straightforward than the one example of Khojaly suggests, although the victimhood of civilians attacked in such cases remains indisputable.

Perhaps inevitably given the extent to which it has been circulated, Adolf Hitler's speech of 22 August 1939 about the Armenian genocide is brought to mind by discussions of Armenians as perpetrators or victims throughout the twentieth century as a whole.

> I have issued the command – and I'll have anybody who utters but one word of criticism executed by a firing squad – that our war aim does not consist in reaching certain lines, but in the physical destruction of the enemy. Accord-

ingly, I have placed my death-head formations in readiness – for the present only in the East – with orders to them to send to death mercilessly and without compassion, men, women, and children of Polish derivation and language. Only thus shall we gain the living space [*Lebensraum*] which we need. Who, after all, speaks today of the annihilation of the Armenians? (in Lochner 1942: 1)

Perhaps it is simply more difficult to firmly designate the Armenians as perpetrators of genocide when they themselves, as a people, have also been victims of genocidal violence; whether or not this should interfere with the commemoration of events in Khojaly as an isolated case requires further debate.

The twinning of Lidice with Khojaly potentially opens up a new supranational context for Holocaust memory. However, crucially, '[s]upranationality presumes some surrender of sovereignty by the member nations' (Etzioni 2001: xix). In other words, within such a body individual nation states potentially agree to be 'bound against their will' (Kembayev 2007: 15) by any weighted majority vote by other members. In a supranational organization, 'sovereignty is shared between central and political bodies' (Heywood 2000: 260). As one of the most prominent features of post-1945 world politics, supranationalism recognizes 'that globalization has perhaps made the notion of nation state sovereignty irrelevant'. Furthermore, advocates of supranational organizations argue that nation-state sovereignty 'produces an anarchical international order that is prone to conflict and war', although its opponents 'stand by the principle of the nation-state, and argue that supranational [organizations] have not, and can never, rival the nation-state's capacity to generate political allegiance and ensure democratic accountability' (Heywood 2000: 260).

Thus supranationality implies a transference of responsibility from individual nations to independent others; certainly the notion that 'shared memories of the Holocaust [harbour] the possibility of transcending ethnic and national boundaries' (Levy and Sznaider 2006: 4) is fundamentally supranational in character. However, the Khojaly massacre, like many Holocaust atrocities, was part of a larger struggle for land, a struggle which continues to motivate border disputes between the Armenians and the Azerbaijanis to date. According to Thomas de Waal:

The cultural and symbolic meaning of Nagorno Karabakh for both peoples cannot be overstated. For Armenians, Karabakh is the last outpost of their Christian civilization and a historic haven of Armenian princes and bishops before the eastern Turkic world begins. Azerbaijanis talk of it as a cradle, nursery, or conservatoire, the birthplace of their musicians and poets. Historically, Armenia is diminished without this enclave and its monasteries and its mountain lords; geographically and economically, Azerbaijan is not fully viable without [Nargorno] Karabakh. (2003: 3)

Whilst the twinning of Lidice and Khojaly may be suggestive of a supranational affinity between the Czech and the Azerbaijani people, the unresolved battle for land in Nagorno-Karabkh undermines any suggestion that either the Azerbaijani or the Armenian groups involved are willing to surrender territorial sovereignty. The Nagorno-Karabakh war, which began in earnest in 1988, ended in 1994, yet up to a million refugees are still living in camps in the affected region. Nagorno-Karabakh remains a contested space. In March 2015, the international media reported a resurgence of violent attacks on civilians (Nigmatulina 2015), and military casualties continue to mount in the border region (Reuters 2015).[7] According to the Azerbaijani national press, the twinning of Lidice and Khojaly was made official by the signing of a protocol document on 26 February 2010 (*Today.az* 2010). The twinning is a polemic act: the Holocaust is mobilized for political ends and sends an uncompromising message to the international community about the nature of what took place in Khojaly in 1992, yet it says little about what happened to the inhabitants of Lidice fifty years earlier, and the existence of a new supranational memory context is problematized by the ongoing struggle for the territorial sovereignty of Nagorno-Karabakh.

This section set out to discuss the dual town twinning of Lidice as a dynamic network of 'glocalisation'; a processual creation of 'new connections that situate … political, economic, and social experiences in a new type of supranational context' (Levy and Sznaider 2006: 27). The idea of town twinning has been considered with a view to its potential as a productive platform for cosmopolitan memory. Whilst different motivations prompted the twinning, or proposed twinning, of Lidice with Khojaly and Stoke-on-Trent respectively, both cases rely, to some extent, on an initial sense of global-local solidarity rendered possible by the mobilization of Holocaust memory. However, the emergence of a 'supranational' context for Lidice's commemoration has not been conclusively indicated; in exploring these cases, it is clear that both communities involved are intensely characterized by the needs of their very distinct constituent groups to reassert particular identities.

In the case of Khojaly, this identity is a national one, based on the Azerbaijani's insistence on their inalienable right to a specific geographic homeland (Nagorno-Karabakh). It is, in fact, motivated by an arguably anti-supranational instinct in which national sovereignty is reasserted rather than surrendered. In the case of Stoke-on-Trent, the identity in question is a regional one, which is also based on an attachment to a particular geographical context. In neither case do the group identities involved transcend their original geographical boundaries, indeed those involved attempt to bind themselves more closely to their particular territories. To what extent the global network they suggest promotes an increased solidarity beyond such boundaries in any sustained way also remains to be seen. They are also not straightforward as examples of supranationalism as defined by political theorists such as Etzioni and Kembayev; in taking part in a larger framework – in this case a memory network – neither community surrenders sovereignty. Place and territory, rather than losing meaning, is reasserted as a central concern in both twinning campaigns.

Furthermore, if we assume, following Welsch and Erll, that a turn *to the other* is an important aspect of transculturalism, and that, following Erll, Levy and Sznaider's project indeed falls within the transcultural sphere – and their interest in 'universal values that are emotionally engaging' does seem to support an interest in an improved self-other relation – then it is also worth noting that neither Stoke-on-Trent or Khojaly's contemporary mobilizations of Lidice's memory seem to consistently fit such a model. In both cases, rooted cosmopolitanism, or a turn towards the other and the fabric of their everyday lives, is to some extent present in the act of twinning; but it occurs, at least in part, as a precursor to self-affirmation. It is not the intention of this analysis to undermine the motivations or actions of those involved in these twinning projects. It is, however, worth considering whether examples such as these may call for a reinterrogation of existing theoretical co-ordinates. For example, in the twinning of Lidice and Khojaly, I have argued that a slippage takes place; the contextual differences between the Holocaust and the Nagorno-Karabakh conflict are necessarily precluded by this action in order for the similarity, rather than the difference between the two cases, to have meaningful political resonance. Yet the twinning also fits a 'glocal' model, as an internalization of the global within a local context. Levy and Sznaider's argument, as already noted, is that glocalization 'does not lead to … convergence or homogenization', and indeed it may not *necessarily* do so; but perhaps in some cases individual contextual specificities are lost during this process, as is arguably the case in the twinning of Lidice and Khojaly.

In considering Khojaly as a case study of glocalization, it becomes apparent that Levy and Sznaider's (2006: 29) model may overestimate the extent to which 'earlier catastrophes become relevant in the present and can determine a future that is articulated outside the parameters of the nation-state'. Whilst Lidice becomes relevant to current perceptions of the Khojaly massacre, Nagorno-Karabakh shows no signs of carving out a future identity beyond the parameters of the national territory. In the case of Stoke-on-Trent, the community is mobilizing Lidice's memory as a way of celebrating their own region and the past activities of those who lived there. The twinning is not concerned with the current suffering of others; it is concerned with memories of suffering only as an element within a larger historical narrative. This is not to say that an engagement with the 'others' of Lidice will not result from the twinning endeavour; indeed such engagement is quite likely to result from the events associated with the campaign. This indicates a need to reconsider transcultural and cosmopolitan memory models as *necessarily* concerned with the human rights of the other; thus the extent to which a *turn to* the other is a definitional element of associated practices is called into question.

Despite their differences as case studies, in drawing attention to the massacre at Lidice, both Khojaly and Stoke-on-Trent's twinning campaigns reinvigorate memory of the village on national and international platforms. Whatever the underlying motivations, and whether or not the campaigns themselves completely fit any particular model of memory practice, in very real terms they continue to defy the Nazis' attempts to obliterate Lidice, and in doing so forge new dialogical connections which promise to shape its future in a globalized world.

This chapter has examined the multifarious ways in which memories of Lidice have remained robust, constituting a refusal of the Nazis' original goal to erase the village from geography and memory. Whilst topographical revision characterized many Nazi campaigns, Lidice's fate was unique in that its destruction was a primary aim rather than an incidental legacy. Beginning at the village itself, I have tracked the development of a diverse memorial complex which calls attention to the various different historical and political factors that have shaped it. In scrutinizing the design and maintenance of the Lidice memorial environment in comparison to those of prominent death camps, I argued that a more-than-representational approach could productively be used to interpret such spaces. I then moved on to consider certain prominent examples of the global network of memory which emerged almost immediately after the village was razed, and which continues to evolve today.

Another way of bringing together the various arguments I have made throughout this chapter is offered by a consideration of the relationship between the microcosmic and the macrocosmic. To return, in the first instance, to the discussion of landscaping techniques; like other scholars who have previously worked through the issues raised by Bauman's link between the ideologies of gardening and National Socialism, I was confronted with what at first glimpse appears to be a conflation of innocence and guilt. All Nazis are not gardeners, and all gardeners are not Nazis. However, as Richard Etlin's introductory note to a collection on Third Reich art and culture suggests:

> On the microcosmic scale, we find a deep penetration of Nazi attitudes towards race, both in the definition of the German essence and in the excoriation of the alien essence, considered typically as Jewish or Slavic, seen as penetrating into the most minute particulars of each domain of human endeavour … The Nazi *Weltanschauung* contained no innocent or neutral detail in any aspect of thought or activity. (2002: xvii)

Whilst there is clearly a danger in putting very different actions on a par without due attention to moral nuance, if we recognize that in some instances the macrocosmic *can* penetrate into the microcosmic we must be willing to consider that possibility in any given context. Crucial to this consideration is that we question how the relationship between the two spheres works; if a racial policy of a nation state can penetrate into the microcosm inhabited by the gardener, is it also true that the microcosmic activity of gardening can lead, as Bauman suggests, to a nation state policy of ethnic cleansing? Perhaps this is in fact an interpenetration which works both ways, and which needs to be teased out carefully in each individual instance.

Similarly, the relationship between the local – the microcosmic – and the global – the macrocosmic – is fundamentally dialogic: when the Nazis razed Lidice, it became global news; the response from another local community (that of Stoke-on-Trent) – resulted in its re-creation; the poetry of Millay and the documentary film of Jennings found a way into dealing with an issue of global concern via attention to the microcosmic environment of the tragedy at Lidice, an environment which could be mobilized to produce a differentiated solidarity capable of transcending national boundaries. There is a palpable need to question the dynamics of the relationship between the macrocosm and the microcosm. In my analysis of the twinning of Lidice with Stoke and Khojaly, I attempted to enact such a scrutiny by examining the variety of mobilizations that are taking place in each respective campaign. These examples simply suggest, I would argue, that the frameworks we generate to examine the future of Holocaust memory – and cosmopolitanism will no doubt continue to be significant in this discourse – need to be flexible enough to take into account the sheer variety and complexity of evolving memory practices as they take place in the world around us; to examine the relationship between macrocosmic and microcosmic activities and environments without assuming that travelling only ever occurs in one direction.

Coda

I visited Lidice in the early spring. One of the first things I asked my guide during my tour was where particular village landmarks had been before its destruction. I had already been shown several photographs of aerial views of the village by the museum curator at my earlier visit to the education centre, each presenting it at a different time: before the massacre, in 1945, and in the present day. The best view for a visitor to the site itself is from the edge of the memorial complex outside the museum, which is where my tour began. My guide pointed out the foundations of the church and the Horák farm, and approximately indicated where other buildings had stood and where the boundaries of the original village had been. She also pointed out the stream that the Nazis had diverted in their topographical alterations.

It is easier to get a sense of where things happened at Lidice than it is at Babi Yar in Kiev; with the foundations of two buildings still present and the photographic images of the village itself to use as a point of comparison, it is possible to visualize something of what it might have looked like in June 1942. In a way, though, the relative absence of ruins here has a disorientating effect; it is tempting to try and fill in the contours of the landscape as it is now – its gentle slopes, hollows, and ridges – with one's eyes, to bring the village back to life in the imagination. It is easy to forget that these contours bear little reference to either the original village or to the results of the Nazi re-landscaping; as I have noted here, the landscape was 'put back' as much as possible to what it had been in the years immediately after the war according to an approximation of its original topography. Sympathizing with my struggle, my guide tells me to come back in winter; when it snows heavily and the sun comes out, she says, the foundations of the original village are faintly visible as the light reflects off the surface, magnifying otherwise hidden contours. I am not sure whether to believe this, but it is an appealing idea: that the snow could, in covering the landscape, uncover its past. It calls to mind Dixon Hunt's (2001: 22) comments about the affective potential of natural materials; their capacity to register the 'passing of the seasons', to continue with 'their own' lives and offer either their 'pathetic sympathy' or a 'consolation of seasonal renewal and regeneration'. In finding the idea of the snow's capacity to show me the past appealing, am I falling prey to something of which I claim to be wary – a sentimental indulgence, an anthropomorphic impulse? Perhaps. After all, what is being renewed as the seasons change? The past cannot be regenerated. But it does impress on me anew how much the weather matters when it comes to how a particular place is experienced. This is something I hear most often from people keen to tell me about their visits to Auschwitz. So familiar with rather ubiquitous images of the camp in the snow, in black and white, and with internees' descriptions of intense cold, the extreme heat suffered by Auschwitz prisoners during the fierce Polish summer seems to be less prominent in people's cultural memories of the camp. Thus those who visit from spring through to autumn are often surprised that there is not, somehow, at least two feet of eternal snow where they have always imagined it to be.

I think again of the weather when the Lidice Memorial website announces its programme for the seventieth anniversary of the massacre, on 10 June 2012. It will be the beginning of the wedding season at Lidice, when the roses are coming into bloom under the early summer sun and the foundations illuminated by the snow are once more invisible. As preparations for the seventieth anniversary of the destruction of Lidice are underway, the 2012 Eurovision Song Contest is hosted in Azerbaijan. A celebration of 'supranational identities' (Stokes 2004: 103), the contest was first held in 1956, the same year the first significantly publicized city twinning in Europe, between Rome and Paris – itself likened to 'a wedding, after a long flirtation' (Vaughan 1979: 208) – was inaugurated. The dignitaries from both cities made an oath to 'to develop, by means of a better reciprocal understanding, a lively sentiment of European fraternity; and to join our forces to promote with all our powers the success of that undertaking so essential for peace and prosperity: the creation of European unity' (in Vaughan 1979: 208). Its stated aims were much like those attributed to the first Eurovision Song Contest; to 'unify post-war western Europe through music' (Raykoff and Tobin 2007: xvii). In the 2012 competition, the Armenian entry withdrew in April, and does not perform at the contest. Their reason for withdrawing is the continued hostility in Nagorno-Karabakh, and the death of another soldier – this time an Armenian – at the border earlier this year (Kramer 2012). The Armenian Public Television network made the following statement:

Despite the fact that the Azerbaijani authorities have given security guarantees to all participating countries, several days ago the Azerbaijani president made a statement that enemy number one for Azerbaijan were the Armenians... There is no logic to sending a participant to a country where he will be met as an enemy. (*Huffington Post* 2012)

One musician from the Azerbaijani entry, Elvin Kerivov, age twenty-nine, expressed relief that things had not been the other way round: 'It's better for Eurovision to be here in Azerbaijan than in Armenia. If Armenia won, our delegation would have to go to Armenia to sing, which is not good for our pride' (in Herszenhorn 2012). Johan Fornäs (2008: 137) has argued that '[s]ome potential may lie hidden in Euro football and the Eurovision Song Contest'; his mention of Euro football reminds me of the controversy that met leaked proposals to build a hotel at Babi Yar, expressly for international visitors for Euro 2012. The dynamics of each case are clearly different: in Kiev, the proposal seemed to be yet another attempt to bury Holocaust memory, whilst for the Armenians, the recent past is still too much in the present to be set aside. As Fornäs (2008: 137) concludes, whatever the potential of events designed to bring Europe together, there are 'few signs of emerging transnational and supranational forms of life and identity' to be observed in reality. It is too early to say the same for the town twinnings discussed in this chapter. Nonetheless, the examples presented are suggestive of one element of supranational activity that demands more interrogation: its selective dynamics. Antonio D'Alfonso (2005: 57) has argued that, in their attempts to create supranational cultures, nations simply 'attract whatever acceptable elements of neighbouring cultures from within and outside their geographical territory, and of course, make sure to expel all undesirable elements of foreign culture'. As far as cultures of memory are concerned, the dawn of supranationalism may do little more than legitimate what has already become the norm: for those with power to decide which memories are to be mobilized and which are best left behind. Like the snow at Lidice, this may, in some cases, reveal pasts which might otherwise have been lost or forgotten; but whereas the snow has no agenda guiding its fall, for those in a position to illuminate the past, the demands of the present will never be far away.

Notes

Sections of this chapter are reprinted by permission of the publishers from 'Mobilising Lidice: Cosmopolitan Memory between Theory and Practice' in Laila Amine and Caroline Beschea-Fasche (eds), Special Edition *Crossroads of Memory, Culture, Theory and Critique* 52(2): 129–45. Copyright © 2014.

1. The phrase 'A Ray of Light Across the Sea' was used to describe the relationship between Lidice and Stoke in the booklet for the Lidice Shall Live Campaign (Stross 1942).

2. The phrase 'different places, same brutality' was used to describe the relationship between Lidice and Khojaly in a press release distributed by the Azerbaijani Embassy in Prague (2010).

3. The Nagorno-Karabakh conflict can be seen as part of a larger struggle for space and resources throughout the Caucasus region after the demise of the Soviet Union (see Krüger 2010: xi–xii).

4. See Parliamentary Assembly Doc. 9066 2nd edition, written declaration no. 324, 2001 ('Recognition of the genocide perpetrated against the Azeri population by the Armenians') and United Nations Economic and Social Council, commission on human rights, 58th session ('Question of the violation of human rights and fundamental freedoms in any part of the world'), republished in Heydarov and Bagiyev (2007: 46–47).

5. When this statement was reported, the journalist – correctly or incorrectly – cited this reference to 'fascists' as relating to Nazi invaders in World War II.

6. Junet's distinction seems to overlook certain aspects of the Nazi campaign involving the deaths of young children and other civilians.

7. Leaders within the region have announced the existence of the 'Nagorno-Karabakh Republic' but '[t]o date the international community has not recognized Nagorno-Karabakh as an independent state or as a part of Armenia'; simultaneously, whilst Azerbaijan still 'asserts that Nagorno-Karabakh is an integral part of its territory', Karabakh Armenians 'reject any part of integration into Azerbaijan' (Krüger 2010: xi).

TRAVELLING TO REMEMBER

I hate conclusions. A good book, essay, course, or lecture should open up
its subject, not shut it down.

—Lawrence Buell, *The Future of Environmental Criticism:*
Environmental Crisis and the Literary Imagination

Memorial texts, like good conclusions, should open up their subjects rather
than close them down. That was an original premise of this book, and throughout each of the three case studies I discussed I have endeavoured to suggest
how such an opening up might work. Primarily, I have done so by travelling.
With travel, as with memory, one thing leads to another. Particular paths do
not await each traveller: rather, as de Certeau suggests, travellers are poets
of their own acts; we all find our own way. John Zilcosky (2008: 6) argues
that both writing and travelling – as forms of 'going where one isn't' – suggest
'the openness of the unimaginable'. In planning a journey, as in planning the
construction of a text, certain co-ordinates can be determined in advance,
but both the journey and the text will always, to some extent, be shaped by
a series of incidental encounters, the nature of which cannot be predicted.

The first part, on Buchenwald, explored a concentration camp in the homeland of the German Enlightenment as a space of a dialogical engagement
between 'victim' and 'visitor'. Via an ecocritical reading of the testimonial project of former inmate Jorge Semprun, this analysis demonstrated landscape
as palimpsest – multilayered, multidimensional and texturized. Following
Semprun's phenomenological immersion in a landscape seemingly saturated
with German cultural history, I explored the potential of textualized topography as facilitative of an intense and reflective empathic unsettlement. In
my discussion of Jacobson's journey to uncover links between the violence
of the Holocaust and post-Katrina New Orleans, the section on Buchenwald
travelled from one ideologically shaped landscape to another in the American
South. This investigation revealed a trajectory between continents as deeply
texturized as the geographically bounded space explored in Chapters 1 and 2.

The following part on Babi Yar examined spatial and literary de-territorial-izations; beginning with Babi Yar's disjointed memorial landscape in Kiev, I traced a trajectory of travelling memory in literature from Kuznetsov's *Babi Yar: A Document in the Form of a Novel* to D.M. Thomas's *The White Hotel*. I argued that this mediation, prompted in part by an evasion of Holocaust memory in Ukraine itself, played a part in the evolution of a new landscape 6,000 miles away: the Babi Yar Park, Denver, Colorado. In examining the relationship between the original mass grave site and its transcontinental counterpart, the chapter interrogated Ukrainian and American public mem-ory of the massacre, and uncovered the centrality of soil and topography within associated discourse and practice. The final part, on Lidice, turned to a complex international memorial network surrounding a landscape which the Nazis infamously attempted to erase from memory and topography and cover with German soil. Again I began with the site itself, examining the possibility of curating nature to appropriately 'landscape' the Holocaust, be-fore moving on to consider memories of Lidice in the global community. I interrogated the twinning of the village with Khojaly, Azerbaijan, and with Stoke-on-Trent, UK, positing the resulting network as an example of cosmo-politan 'glocalization'. In, both cases, I suggested, despite their motivational specificities, the twinnings rely on a sense of global-local solidarity rendered possible by the mobilization of Holocaust memory.

As a way of concluding, I turn to the encounters that have shaped my own engagement with the landscapes of memory discussed throughout. As Susannah Radstone 2011: 111–12) contends in a recent review of emerging models of memory scholarship: 'One of the fundamental insights provided by memory research ... is that memory constructs the past *in the present*. So any story that I might tell about the history and development of mem-ory studies will be a story that I tell from, and inside, not just the present, but my present'. Thus in attempting to better define the intervention I have pursued within this field, it is inevitable that at least part of the story comes from my own present. As stated in the introduction, the final challenge of this project is to situate not only an abstract idea of *the* self, but also *my*self, in relation to the Holocaust and its landscapes. I consider this story here alongside the work of a writer whose methodologies perhaps most closely embody that advocated here: W.G. Sebald. Sebald's literature is concerned with the 'history of modernity' and frequently the Holocaust in particular (Long 2007a: 14–16) and with the workings and ethics of memory in relation to and beyond particular historical contexts. Whilst likened to travel writing, his works have also been interpreted as inversions of the paradigms of travel (see Zilcosky 2004; Theisen 2004); as Wylie (2007: 208) has argued, Sebald's writing is unique in its 'treatment of landscape's essential tension in-between movement and dwelling, outsider and insider ... Caught precisely between staying and moving on, Sebald's writing is *of* landscape, not simply about landscape.' Characterized by a denial of 'redemptive closure' (Kilbourne 2007: 140) and 'an ethos of embodied uncertainty' (Walkowitz 2007: 169), Sebald presents us with travels structured by what Jessica Dubow (2004: 2007) names a condition of incompleteness. These travels, however, are not evacuated by their open-ended nature. The places encountered in Sebald's texts are co-ordinates that both reveal imbrications of past narratives and invite their implication within new trajectories of thought and response. Sebald presents landscape as a 'medium of exchange' (W.T.J. Mitchell 1994: 1), always becoming but never completed.

In order to elucidate in precise terms how this book unfurled, I here discuss the encounters that have structured the experience behind it alongside examples from Sebald's *The Rings of Saturn* (2002). The purpose of this discussion is not to provide a new reading of a novel of which so many thorough and nuanced readings already exist. Indeed, scholarly discourse on Sebald, now almost a subdiscipline of literary criticism in itself, better enables me to elucidate a particular conceptual model; Sebald scholarship is a rare instance in which literary critics have brought cultural geography and cultural memory together. Neither is my intention for this conclusion to function as a chapter on Sebald as such. Whilst many of the methodologies utilized and perspectives taken throughout echo those present in Sebald's literature of landscape, it is his creation of textualized network of many places – as opposed to illuminating one place in isolation – that renders it so suited as a structural device for this conclusion, which attempts to bring three places together as well as to articulate the relationship between landscape, literature and memory proposed throughout *Topographies of Suffering*.

Apparently from a hospital bed, the narrator of *The Rings of Saturn* recalls a walking tour through East Anglia. Like many other protagonists in Sebald's texts, his subject position in relation to the histories revealed by the text is fundamental to the author's treatment of landscape. Sebald, as Eric Santner (2006: 138) suggests, presents a 'narrator-witness-listener', a subject who 'takes on the responsibility of mourning' (Schlesinger 2004: 54) without lapsing into nostalgia; a 'subject of the age of mass-mediated reality [constituted] in the awareness that any nostalgia for lost authenticity is a myth and that there could be no comfort in this awareness' (Kilbourne 2007: 139). Each place he visits – and the walks that link them – anchors new stories. He does not go in search, as I did, of atrocity beneath the surface, yet a history of destruction haunts his travels. Each story leads the reader to a place and time far from the East Anglian coast in 1992 as experienced by this narrator, and as such a historical metanarrative shadows the tour from start to finish. The stories told in *The Rings of Saturn* are generated by a diverse range of encounters and scrutinized with reference to a plethora of mediated and remediated sources. Whilst the initial journey is structured according to predetermined co-ordinates and existing routes, the experience of the narrator is shaped by the incidental encounters that occur along the way. As such, it echoes my own journey – one which is left open-ended, here, as much as concluded. I use three guiding principles of Sebald's text to structure this overview of *Topographies of Suffering*: a transition from *lieux de mémoire* to landscapes of memory, based on recognition of their evolving nature, and their subjection to mediation and remediation; the potential of such sites for the facilitation of cosmopolitan engagement; and the value of seeing Holocaust texts through an ecocritical lens that situates Others as part of the world around us, a world for which we have a universal and ineluctable responsibility.

Landscape Beyond the Lieu: Mediation, Remediation and Incidental Encounters

A key aim of this book is to demonstrate the dialogic and evolving nature of memorial landscapes in order to overcome a critical sense of monument fatigue. Sebald's narrator reveals much about the problems that may face a visitor to a commemorative site who tries to recapture the past, problems which have perhaps contributed substantially to this fatigue. He recalls a visit to an official memorial for the Battle of Waterloo, a 'circus-like structure' where the battle has been recreated with wax figures in authentic uniform:

> This then, I thought as I looked round me, is the representation of history. It requires a falsification of perspective. We, the survivors, see everything from above, see everything at once, and we still do not know how it was. The desolate field extends all around where once fifty thousand soldiers and ten thousand horses met their end within a few hours. The night after the battle, the air must have been filled with death rattles and groans. Now there is nothing but the silent brown soil. Whatever becomes of the corpses and mortal remains? Are they buried under the memorial? Are we standing on a mountain of death? Is that our ultimate vantage point? Does one really have the much-vaunted historical overview from such a position? (2002: 125)

As Simon Cooke (2009: 16) suggests, the example demonstrates the Sebaldian logic that 'official or institutional storage sites for cultural memory … serve, literally as well as figuratively, as cover-ups of the past'. Hence, perhaps, Confino and Fritzsche's (2002: 5) suggestion that it is time to focus on memory 'out of the museum and away from the monument'. I have argued, however, that official sites of memory can be experienced, as Crownshaw suggests, 'against the grain'; that by focusing on the dialogical, processual and social interactions that take place in and around the memorial environment, we may better recognize their potential to facilitate an empathically unsettling engagement with the past which is of some ethical value. This is precisely the way in which Sebald's narrator in *The Rings of Saturn* travels through and encounters landscape, as his 'mental wanderings [take] cultural memory so persistently on the move' (Cooke 2009: 27).

The Sebaldian narrator is a rather particular traveller, who self-consciously distinguishes his own activities from those of 'holidaymakers' who 'cross the threshold' only to 'leave again after they have taken a brief look around in the uncomprehending way characteristic' to them (2002: 92–93). In lingering over details about each place on his route, he becomes immersed in them and their particular histories. Whilst his larger trajectory itself is determined by pre-existing routes, such as an old diesel train track that runs from Nor- wich to Lowestoft (2002: 29), his choice of destinations pays heed to no conventional hierarchy of popular attractions. In spending so much time in the places others merely dismiss after a 'brief look around', he constructs his own unique path through the East Anglian landscapes. His selection of stops, such as the Sailor's Reading Room in Southwold, or a deserted hotel in Lowestoft recommended from a guidebook 'published shortly after the turn of the century' (2002: 42), takes him away from the tourist route as often as it coincides with it. As such Sebald alerts us to what we may gain from an exploration of the larger context, be it cultural, social or geographic, in which a particular place exists. Accordingly he pays close attention to the artefacts he stumbles across, such as a *Daily Express* photographic history of the Sec- ond World War, frequently relying on sources of 'unofficial knowledge' and 'public history' such as Raphael Samuel (1994: 1–6) has argued must be sought in order to comprehend not only historical events but the memo- ries that circulate around them. This book has deliberately relied on both official and unofficial sources, both sought and stumbled across: archives, guidebooks, testimonies, fictions, internet forums, newspapers, magazines, interviews and informal conversations. The importance of the latter, in par- ticular, is clearly indicated in *The Rings of Saturn,* in which the narrator falls into conversation with people as he travels, from the gardener at a country house (2002: 38) to a property investor in a hotel bar (2002: 193–4). These encounters offer him new perspectives on the landscapes through which he travels and tell him stories that send his imagination to landscapes far away. Throughout the sections that follow, I briefly introduce some examples of the encounters I have had during my research, to elucidate the ways in which 'the gloriously unavoidable nature of human interaction' (MacDonald 2009: 21) facilitates memory-work. It is these encounters, alongside those mapped out in advance, that have mediated and remediated my own experiences of place, and which subsequently alerted me to the ways in which memories of them have travelled.

It is in part this approach to travel that allows Sebald's narrator to reveal the intricately textured and textualized nature of place; at Somerleyton Hall, residence of Her Majesty's Master of the Horse, for example, one cannot 'readily say which decade or century it is, for many ages are superimposed … and coexist' (2002: 36). Such a superimposition of many ages has been revealed in discussions of each of the three case studies considered here. At Buchenwald, the ages of the dukes of Saxony-Weimar, Goethe and Eckermann, the SS and their prisoners, Soviet and post-reunification commemoration are laid bare in topography and narrated by Semprun's testimonial project. At Babi Yar in Kiev and across the Ukraine, despite new vegetable gardens and the construction projects of the Soviet government, a landscape transformed by years of mass death and burial awaits close scrutiny. At present day Lidice, where the razed village and its replacement sit either side of Barnett Stross's rose garden, three temporalities are imbricated in one diverse landscape.

That literature both prompts and mediates experience of inhabiting and travelling through landscape is an essential premise of this enquiry that is also evident in Sebald's work. The writings of Thomas Browne, a seventeenth-century doctor and son of a silk merchant, provide an initial point of departure for the narrator of *The Rings of Saturn*. Browne's view of the world, 'as no more than a shadow image of another far beyond' (2002: 18), also grounds the metahistorical perspective of the text. It is in this spirit that the narrator records his travels; the histories behind the places he visits take over the description of his journey. Semprun's writing, D.M. Thomas's novel, and Peter Herbstreuth's passing comment about discoloured crops at the Lidice mass grave were my own points of departure. Each set in motion a unique trajectory. Semprun led me not only to Buchenwald, but to Goethe, as writer, traveller, meteorologist, and cultural symbol, to the cultural dichotomy of Weimar's legacy, and eventually to New Orleans. *The White Hotel* led me, not only to Babi Yar, but to Pronicheva and Kuznetsov, to the experiences of *holodomor* victims, and ultimately to the Babi Yar Park in Denver. In my search for Lidice's discoloured crops, I went from the site itself to Stoke-on-Trent's fundraising campaign, to Millay's poem and Jennings's *Silent Village*, and from these texts to a global network of twinning and renaming from Illinois to Azerbaijan.

The way one thing leads to another in travel is exemplified by my first evening in Weimar, where I met two English people living and working in the city: Sonja Bruendl and Howard Atkinson, who heard me speaking in English and stopped to say hello. I invited them to accompany me on a visit to a restaurant called *Zum Zwiebel* [the Onion]. I was interested in *Zum Zwiebel* because I had heard a rumour that Hitler had been there for a drink, and I was interested in Sonja and Howard because they lived in Weimar. Citizens

of Weimar, they told me, were very conscientious about Buchenwald. Howard suggested that this is easier in Weimar than it might be in other cities
with a shameful element to their pasts because here there are so many positive narratives to counteract it. It was Howard, as much as Semprun and his
imaginary Goethe, who prompted me to consider the dichotomous nature of
the memories circulating between the city and the camp, Gorra's (2004: 16)
'coincidence in something more than space'. I became interested in how this
dichotomy was played out, not initially via academic commentary, but whilst
walking around Weimar's marketplace and noticing a post box commemorating the twinning of the city with Stratford-Upon-Avon as part of the Weimar
1999 Capital of Culture programme. Similarly, it was an incidental visit to
the *holodomor* Memory Candle in Kiev where I saw so many images that
reminded me of the pastoral destruction described in Kuznetsov's text that
suggested the value of pursuing a multidirectional comparison of Holocaust
and *holodomor* experience.

As Sebald's narrator demonstrates in his walk around East Anglia, whilst
you do not always find that which you set out in search of,[1] there is a value
to simply getting lost in landscapes. Long (2007b: 140) has referred to Sebald's walkers as 'deliberately inefficient', and argues that the tendency to
'explore byways rather than make beelines' is best understood as a response
to the 'increased efficiency in economic and bureaucratic life' germane to
modernity. As happens 'so often in unfamiliar cities' (2002: 84), I went the
wrong way in Kiev many times, not in a purposeful response to modernity but
purely by mistake. The city's metro system, which has the deepest tunnels in
the world, is a spectacular but confusing place for the non-Ukrainian visitor.
The signs are all in Cyrillic script; there is no condescension to the West in
Kiev's sprawling underground marble halls. Street signs, too, are not in abun-
dance. Maps are either in English or Ukrainian, but never both, it seems, so
cross-referencing is difficult. Navigating the city demands encounters, if only
because it is necessary to keep asking someone where you are. I came to appreciate the value of the byway over the beeline. One of the many places we
got lost was in the hillside of the Pechersk Lavra, on the way to the Museum
of the Great Patriotic War. This is not a museum that should be difficult to
find. A 62m-high titanium statue, *Rodina Mat* (literally 'Nation's Mother',
formally referred to as the 'Defence of the Motherland Monument'), stands
on the hillside over the museum, visible from miles around. However, when
standing at the bottom of the Lavra, a veritable maze of monks' vegetable
gardens, chapels and paths lies between the approaching visitor and the Iron
Lady. The long walk put me behind schedule and I arrived at the museum
later than planned. The museum is a hangover from the Soviet era, a gloomy
and forbidding place where museum employees follow visitors from room
to room. The rooms are lined with glass cases of exhibits. Captions are in

Ukrainian only. In one of the dimly lit rooms a man was setting up a table of books in front of several rows of chairs. One of the titles looked familiar, and upon talking to the man – who spoke a little English – we learned that he was the son of Anatoli Kuznetsov, there to launch a French translation of his father's book. He showed us a typewriter in a case in the corner of the room: the typewriter on which Kuznetsov had written *Babi Yar*. He pointed to the machine with pride. This was the typewriter Kuznetsov risked his life to collect, along with his manuscript for *Babi Yar* and his Cuban cigars, before escaping from his escort when he defected to Britain. I was left thinking about how getting lost in the labyrinthine Lavra had resulted in this chance meeting. Ten minutes before or after I would have missed that window of opportunity, to see that famous typewriter and shake hands with a descendant of Kuznetsov, whose writing was one of my central co-ordinates and whose stories were in my head as I had walked through the city.

This encounter demonstrated a way in which the museum environment can become dynamic through social mediation. In the room next door to that in which I saw the typewriter are displays relating to the Holocaust in Ukraine. A spotlight illuminates a hangman's noose. A glass case on the wall contains two exhibits rarely exposed to the light of the public museum: a shrivelled glove and a desiccated fragment of soap, both apparently made from human remains. Unlike Jacobson's lampshade, with no available means of contextualizing these objects they appear to refer only to themselves. Some encounters open up the imagination; others close it down.

Later that night we saw protestors with tents lining Kiev's main street, Kreschatik. Encountering protest creates a singular awareness of individual and group values and affinities. I recognized one of the words in a repeated chant by a group in Kreschatik as the name of the former Ukrainian Prime Minister, Yulia Tymoshenko, who was at that point in court being tried for abuse of office.[2] Seeing the protestors had made me interested in the case and I followed it after returning to England. Tymoshenko was sentenced less than two weeks later, to seven years in prison, a conviction which the European Union has called 'justice being applied selectively under political motivation' (BBC News 2011). To reduce ten years of complex political change to brief summary, Tymoshenko was a leading figure in the Orange Revolution of 2004 (Herb 2008: 1629). Whether guilty or innocent of abusing her position, she was key to securing Ukrainian independence (Herb 2008: 1629). The protests against her trial and conviction suggest her role in that process has not been forgotten. It is impossible to go 'travelling in search of the past', to borrow from Martin Gilbert (1997), without incidentally encountering present concerns. Tymoskenko's husband, Oleksandr Tymoshenko, was granted political asylum in the Czech Republic. He bought a house in Lidice, which

I had visited myself in April 2009, seven years after reading Peter Herb-streuth's comment about crop discolouration over the mass grave.

Due to a broken metro train, I got a taxi from Prague to Lidice. This was not a completely straightforward operation. Lidice is not pronounced as it is spelt. When journalist Howard Brubaker covered the renaming of Stern Hill as Lidice for the *New Yorker,* he remarked that 'the name which Nazis thought they had extinguished' would be 'mispronounced for all time' in Illi-nois (*Time* 1942). But perhaps it is better to be mispronounced than forgot-ten. To my disappointment, my guide at the memorial did not know about the discoloured crops, just that the Red Army had put a temporary monu-ment in place over the grave at the end of the war. Whilst reading all available accounts about Lidice to search for the origin of this rumour, I noted that the young Germans drafted in to destroy the Lidice graveyard were from Thuringia (Bradley 1972: 114), where the forests had been cut down to build Buchenwald. Once you start seeking connections, they will never stop ap-pearing. They are like the quirks of fate that structure life and history, which Semprun revelled in exposing: 'The history – the stories, the narratives, the memories, the eyewitness accounts in which it survives – lives on. The text, the very texture, the tissue of life' (*WBS* 39). These are the co-ordinates upon which cultural memory, like life itself, is formed, and in embracing them we may reinvigorate both our experiences at and our interpretations of memorial environments.

Margaret Bruzelius's (2007: 198) discussion of Sebald draws attention to his compulsive tangential connection of 'wildly different disparate people and events'. Not unlike the quirks of fate in Semprun's texts, in *The Rings of Saturn* these result in the creation of 'networked' and 'cosmological spaces' with 'expansive and complex' 'spatial and temporal dimensions' (Hui 2010: 277). In expanding on the nature of these spaces, Barbara Hui brings together two key thinkers on place from the fields of cultural geography and cultural memory: Doreen Massey and Andreas Huyssen. Massey's understanding of space acknowledges that 'its specificity is not some internalized history but the fact that it is constructed out of a particular constellation of social rela-tions, meeting and weaving together at a particular locus' (in Hui 2010: 279), whilst Huyssen's 'present pasts' articulate something of how Sebald is most concerned with 'investigating and exposing history' (in Hui 2010: 283). For Hui, the result is distinctly cosmopolitan, a 'travelogue narrative' that 'builds for the reader a sense of the local that is neither inward looking nor bounded but rather shows the area's particular character of place to be fundamen-tally defined and shaped by its location at the intersection of multiple global histories' (Hui 2010: 283). It is to this dimension of Sebaldian space – its exposure of a local-global nexus – to which I now turn.

Cosmopolitan Engagement

Travelling through and immersion in landscape forces a re-evaluation, both of what we know about ourselves and our own culture and what we think we know about others. Debbie Lisle (2006: 4) suggests that the most interesting of travel writing exposes a confrontation, for both readers and writers, 'with the problem of global community – of what values might cut through cultural difference and make it possible to develop a global order based on shared understandings, norms and sensibilities'. In *The Rings of Saturn,* landscape is presented as an affective medium central to the emotional life of the narrator; it forces a *positioning of a self* in relation not only to history but also to others, whilst remaining constantly aware of the caesura between past and present, self and Other. The networked and cosmological spaces Hui observes are shaped by the Sebaldian narrator's consciousness (Hui 2010: 260), thus one landscape will often lead to others which are spatially and temporally distant: a bridge he sees over the river Blyth between Southwold and Walberswick, for example, prompts him to recall the Taiping revolution in the 1850s and 1860s and the subsequent fall of Nanking: the 'bloody horror' of the Chinese landscape, (2002: 140) mass suicide (2002: 141) and violent destruction (2002: 144–55); all this stems from the narrator's realization that the train that used to run over the Blyth bridge 'had originally been built for the Emperor of China' (2002: 138). Thus landscape experience as presented in *The Rings of Saturn* suggests both the affective impact of place and its potential to facilitate a cosmopolitan ethics and productive multidirectionality. A cosmopolitan value system is intrinsic to Sebald's work, borne out in part by his efforts to 'consider how the lives of people in one place rely on, exploit, or benefit the lives of people elsewhere' and to 'compare, distinguish and judge among different versions of thinking beyond the nation' (Walkowitz 2007: 169). Faced with the empty expanse of coast at Lowestoft, he thinks of dying fishermen whose boats have vanished and in whose legacy '[n]o one is interested' (2002: 53). Sebald thus forces us to question that which I attempted to unravel at Buchenwald through the work of Semprun, in the Ukraine through the testimony of witnesses to the *holodomor* and the Holocaust, and in the case of Lidice's twinning with Stoke and Khojaly, asking: 'Across what distances in time do the elective affinities and correspondences connect? How is it that one perceives oneself in another human being, if not oneself, then one's own precursor?' (2002: 182). The importance of being able put oneself in the place of another, without either losing one's own self or vicariously inhabiting that of an Other, I have argued, is central to the creation of differentiated solidarity – in terms of both local and global dynamics – in the examples discussed in this book.

Throughout my travels, I have encountered barriers which I have been unable to overcome, but on many more occasions I have discovered the existence of values that cut through cultural difference. One of the many incidental conversations I have had with visitors to memorial sites foregrounded my own interrogation of cosmopolitanism. Returning from Buchenwald to Weimar on the bus, I met two history teachers from Los Angeles: Elizabeth Azedoohi Kocharian and Yim Tam. They were making a stop on their journey across Germany to see the camp; they had ideally wanted to take a detour to Poland and see Auschwitz but the proximity of Buchenwald to Frankfurt, one of the predetermined stops on their journey, made it a more practical option. Their students, they told me, were deeply interested in the Holocaust:

> Elizabeth Azedoohi Kocharian (EK): Teaching history is a struggle, but whenever we talk about the Holocaust students pay attention, and students want to learn more.
>
> Yim Tam (YT): I think the students are so intrigued by it because it's so horrific. And I teach in an area where there is quite a lot of violence, and I think to see something a little bit more extreme than what their daily life is, is fascinating for them.
>
> EK: Our kids only associate the Holocaust with attacks on the Jews, and when I tell them about, that other groups were there, they're extremely surprised, our young homosexual kids in high school, they're just starting to come out of the closet, and when they find out that homosexuals had been persecuted and were sent to the camps years before the actual Holocaust began, they do identify with that…

For Elizabeth and Yim, a visit to Buchenwald was an opportunity to engage anew, for themselves and their students:

> YT: We teach students about the Holocaust, they're usually familiar with the book *Night*, and familiar with Elie Wiesel … I'll take pictures and go back to school and tell the kids, he stayed at this camp, it's going to mean so much more … for us there's a definite purpose, I mean, we teach it, and I think it becomes more real to us if we've seen it. I feel emotionally connected to this place now, and I think I would teach it a lot better, and I definitely want to go back home and re-read *Night*. I want to look up Weimar a little bit more and find out more about the history and how it's tied to Hitler, why it was named the Weimar Republic, you know, all these questions start to pop up.

The Holocaust, it seems, creates opportunities for the students to define themselves, be it with or against a particular identity. Their students, Elizabeth explains, are obsessed with Hitler, as the 'ultimate evil power. And it's not that the kids really want to be him, but they want to know a lot about him because he was so charismatic and was able to lead so many people, even if they recognised how wrong [he was]. And so anything that has to do with Hitler they're very impressed with.' I tell them they should visit the Hotel Elephant, and offer to take them to *Zum Zwiebel,* where Hitler might have been for a drink. Here I ask them what the difference is between visiting a site where something actually happened, to visiting somewhere like the U.S. Holocaust Memorial Museum; does it provoke a different feeling?

> YT: I kept on telling Elizabeth, this is unreal. I feel like this [the camp] is fake almost, and the reason why I say this is that back home in LA we do have so many fake things, we do have replicas of stuff, and I almost felt like I was walking on a movie set, something unreal. When I'm in a museum, in the Holocaust Memorial at Washington, D.C., it's alive for me, because you see all these pictures, and I guess maybe it's an American way of displaying things, every angle you turn there's something screaming at you, it's much louder, it's much, I want to say it's much more Hollywood and flashy, everything draws your attention. And I guess it hasn't quite sunken in yet ... why I was here, in that many people died [here].

What creates an experience of the real may be to some extent culturally (and in this case nationally) conditioned. Yet the motivations behind seeking this experience may lead outwards, to the fostering of concern for Others:

> EK: We just finished our study of World War II and what we ended up doing is we had a member from a group called STAND which is the organization that's trying to alleviate the genocide in Darfur come to our room and talk to the kids and they collected money and they encouraged a lot of students to join the STAND group at school. So in a way it got them affected and interested in something current. But then when it comes to the war they'd rather ignore it because they don't really understand what it's about, it doesn't make sense to them at all.
>
> YT: It's sad that many of our students forget that we're at war right now, because it's not on our soil, you know. And it's awful. It's awful. I would say our students don't understand war, because we've never had it in our country. And even what happened on September 11th doesn't affect our students the same way ... most of them don't have any connections to New York. They saw the bombing, but you know, we see so many horrific things on television anyway, a lot of our kids are desensitized to what's reality and what's not and how it's really affecting us.
>
> EK: Mine forget that we're currently fighting two wars right now, and part of it is that they haven't sacrificed anything.

In attempting to mobilize their students' fascination with Holocaust victims and perpetrators in order to make them recognize the atrocities taking place around them, including those in which their own government was complicit, Elizabeth and Yim contributed to my own sense that multidirectional memory should be approached as Rothberg (2009: 19) presents it; 'under the sign of optimism', but an optimism which remains vigilant of contextual specificities. This encounter at Buchenwald shaped my experience and analysis of the sites and memory work I discovered later, at the Babi Yar Park in Denver and in the global memorial network surrounding Lidice.

Another of the encounters that contributed to my understanding of multidirectional memory work in practice occurred in Denver. Denver does not feel as easy a place to have incidental encounters as Weimar. You can walk from one end of Weimar to another in an hour accompanied by tourists from every part of the globe; you can walk for an hour in Denver and not see another person. The Denver Metro area is 8,414 square miles to Weimar's 32. You almost certainly would not walk for an hour in Denver, in any case, because everyone drives everywhere.[3] Having toured the Babi Yar Park with Ellen Premack and Helen Ginsburg, we had lunch together in a restaurant across the road, which we drove to from the memorial's car park. Walking is anathema in Denver. From a theoretical perspective I found Ellen and Helen's comments – made over lunch – that the inclusion of World Trade Center steel at the Babi Yar Park could remain free of political connotations, somewhat difficult. Nonetheless, it would be impossible to talk to Helen and not recognize the importance of looking beyond politics. It is hard to reconcile her with the label of memorial entrepreneur; it says so little about her emotional involvement with the Babi Yar Park. She described the initial phase of her work for the project as the most wonderful and painful time of her life. Even the 'official' documents relating to the Babi Yar Park, in archives held at the Mizel Museum and the Penrose Special Collection at the University of Denver library, are full of Helen's life; the letters and speeches she wrote to raise funds and awareness about the project; the photos of her: at the unveiling of the first sign at the park, with Denver Mayor William McNicholls in 1974; garnering support at the White House with Jimmy Carter in 1978; at the inauguration of the park in 1983 with another Denver Mayor, Federico Pena. Helen's distinctive handwriting runs through the archives, a point of continuity across diverse documents spanning forty years of planning, developments, setbacks and achievements. Visiting sites of memory may alert us to the motivations of those that shaped them, whether their involvement has been elected or forced, politically or emotionally grounded.[4]

Helen's self-imposed role in the creation of the Babi Yar Park, her desire that it should '[thrive] on its message of freedom and dignity for all men, regardless of religion, race, ethnicity or national citizenship' and 'speak out against anti-humanism anywhere in this world of ours' relies on the premise that 'whenever a man is harmed, we are all hurt'. Whilst I could not share

Helen's suggestion that to align the Holocaust with 9/11 carried no political implication, and her belief that such an implied parallel did not erode the specificity of each event, I could share her optimistic insistence on cosmopolitan ethics. Similarly, whilst I may doubt whether the twinning of Stoke-on-Trent with Lidice really constitutes an example of outward-facing supranational engagement, its facilitation of increased involvement of the children of that city with the International Children's Exhibition of Fine Arts, Lidice (ICEFA) is encouraging.

The ICEFA project itself deserves more scrutiny than I have been able to give it in the context of this book, not least because, as the number of children entering each year increases, along with the number of countries involved, it becomes increasingly global in scope. Each year the organizers set a theme, recommended by UNESCO, to inspire entrants. Whilst the competition was established to 'commemorate the child victims from the Czech village of Lidice murdered by German Nazis as well as all other children who have died in wars' (ICEFA 2011), the themes are not specifically related to these subjects (given the age range of entrants – between four and sixteen – this would clearly raise innumerable issues). Rather the competition aims 'to enable children from all over the world to express themselves through art, demonstrating their desire to live in a world without wars where there is room for realising children's wishes' (ICEFA 2011). Thus in recent years themes such as 'Happiness' (2005), 'the Universe' (2009) and 'This is where I live, that is me' (2011) have been typical. The theme for 2010 was 'Biodiversity'. I am interested to find that, whilst the theme apparently inspired many entries depicting 'living nature in its diversity', 'the sad fact' remained that 'the children from war-stricken countries painted pictures that are full of suffering, pain and despair' – 'in spite of the recommended theme' (ICEFA 2011). In the context of my own enquiry the idea that 'in spite of the theme' of biodiversity, some children did not simply respond by representing 'living nature' takes on intriguing dimensions; for there is more than an incidental link between war and biodiversity, albeit the destruction rather than the celebration of diverse living forms. To unpack the centrality of this connection to my own argument, I turn again to the world as inhabited by the Sebaldian narrator.

Encountering Nature and History: Towards a Holocaust Ecocriticism

The third aim of *Topographies of Suffering* was to demonstrate something of what might be gained by taking an ecocritical perspective on memorial texts, particularly but not solely within the Holocaust context. Episodes throughout *The Rings of Saturn* consistently direct attention to the complexity of human emotions with regards to the natural world, and the narrator takes an ecological approach to landscape; that is, one 'concerned with the limits of nature, and with our need to value, conserve and recognize our dependence upon it' (Soper 1995: 7), a discourse which focuses on 'the 'nature' that we are destroying, wasting and polluting' (Soper 1995: 4). Anne Fuchs' (2007: 122) discussion of 'perspective and subjectivity from a phenomenological perspective' outlines the opposition constructed by Sebald between two paintings. In Rembrandt's *The Anatomy Lesson,* contemplation of which distresses the narrator, a surgeon dissects the cadaver of a thief for an audience of other surgeons. The gaze of the viewer is directed to the corpse. The audience of surgeons in the painting gaze, not on the body, but on a set of charts beyond it. The surgeons present a Cartesian model of perception, highlighting an opposition between the body and the mind and a devaluation of biological life and resulting in the reduction of animal to automata. Flesh is categorized according to utility; 'unnecessary' flesh may be discarded. Fuchs links this perspective to the trajectory of European rationalism and biopolitics, which, as suggested by Agamben, has resulted in a climate in which 'Auschwitz' (as a metonym for the concentration camps) was – and remains – possible. He articulates the problem as a matter of perspective, in this case a falsification as discussed in relation to the 'impossible' view represented in van Ruisdael's *View of Haarlem with Bleaching Fields.* Whilst contemplating the Cartesian objectivity displayed in the Rembrandt highlights man's responsibility for a 'historical acceleration of natural destruction' and distresses Sebald's narrator (Fuchs 2007: 123), he is temporarily calmed when he moves on to study van Ruisdael's pastoral landscape. *View of Haarlem* is able to relieve his distress because it poses, unlike *The Anatomy Lesson,* a harmonious relationship between man and the natural world. The painting shows 'an almost imperceptible transition from the cultivated landscape to the cityscape on the horizon [which] suggests unity between the two spheres' (Fuchs 2007: 128); the man/nature relation is depicted as one of transcendental promise and imaginary unity. The ultimate evacuation of this perception of unity is highlighted by Long's analysis of the context in which the paintings are viewed: that of the Mauritshaus in The Hague, 'initially a private display of personal wealth and power, but one that also embedded this individual power in the geopolitical framework of national colonial interests' (2007b: 32).

Each site examined in this book has demonstrated ways in which the Holocaust radically altered the human relationship with the natural world, presenting an interruption of perceived harmony. In all three sections a trope emerged – the Holocaust has been conceptualized, across cultures, within a framework of the disrupted pastoral. At Buchenwald, the deforestation of the Ettersburg to build a concentration camp revealed the emptiness of National Socialist forest protection, birds fled and forest hangings ruptured the 'time-

less' woodlands; in Ukraine, ethnic cleansing policies disrupted a long-stand-
ing productive relationship between man and nature to leave behind a
landscape of mass graves, a place presented by Kuznetsov and Desbois as
'no longer blessed', where the beauty has been 'taken from everything'; and at
Lidice, a rural village was razed to the ground and covered with German soil,
prompting the use of imagery in which the destruction of rural peace and
seasonal continuity communicate a sense of what was lost in the massacre;
Millay's poem and Jennings's filmic rendition both cast the destruction of
Lidice within a frame of a disrupted pastoral. It must be noted, however, that
the calm achieved by Sebald's narrator is undermined by his own acknowledgement that van Ruisdael's vantage point could only have been from 'an
imaginary position some distance above the earth. Only in this way could he
see it all together' (2002: 83). Indeed, according to Fuchs, Sebald knowingly
invokes the affectiveness of contemplating a harmonious nature/culture relationship whilst well aware of its roots in an obsolete artistic tradition, thus
highlighting the narrator's fundamental 'awareness' as noted by Kilbourne
(2007: 139): 'that any nostalgia for lost authenticity is a myth' which offers
no comfort. In invoking the notion of a pre-Holocaust pastoral, the above-
mentioned texts inevitably elide the fact that a harmonious balance between
man and nature is rarely found throughout human history, ignoring the obsolete nature this particular mode of representation, but they also testify to the
affective properties of such imagery in connection with human-perpetrated
destruction. A reliance or mobilization of this affectivity in memorial landscapes has been identified at various points throughout this book.

Furthermore, there may be a value to mourning a lost harmony, whether
it ever existed or not, if it prompts 'an ability to see ourselves in an environmental context and to think in connective processes' fundamental to ecocentric thought (Riordan 2007: 108); for this in itself may contribute to the development of an inclusive humanity. This, I have argued, is what Semprun's
project advocates. He immerses himself in the natural world, and seeks encounters within it which he wishes others to share. Only in this way could
the Nazis' biopolitical territorialization of the Ettersburg be uprooted. An
ecological perspective, which highlights a historical acceleration of natural
destruction (Fuchs 2007: 124) dominates *The Rings of Saturn*. The notion
of this process, the place of the Holocaust within it, and how this might
conceivably be related to commemorative space is something I have begun
to explore here but of which, in many ways, I have as yet only been able to
scratch the surface within the remit of this exploration. In order to offer a
little more exposition of what seems to me to be an infinitely rich area for
future consideration, and one with a potentially urgent dimension, I turn to
Sebald's text in a little more detail; taking, perhaps, a byway rather than a
beeline towards a final concluding statement.

The world of the Sebaldian narrator echoes many of those I have discussed in this book, constituting as it does 'a historically marked space that
provides a living archive of the history of catastrophes for which mankind
is responsible ... a disruptive space which carries the traces of its ongoing
destruction' (Fuchs 2007: 129). Whilst beauty still exists in nature, 'the encounter is generally accompanied by or related to historical factors of disruption' (Fuchs 2007: 130); only a world in which the subject is '[f]reed
from the restraints of Cartesian reality' – one which, for Sebald, only exists
in a 'time after the end of time' – can come the 'end of man's exploitative
relationship with nature' (Fuchs 2007: 135). There is a suggestion here of a
dialectical disjuncture between ecocritical and biopolitical logic, which is explicitly interrogated elsewhere in *The Rings of Saturn*. Mary Cosgrove (2007:
109), for example, argues that the text instantiates the new branch of genocide research conducted from this standpoint (including the work of Davis
and Levene), linking global warming, natural hazards and 'the creation of
conditions favourable to genocide'. In Sebald's retelling of the life of Joseph
Conrad, love of the sea prompts the explorer to travel to the Congo, where
he becomes ill. This, it is implied, is a reaction to his contemplation of the
atrocities committed under the colonial banner.

> There is an urgent political dimension to this reminder ... that is not exclusively
> focused on the destruction of nature as a tragedy in itself. Taken alongside Se-
> bald's interest in twentieth century genocide, in particular the Holocaust, his
> discourse on the human harnessing of the environment, its natural resources
> and its physical space during the period that A. Dirk Moses terms the racial
> century of 1850–1950, can be seen not just in the economic terms of peripher-
> alisation ... but more disturbingly as a basic premise of the political struggle for
> more land, territory, lebensraum that goes hand in hand with the perpetration
> of genocide. (Cosgrove 2007: 109–10)

As Cosgrove notes, research that attempts to concretize these links has
begun to advance this theory beyond metaphor and rhetoric. In reference to
Davis's *Late Victorian Holocausts,* she argues:

> Both Davis's and Sebald's respective historical enquiries acknowledge the nat-
> ural environment as the 'ultimate context': the insight that we in the Western
> (and westernized) world do not entirely run the show on planet earth ... This
> view serves as a sobering reminder that historical understanding of the twenty-
> first century should expand 'ecocentrically' to take account of human interac-
> tion with and exploitation of nature. (2007: 109)

Such an ecocentric view of the Holocaust emerges in *The Rings of Saturn*.
The history of the production of silk is a theme that runs through several stories in the text, including the Empress of China's love of the silk worm, and

in a final passage on silk towards the end of the book, the narrator recounts a drive towards national self-sufficiency in 1930s Germany which included a plan to launch a new era of national silk cultivation. The production of silk was considered likely to become an increasing priority because of 'the importance [it] would have in the dawning era of aerial warfare and hence in the formation of a self-sufficient economy of national defence' (2002: 293). The narrator comes across a pamphlet and a film promoting German silk cultivation, made for primary schools; part of the drive to increase the practice of sericulture, which suggests that silkworms, 'quite apart from their indubitable utility value', were:

> an almost ideal object lesson for the classroom. Any number could be had for virtually nothing, they were perfectly docile and needed neither cages nor compounds, and they were suitable for a variety of experiments. They could be used to illustrate the structure and distinctive features of insect anatomy, insect domestication, retrogressive mutations, and the essential measures which are taken by breeders to monitor productivity and selection, including extermination to preempt racial degeneration. (2002: 293–94)

The corresponding film showed 'a silk-worker receiving eggs despatched by the Central Reich Institute in Celle, and depositing them in sterile trays' (2002: 294). Celle is the nearest city to the famous Bergen-Belsen camp, and the two are historically connected. Celle was an important garrison location and the seat of a military district command during World War II. The only serious bombing attack on the city hit a train which had been transporting prisoners to Bergen-Belsen; the SS officers and the citizens of Celle hunted down several hundred of the prisoners who managed an initial escape. Today tourists to the Bergen-Belsen memorial site will generally stay in the city, the closest place to the camp with large hotels. None of this is mentioned by Sebald, who focuses on the lives and deaths of the worms in Celle as shown in the film.

> We see the hatching, the feeding of the ravenous caterpillars, the cleaning out of the frames, the spinning of the silken thread, and finally the killing, accomplished in this case not by putting the cocoons out in the sun or in a hot over, as was often the practice in the past, but by suspending them over a boiling cauldron. The cocoons, spread out on shallow baskets, have to be kept in the rising steam for upwards of three hours, and when a batch is done, it is the next one's turn, and so on until the entire killing business is completed. (2002: 293)

These deliberately unemotional and reductive descriptions of the silk worms bring to mind the relationship between European rationalism, biopolitics and the Holocaust noted by Fuchs in relation to the narrator's experience of viewing the Rembrandt and Agamben's discussion of the same terrain in *Homo Sacer*. A parallel between his model of Third Reich biopolitics – as reliant on the construction of a category of 'life that does not deserve to be lived', and which should in fact be destroyed if it may be damaging to the German race – and Sebald's silk worms – on which 'essential measures' were taken 'to monitor productivity and selection, including extermination to preempt racial degeneration' (2002: 294) – is palpable. Sebald's description of the silk worms' extermination as shown on the video constitutes another implicit Holocaust parallel, highlighting as it does the development of a new method of destruction. They are exposed to steam in batches, and the gas chambers may be present in the reader's imagination.

Fuchs's analysis explores the farming of herrings earlier in the book in a similar biopolitical context which also prompts a connection to Belsen. In this story, the steady flow of toxins into the sea from irresponsible industrial actions results in the death of much sea life. The narrator recalls: 'It was not without reason that the herring was always a popular didactic model in primary school, the principal emblem, as it were, of the indestructibility of Nature' (2002: 53). The poisoning of landscape which marks an end to this reliable promise of cyclical nature encapsulates the overall text's presentation of an accelerated history of destruction. Indeed the narrative immediately moves on from the fate of the herrings to a story about a man who had been among the liberators at the Bergen-Belsen camp. Five pages after a photograph of a pile of dead herrings, a photograph of bodies at Belsen appears. Whilst this may be 'a daring juxtaposition' (Fuchs 2007: 126), there is a fundamental rationale to it, one which is echoed in Robert Pogue Harrison's (2003: 31) decision to employ the term 'holocaust' in a discussion of capitalist economies: 'The daily holocausts that supply the world markets' demands for meat, fish and poultry take place in another world than the one most of us inhabit. And yet we live off such holocausts, inevitably.' Legitimating these juxtapositions is the premise that the Holocaust's victims were perceived by their persecutors to live on a purely biological plane. The destruction of the natural world and its animal population therefore resonates, in Sebald's fiction, with the destruction of people, and both forms of destruction are intimately bound to the way in which modern society sought to produce and master the natural world. At its most nuanced, ecocritical logic draws together, but does not conflate, the destruction of nature and of people.

Sebald's work renders the question of human value within nature meaningless; nature can never be external to us because it is central to our affairs. In Sebald, Riordan has argued, the problematic modern understanding of nature is revealed: we fail to see ourselves in context and our value judgements are perverted by self-obsession. As previously discussed, nature is not traumatized by human action; catastrophe, stresses Riordan, is always human. Modern views see nature as either malleable to human will or indifferent to it, hence Riordan's (2007: 52) point that Sebald succeeds in maintaining an ecocritical perspective: 'In refusing to acknowledge the value of the non-human world, we are simultaneously devaluing ourselves.' Hans-Walter Schmidt-Hannisa's (2007: 59) essay on the relationship between man and animals in Sebald's work similarly argues that he constantly displays an anti-Cartesian recognition of and respect for animals' ability to suffer. On the herrings sequence he notes that a reduction of animals to a series of quantities, revealing 'the perverted relationship of a civilization which has succumbed to the dialectic of the Enlightenment' is countered by the Sebaldian narrator's empathic perspective when considering the vast numbers of these fish that were caught annually:

> the natural historians sought consolation in the idea that humanity was responsible for only a fraction of the endless destruction wrought in the cycle of life, and moreover in the assumption that the peculiar physiology of the fish left them free of the fear and pains that rack the body and souls of higher animals in their death throes. But the truth is that we do not know what the herring feels. (2002: 59)

This passage not only raises the possibility of empathy but highlights the inherent difficulty of achieving it – the problem of not being able to *know*. He goes on to describe the unique physiology of the herring. Sebald's narrator makes a distinction between the kind of knowledge that results from learning and the more complex endeavour to 'know' the experiences of others. The standpoint of the narrator strikes a balance between attempting an empathic relationship with the unknowable other and acknowledging that that the endeavour may eventually be impossible; that he continues to relay details about the life of the herring is testament to his attention to its specificity.

I proposed initially that encounters with nature in topographies of suffering could potentially be of ethical worth; this relies, perhaps more than anything, on maintaining such specificity. This notion was drawn out in some detail in discussing Semprun's engagement with one of the many beech trees on the outskirts of the camp at Buchenwald, his 'willingness to look at and listen to the world ... a letting go of the self which brings the discovery of a deeper self' (Bate 2000: 155). I continued to push the notion that nature should be attended to in the second and third chapters; in my consideration of the topography of Holocaust memory in Ukraine, it was by attending to the experiences people had with nature that I was able to suggest a way of diluting the existing memory competition. The aforementioned affective properties of natural forms, natural growth and topographical resonance has been considered in some detail in chapters 2 and 3; in the present landscape of the Babi Yar Park in Denver, where topography and soil are perceived as having unique symbolic value, and at Lidice, where I took the opportunity to examine the various theoretical questions raised by this kind of signification for both curators and visitors. I conclude from this exploration that it would be undesirable to echo what Bate (2000: 272) has called Heidegger's 'appalling error of judgement' by comparing practices which are intrinsically very different, and that do so is to 'fail to grasp the unique evils of the Holocaust'. Yet in considering Bauman's argument about the confluent logic of gardening and ethnic cleansing, we can use the comparison permitted by Celan: that which recognizes the importance of diversity in a stable world. At the Babi Yar Park and Lidice, perhaps it does not matter so much which practices are utilized, as long as we attend to the specificity of each form – be it a rose, a tree, or a handful of soil – alongside that of those whom their presence is employed to commemorate.

Topography beyond the Ineffable

In the above integration of *The Rings of Saturn* and my own case studies, I have attempted to demonstrate a particular model of approaching memorial landscapes, as both writer and visitor. I have advocated an evolution from the conceptualization of such landscapes as *lieux de mémoire,* in order that we may better recognize the ways in which encounters and texts mediate an ever-evolving experience of memorial sites. I have also suggested that we examine, accordingly, their potential to create an ethically oriented cosmopolitan engagement. I have taken this point further, advocating a specifically ecocritical cosmopolitanism, predicated in 'our ability to see ourselves in [an] environmental context' that we share with others, 'and to think in connective processes' in which those others are also intimately involved. Each of the three sites discussed has addressed these issues in different ways.

In Chapter 1, I presented Semprun's testimonial project as an example of the ways in which a landscape may invite an immersive, phenomenological engagement with nature and cultural history through a literary mediation that both constitutes and urges a de-territorialization of rooted superorganicism, biopolitics and exclusive humanism. Semprun, dispossessed like Celan, managed to imaginatively reanimate the Buchenwald landscape, and invites us to do the same. His work compels us to attend to the trees, the wind, the snow and the seasons. Like that of Celan, his work opens itself to multiple readings. Unlike Celan, however, Semprun managed to find an earth which he could, if not dwell, at least de-territorialize from the clutches of his persecutors. The result is an inclusive space which, even if it does not provide us with the elusive 'sense of what it was like to be there' as a victim (Bernard-Donals and Glejzer 2001: 2), presents opportunities for 'acts of remembrance' which are worth pursuing nonetheless.

Chapter 2 discussed another site rendered dynamic through literary mediation, in this case via a series of texts from testimony to fiction which introduced the events at one ravine in Kiev to the global imagination. This mediation, I suggested, was central to the way in which cultural memories of Babi Yar travelled to Denver. That Babi Yar in Kiev and the Babi Yar Park in Denver share a particular biosphere and topography was presented as an example of the perceived significance of landscape for the representation of atrocity and a singular ability to act as a carrier of the essence of atrocious experience. I identified the emergence of a mode of transcultural identification, visible in the very creation of the Denver park and also central to its current attempt to draw implicit parallels between the Holocaust and the War on Terror. Such a mode of identification is refused within Ukraine in terms of any recognition of the shared ground between Holocaust and *holodomor* memory. I concluded that there is something to be gained from a focus on actual experience as far as drawing events into a multidirectional nexus is concerned; that one way we might overcome zero-sum logic is to pay attention to something that draws apparently disparate cultures together: in this case, the experience of landscape as disrupted by atrocity and the disconnection of people from their lived environments.

Such a disruption, I have suggested via Millay and Jennings, was implicit to the way the destruction of Lidice was presented to the world in 1942. The Nazis' attempt to territorialize the land on which it stood can be understood within a similar framework of ruptured pastoral. I took the opportunity, in a scrutiny of curatorial practice at Lidice, to consider the impact and implications of mobilizing particular landscaping approaches at places of such disruption. Whilst aware of the despecification that might result from putting very 'different types of activities on a par' (Uekötter 2006: 206–7), thus overall rejecting a purely representational approach to decoding landscape and landscape practice, I came to the conclusion that ecological considerations may yet have a place in the future of sites such as Lidice – to do so represents another step towards recognizing the interconnectedness of all things. I further presented Lidice as a central co-ordinate in a nexus of transnational memory-activity which is suggestive of various attempts to develop and affirm such interconnectedness amongst people from diverse cultures. Whilst a scrutiny of the background and motivations of each instance examined suggested that such activities must be approached with due attention to the polemic motivations that may lurk behind cosmopolitanism, there can be no doubt that Lidice is remembered on a global level as a result; the Nazis' attempt to erase it from history continues to be refused.

Throughout the three case studies, I have demonstrated the diversity of Holocaust topographies, taking my analysis beyond the death and concentration camps to places where there is no architecture of destruction. I have argued that that these topographies of suffering can offer meaningful spaces for ethically oriented memory work, which may take place both within the landscape itself and away from it. *Topographies of Suffering* has defined three trajectories of mediation and remediation – through literature, film, twinning, networks, new memorial spaces, and examined the potential and the limitations of the multidirectional networks that have appeared as a result. Throughout I have emphasized that an awareness of a site's history within a particular cultural context can enrich our encounters with it. In undertaking this analysis, I aimed to demonstrate the potential of landscape for facilitating an ethically motivated encounter with Holocaust history according to the Levinasian demand that we enter into relationship with others without immediately divesting them of their alterity. Inevitably, in limiting the analysis to three landscapes, I cannot as a result claim to make any generalizations about the way such places 'work'. Each is open to different ways of reading and habitation, according to the way in which it is approached. Yet it is through their very openness that landscapes are rendered productive; they are endlessly open to us, and our interventions within them have the potential to change us just as we change them. These topographies of suffering, in their dynamism, refuse the possibility that there is a massive, passive memory awaiting us when we confront the past; as spaces of encounter, they present us with realms in which we may be touched but never completed.

Notes

1. In *Rings*, for example, the narrator sets out to discover the whereabouts of Browne's skull, which by coincidence is said to be stored where he had been a patient; whilst he fails to find the object itself, he goes on to trace its history.
2. The accusation being that Tymoshenko's 2009 deal with Russian energy suppliers was politically motivated (see BBC News 2011).
3. Nonetheless, it was in Alan Gass's car, travelling through the grey urban landscape between the Babi Yar Park and the Mizel Museum, later that afternoon that I heard about his childhood memories of the Denver landscape around the park before it was built up and neat lawns and flower beds replaced the native prairie grass. That to this day the landscape of his memory is preserved at the park can be partly put down to his involvement.
4. As a counterexample, I fell into conversation with a man at Buchenwald who has been ordered, as a member of the Weimar's population in the 1950s, to lay the gravel over the muster ground; part of an initiative to both landscape the camp as a memorial and make local people atone for having lived alongside it.

BIBLIOGRAPHY

Abrams, D. 1996. *The Spell of the Sensuous*. London: Vintage.

Addis, M. and A. Charlesworth. 2002. 'Memorialisation and the Ecological Landscapes of Holocaust Sites: The Cases of Plaszow and Auschwitz', *Landscape Research* 3: 229–51.

Adorno, T. 1965. 'Engagement', in *Noten zur Literatur* 3: 125–27. Frankfurt: Suhrcamp Verlag.

Adorno, T. and M. Horkheimer. (1944) 2002. *Dialectics of Enlightenment: Philosophical Fragments*, trans. E. Jephcott. Stanford, CA: Stanford University Press.

Agamben, G. 1995. *Homo Sacer: Sovereign Power and Bare Life*, trans. Daniel Heller-Roazen. Stanford, CA: Stanford University Press.

Agnew, H. 2010. *The Czechs and the Lands of the Bohemian Crown*. Stanford, CA: Hoover Institute.

Allen, J. 2000. *Without Sanctuary: Lynching Photography in America*. Santa Fe, NM: Twin Palms.

Alperin, M. 2012. 'With Iran in Mind, Babi Yar Remembered as 'Evil at its Worst', *Jewish Journal*. Retrieved 3 April 2012 from http://www.jewishjournal.com/israel/article/with_iran_in_mind_babi_yar_remembered_as_evil_at_its_worst_20120130/

Applegate, C. 1990. *A Nation of Provincials: The German Idea of Heimat*. Berkeley, Los Angeles and Oxford: University of California Press.

Arnold, E.T. 2012. *What Virtue There Is in Fire: Cultural Memory and the Lynching of Sam Hose*. Athens: University of Georgia Press.

Atkinson, D. et al. (eds). 2005. *Cultural Geography: A Critical Dictionary of Key Concepts*. London and New York: I.B. Taurus.

Atkinson, H. and S. Bruendl. 2008. Unpublished data (interview with J. Rapson, 9 April.)

Azaryahu, M. 2003. 'Re-Placing Memory: the Reorientation of Buchenwald'. *Cultural Geographies* 10: 1–20.

Azerbaijani Embassy in Prague. 2010. 'Lidice and Khojaly: Different Places, Same Brutality'. Retrieved 3 May 2010 from http://www.azembassyprague.az/eng/news/press_releases/2010/press_release_003.shtml

Babi Yar Park Foundation. n.d. Planning document. Archives of the Mizel Museum, Denver.

Bachelard, G. (1958) 1969. *The Poetics of Space*, trans. Orion Press. Boston: Beacon Press.

Baedeker, K. 1925. *Northern Germany Excluding the Rhineland: Handbook for Travellers*, 17th ed. Leipzig: Karl Baedeker.

Baer, U. 2002. *Spectral Evidence: The Photography of Trauma*. Cambridge, MA: MIT Press.

Ball, K. 2008. *Disciplining the Holocaust*. Albany: State University of New York Press.

Bartov, O. 1996. *Murder in Our Midst: The Holocaust, Industrial Killing, and Representation*. New York and Oxford: Oxford University Press.

———. 2007. *Erased: Vanishing Traces of Jewish Galicia in Present Day Ukraine*. Princeton: Princeton University Press.

———. 2011. 'Review'. *Slavic Review: Interdisciplinary Quarterly of Russian, Eurasian, and East European Studies* 70(2): 424–28.

Barnshaw, J. and J. Trainor. 2007. 'Race, Class, and Capital amidst the Hurricane Katrina Diaspora', in D.L. Brunsma, D. Overfelt and J.S. Picou (eds), *The Sociology of Katrina: Perspectives on a Modern Catastrophe*. Plymouth: Rowman and Littlefield, pp. 91–106.

Baruch Stier, O. 2003. *Committed to Memory: Cultural Mediations of the Holocaust*. Amherst: University of Massachusetts Press.

Bate, J. 2000. *The Song of the Earth*. London, Basingstoke and Oxford: MacMillan/Picador.

Bauman, Z. 2000. *Modernity and the Holocaust*. Cambridge and Maldon, MA: Polity.

BBC News. 2001. 'Mass Graves Found at Nazi Camp'. Retrieved 10 July 2008 from http://news.bbc.co.uk/1/hi/world/europe/1673471.stm

———. 2009. 'Babi Yar Hotel Decision Condemned'. Retrieved 3 April 2012 from http://news.bbc.co.uk/1/hi/world/europe/8274043.stm

———. 2011. 'Ukraine Ex-PM Yulia Tymoshenko Jailed Over Gas Deal'. Retrieved 4 May 2012 from http://www.bbc.co.uk/news/world-europe-15250742

Beaumont, P. 2009. 'Anger as Kiev Council Plans to Build Hotel at Biggest Holocaust Shooting Site'. *Guardian*. Retrieved 3 April 2012 from http://www.guardian.co.uk/world/2009/sep/24/hotel-kiev-holocaust-germany-babi-yar

Beck, U. 2004. *Der Kosmopolitische Blick oder Krieg ist Frieden*. Frankfurt: Suhrkamp.

Bendersky, J. W. 2007. *A Concise History of Nazi Germany*. Lanham, Maryland and Plymouth: Rowman and Littlefield.

Bennett, J. 2005. *Empathic Vision: Affect, Trauma and Contemporary Art*. Stanford, CA: Stanford University Press.

Berghahn, K. 2001. 'Patterns of Childhood: Goethe and the Jews', in K. Berghahn and J. Harmand (eds), *Goethe in German-Jewish Culture*. Rochester, NY and Woodbridge, Suffolk: Camden House, pp. 3–15.

Berkhoff, K. 2008. 'Dina Pronicheva's Story of Surviving the Babi Yar Massacre: German, Jewish, Soviet, Russian, and Ukrainian Records', in R. Brandon and W. Lower (eds), *The Shoah in Ukraine: History, Testimony, Memorialization*. Bloomington: Indiana University Press, pp. 291–317.

Berkley, G.E. 1993. *Hitler's Gift: The Story of Theresienstadt*. Boston: Branden Books.

Bernard-Donals, M. 2005. 'Conflations of Memory, or What They Saw at the USHMM After 9/11', *New Centennial Review* 5(2): 73–106.

Bernard-Donals, M. and R. Glejzer. 2001. *Between Witness and Testimony: The Holocaust and the Limits of Representation*. Albany: State University of New York Press.

Blanton, C. 2002. *Travel Writing: The Self and the World*. London and New York: Routledge.

Bond, L. 2011. 'Compromised Critique: A Metacritical Analysis of American Studies after 9/11', *Journal of American Studies* 45(4): 733–56.

Bond, L. and J. Rapson. 2014. 'Introduction', in L. Bond and J.Rapson (eds), *The Transcultural Turn: Interrogating Memory Between and Beyond Borders*. Berlin: de Gruyter, pp. 1–26.

Bonder, J. 2009. 'On Memory, Trauma, Public Space, Monuments, and Memorials', *Places* 21(1): 62–70.

Bonder, J. and K. Wodiczko. 2009. 'A Working Memorial at Babi Yar Park', in *Babi Yar Memorial Park Brochure*. Retrieved 6 February 2011 from http://www.mizelmuseum .org/pdfs/BabiYar.pdf

Bradley, J. 1972. *Lidice: Sacrificial Village*. New York: Ballantine Books.

Brandon, R. and W. Lower. (eds). 2008. *The Shoah in Ukraine: History, Testimony, Memorialization*. Bloomington: Indiana University Press.

Brodzki, B. 2007. *Can These Bones Live? Translation, Survival and Cultural Memory*. Stanford, CA: Stanford University Press.

Browne, S.D. and D. Middleton. 2011. 'Memory and Space in the Work of Maurice Halbwachs', in P. Meusberger, M. Heffernan and E. Wunder (eds), *Cultural Memories: The Geographical Point of View*. Dordrecht, Heidelberg, London and New York: Springer, pp. 29–50.

Bruce-Mitford, M. 2008. *Signs and Symbols: An Illustrated Guide to Their Origins and Meanings*. Munich, Melbourne and Delhi: Dorling Kindersley.

Bruzelius, M. 2007. *Romancing the Novel: Adventure from Scott to Sebald*. Cranbury, NJ: Associated University Presses.

Buchenwald.de. 2012a. Untitled. Retrieved 24 July 2013 from http://www.buchenwald .de/en/751/

———. 2012b. 'Elementary Testimony to the National Socialist Crimes and the History of the Twentieth Century to Be Included on the UNESCO World Heritage List'. Retrieved 24 July 2013 from http://www.buchenwald.de/en/753/

Buell, L. 2005. *The Future of Environmental Criticism: Environmental Crisis and the Literary Imagination*. Maldon, Oxford and Carlton, AU: Blackwell.

Bugajski, J. 1995. *Ethnic Politics in Eastern Europe: A Guide to Nationality Policies, Organizations, and Parties*. New York: M.E. Sharpe.

Burton, R.D.E. 2003. *Prague: A Literary and Cultural History*. Oxford: Signal.

BusinessWire.com. 2011. 'M&A PROPERTY INVESTORS Closes a JV in Czech Republic'. Retrieved 9 April 2012 from http://www.businesswire.com/news/home/ 20111018005782/en/MA-PROPERTY-INVESTORS-Closes-JV-Czech-Republic

Byron, G. and H.L. Bulwer. 1841. *The Complete Works of Lord Byron: Reprinted from the Last London Edition*. Paris: A. and W. Galignani.

Campbell, N. 2008. *The Rhizomatic West: Representing the American West in a Transnational, Global, Media Age*. Lincoln: University of Nebraska Press.

Carson, R. 1962. *Silent Spring*. Middlesex: Penguin.

Caruth, C. 1996. *Unclaimed Experience: Trauma, Narrative and History*. Baltimore and London: Johns Hopkins University Press.

Caruth, C. and G. Hartman. 1996. 'An Interview with Geoffrey Hartman', *Studies in Romanticism* 35(4): 630–52.

Casey, E. 1996. 'How to Get from Space to Place in a Fairly Short Stretch of Time: Phenomenological Prolegomena', in S. Feld and K. Basso (eds), *Senses of Place*. Santa Fe: School of American Research Press, pp. 13–52.

Casey, T. 2002. *The Social Context of Economic Change in Britain: Between Policy and Performance*. Manchester and New York: Manchester University Press.

CELL. 2011. *Anyone Anytime Anywhere: Understanding the Threat of Terrorism – Visitors Guide.* Denver: Denver Post.

de Certeau, M. 1988. *The Practice of Everyday Life,* trans. S. Rendall. Berkeley, Los Angeles and London: University of California Press.

Chandler, R. 2006. 'Introduction: "Speaking for Those Who Lie in the Earth": The Life and Work of Vasily Grossman', in Vasily Grossman, *Life and Fate,* London: Vintage, ix–xxvi.

Chape, S. et al. 2008. *The World's Protected Areas: Status, Values and Prospects in the 21st Century.* Berkeley and Los Angeles: University of California Press.

Chiras, D. 2004. *Environmental Science.* Sudbury, MA: Jones and Bartlett.

Claviez, T. 1999. 'Pragmatism, Critical Theory, and the Search for Ecological Genealogies in American Culture', *Yearbook of Research in English and American Literature: REAL* 15: 343–80.

Clark, S.H. 1999. *Travel Writing and Empire: Postcolonial Theory in Transit.* London and New York: Zed Books.

Cloke, P. and O. Jones. 2001. 'Dwelling, Place and Landscape: An Orchard in Somerset', *Environment and Planning A* 33: 649–66.

Closmann, C.E. 2009. *War and the Environment: Military Destruction in the Modern Age.* College Station: Texas A&M University Press.

Coates, P., T. Cole and C. Pearson. 2010. *Militarized Landscapes: From Gettysburg to Salisbury Plain.* London and New York: Continuum.

Cole, T. et al. 2009. 'Geographical Record: Geographies of the Holocaust', *The Geographical Review* 99(4): 563–74.

Confino, A. 1997a. 'Collective Memory and Cultural History: Problems of Method', *American Historical Review* 105(2): 1386–403.

———.1997b. *The Nation as a Local Metaphor: Württemberg, Imperial Germany, and National Memory, 1871–1918.* Chapel Hill: University of North Carolina Press.

Confino, A. and P. Fritzsche. 2002. *The Work of Memory: New Directions in the Study of German Society and Culture.* Champaign: University of Illinois Press.

Conquest, R. 1986. *The Harvest of Sorrow: Soviet Collectivization and the Terror-Famine.* Oxford and New York: Oxford University Press.

Cooke, S. 2009. 'Cultural Memory on the Move in Contemporary Travel Writing: W.G. Sebald's *The Rings of Saturn*', in A. Erll and A. Rigney (eds), *Mediation, Remediation, and the Dynamics of Cultural Memory.* Berlin: de Gruyter, pp. 15–30.

Cooper, C. 2006. *Ukraine,* 2nd ed. New York: Infobase.

Cosgrove, D. [1984] 1998. *Social Formation and Symbolic Landscape.* Madison: University of Wisconsin Press.

Cosgrove, D. and S. Daniels. 1988. 'Introduction', in D. Cosgrove and S. Daniels (eds), *The Iconography of Landscape.* Cambridge: Cambridge University Press, pp. 1–10.

Cosgrove, M. 2007. 'Sebald for Our Time: The Politics of Melancholy and the Critique of Capitalism in his Work', in A. Fuchs and J.J. Long (eds), *W.G. Sebald and the Writing of History.* Würzburg: Königshausen & Neumann, 91–110.

Craps, S. and M. Rothberg. 2011. 'Introduction: Transcultural Negotiations of Holocaust Memory', *Criticism: A Quarterly for Literature and the Arts* 53(4): 517–21.

Cravens, C.S. 2006. *Culture and Customs of the Czech Republic And Slovakia.* Westport, CT: Greenwood.

Crowe, D.M. 1994. *A History of the Gypsies of Eastern Europe and Russia.* Basingstoke and New York: Palgrave Macmillan.

Crownshaw, R. 2010. *The Afterlife of Holocaust Memory in Contemporary Literature and Culture*. Basingstoke: Palgrave Macmillan.

Cushman, R.C. and S.R. Jones. 2004. *A Field Guide to the North American Prairie*. New York: Peterson.

Czechoslovak American Congress. 2012. 'Community Calendar'. Retrieved 20 April 2012 from http://www.bohemianlawyers.org/CAC-Calendar-JUNE-2010.pdf

D'Alfonso, A. 2005. *Gambling with Failure*. Toronto: Exile Editions.

Dalton, D. 2009. 'Encountering Auschwitz: A Personal Rumination on the Possibilities and Limitations of Witnessing/Remembering Trauma in Memorial Space', *Law-Text-Culture* 13: 187–226.

Davis, M. 2002. *Late Victorian Holocausts: El Niño Famines and the Making of the Third World*. London and New York: Verso.

Davis, T. 2006. *A Failure of Initiative: Final Report of the Select Bipartisan Committee to Investigate the Preparation for and Response to Hurricane Katrina, February 15, 2006*. Washington DC: House, Select Bipartisan Committee to Investigate the Preparation for and Response to Hurricane Katrina.

Davis, T.M. 2011. *Southscapes: Geographies of Race, Region, and Literature*. Chapel Hill: University of North Carolina Press.

Dean, M. 2003. *Collaboration in the Holocaust: Crimes of the Local Police in Belorussia and Ukraine, 1941–44*. Basingstoke, London and New York: Macmillan Press.

Denber, R. and R. Goldman, with Human Rights Watch (formerly Helsinki Watch). 1992. *Bloodshed in the Caucasus: Escalation of the Armed Conflict in Nagorno Karabakh*. Vienna: Human Rights Watch.

Desbois, P. 2008. *The Holocaust by Bullets: A Priest's Journey to Uncover the Truth Behind the Murder of 1.5 Million Jews*, trans. C. Spencer. Basingstoke and New York: Palgrave Macmillan.

Di Giovine, M.A. 2009. *The Heritage-scape: UNESCO, World Heritage, and Tourism*. Plymouth: Lexington Books.

Dixon Hunt, J. 2001. '"Come into the Garden, Maud": Garden Art as a Privileged Mode of Commemoration and Identity', in J. Wolschke-Bulmahn (ed.), *Places of Commemoration: Search for Identity and Landscape Design*. Washington, DC: Dumbarton Oaks, pp. 9–24.

Dorrian, M. and G. Rose. 2003. *Deterritorializations: Revisioning Landscape and Politics*. London and New York: Black Dog Publishing.

Drescher, S. 2009. 'From Consensus to Consensus: Slavery in International Law', in Jean Allain (ed.), *The Legal Understanding of Slavery: From the Historical to the Contemporary*. Oxford: Oxford University Press, pp. 85–104.

Dubow, J. 2004. 'The Mobility of Thought: Reflections on Blanchot and Benjamin', *Interventions: International Journal of Postcolonial Studies* 6(2): 216–88.

Duncan, J. 1980. 'The Superorganic in American Cultural Geography', *Annals of the Association of American Geographers* 70(2): 181–98.

Ellingworth, J. 2009. 'Kiev Mayor Vetoes Hotel on Babi Yar Massacre Site', *The Telegraph*, 29 September.

Ellman, M. 2007. 'Stalin and the Soviet Famine of 1932–3 Revisited', *Europe-Asia Studies* 59(4): 663–93.

Erll, A. 2011a. 'Travelling Memory', *Parallax* 17(4): 4–18.

———. 2011b. *Memory in Culture*, trans. S.B. Young. Basingstoke and New York: Palgrave Macmillan.

Erll, A. and A. Rigney. 2009. *Mediation, Remediation, and the Dynamics of Cultural Memory*. Berlin: de Gruyter.

Etlin, R. 2002. *Art, Culture and Media under the Third Reich*. Chicago and London: University of Chicago Press.

Etzioni, A. 2001. *Political Unification Revisited: On Building Supranational Communities*. Lanham: Lexington Books.

Farmer, S. 1995. 'Symbols That Face Two Ways: Commemorating the Victims of Nazism and Stalinism at Buchenwald and Sachsenhausen', *Representations* 49: 97–119.

Felman, S. and D. Laub. 1992. *Testimony: Crises of Witnessing in Literature, Psychoanalysis and History*. New York: Routledge.

Findling, D. and S. Schweber. 2007. *Teaching the Holocaust*. Los Angeles: Torah Aura.

Fogarty, M.P. 1945. *Prospects of the Industrial Areas of Great Britain*. London: Methuen.

Ford, M. 2014. 'Good News From Ukraine: Everyone Still Hates Hitler', *Atlantic*, 20 March.

Fornäs, J. 2008. 'Meanings of Money: The Euro as a Sign of Value and Cultural Identity', in W. Uricchio (ed.), *We Europeans? Media, Representations, Identities*. Bristol and Chicago: Intellect Books, pp. 123–40.

Francis, H. 2012. 'Hywel in Parliament: Debates'. Retrieved 20 March 2012 from http://www.hywelfrancis.co.uk/inparliament/debates/debates_300112.php

Friedlander, S. 1993. *Memory, History, and the Extermination of the Jews of Europe*. Bloomington: Indiana University Press.

Fuchs, A. 2007. '"Ein Hauptkapital der Geschichte der Unterwerfung": Representations of Nature in W.G. Sebald's *Die Ringe des Saturn*', in A. Fuchs and J.J. Long (eds), *W.G. Sebald and the Writing of History*. Würzburg: Königshausen and Neumann, pp. 121–38.

Fussell, P. 1989. *Wartime: Understanding and Behavior in the Second World War*. Oxford and New York: Oxford University Press.

Gass, A.G. 2010. 'How Babi Yar Park Came to Be', in *Mizel Tov: Good News from the Mizel Museum*, Spring/Summer. Retrieved 10 September 2011 from http://www.mizelmuseum.org/pdfs/MizelTovMarch2010.pdf

Gay, V.P. 1992. *Freud on Sublimation: Reconsiderations*. Albany: State University of New York Press.

Gedenkstätte Buchenwald. 1993. *Buchenwald: A Tour of the Memorial Site* (BTM), trans. J. Gledhill and T. Gohlke. Göttingen: Wallstein Verlag.

———. 2004. *Buchenwald Concentration Camp 1937–1945: A Guide to the Permanent Historical Exhibition* (BGE), trans. J. Rosenthal. Göttingen: Wallstein Verlag.

Gedenkstätte Buchenwald and Härtl, U. 2006. *K.L. Buchenwald, Post Weimar: The Former Buchenwald Concentration Camp, Photographed by Jürgen M. Pietsch in 1998 and 1999*, 2nd ed. (KLB), trans. J. Rosenthal. Göttingen: Schwarz Weiss.

Gerrard, A. 2011a. 'The Twinning of Lidice with Stoke-on-Trent', unpublished data (interview by email with J. Rapson, March 22).

———. 2011b. 'Historic Link Is a Part of Our Future', *This Is Staffordshire*. Retrieved 12 January 2012 from http://www.thisisstaffordshire.co.uk/Historic-link-future/story-12490003-detail/story.html

Gerrard, A. and C. Gerrard. 2011. 'Lidice & Stoke-on-Trent'. *Staffordshire Fine Arts*. Retrieved 23 March 2011 from http://www.creativestoke.co.uk/80430/info.php?p=39

Gifford, T. 1999. *Pastoral*. Abingdon, Oxon and New York: Routledge.

Gilbert, M. 1997. *Holocaust Journey: Travelling in Search of the Past*. New York and Chichester: Columbia University Press.

Ginsburg, H. 1974. Speech draft (sign unveiling). Archives of the Mizel Museum, Denver.

———. n.d., ca. early 1970s. Speaker system narrative. Archives of the Mizel Museum, Denver.

———. n.d., ca. early 1970s. Speech draft. Archives of the Mizel Museum, Denver.

———. n.d., ca. early 1970s. Voiceover transcript. Archives of the Mizel Museum, Denver.

Glaser, H. 1978. *The Cultural Roots of National Socialism*, trans. E.A. Menze. Austin: University of Texas Press.

Goethe, J.W. von. (1774) 1989. *The Sorrows of Young Werther*, trans. Michael Hulse. London and New York: Penguin.

Golson, G.J., S. Penuel and K. Bradley. 2011. *Encyclopedia of Disaster Relief*. Thousand Oaks: Sage.

Gorra, M. 2004. *The Bells in Their Silence: Travels through Germany*. Princeton and Oxford: Princeton University Press.

Gross, A.S. and M.J. Hoffman. 2004. 'Memory, Authority and Identity: Holocaust Studies in the Wake of the Wilkomirski Debate', *Biography* 27(1): 25–47.

Grossman, V. (1985) 2006. *Life and Fate*, trans. R. Chandler. London: Vintage.

———. (1994) 2011. *Everything Flows*, trans. R. Chandler. London: Vintage.

Gulliver, T. 2010. 'Broken Pieces, Shattered Lives: The Lasting Legacy of Hurricane Katrina', in L.A. Sandberg and T. Sandberg (eds), *Climate Change: Who's Carrying the Burden? The Chilly Climates of the Global Environmental Dilemma*. Ottawa: Canadian Centre for Policy Alternatives, pp. 173–84.

Hachmeister, G. L. 2002. *Italy in the German Literary Imagination: Goethe's 'Italian Journey' and Its Reception by Eichendorff, Platen, and Heine*. Rochester, NY Camden House.

Halbwachs, M. (1950) 1980. *The Collective Memory*. New York: Harper Colophon.

———. (1925) 1992. *On Collective Memory*, ed. and trans. L. Coser. London and Chicago: University of Chicago Press.

Harding, L. 2014. 'Kiev's Protesters: Ukraine Uprising Was No Neo-Nazi Power-Grab', *Guardian*, 13 March. Retrieved 25 March from http://www.theguardian.com/world/2014/mar/13/ukraine-uprising-fascist-coup-grassroots-movement

Henri-Lévy, B. 2011. 'A Tribute to Jorge Semprun', *Huffington Post*. Retrieved 7 June 2011 from http://www.huffingtonpost.com/bernardhenri-levy/jorge-semprun_b_877342.html

Herb, G.H. 2008. *Nations and Nationalism: A Global Historical Overview*. Santa Barbara: ABC-CLIO/Greenwood.

Herbstreuth, P. 2000. 'Monuments and Memorials', in B. Nemitz (ed.), *Trans-Plant: Living Vegetation in Contemporary Art*. Ostfildern and Berlin: Hatje Cantz, pp. 150–55.

Herszenhorn, D.M. 2012. 'Azerbaijan Delights in Taking the Stage as Eurovision Host', *New York Times*. Retrieved 29 May 2012 from http://www.nytimes.com/2012/05/28/world/asia/azerbaijan-revels-as-host-of-eurovision-song-contest.html

Hetnov, D and I. Yukhnovskiy. 2008. *The Holodomor 1932–1933: Genocide against the Ukrainian People*. Kiev: Olena Teliha.

Heydarov, T. and T. Bagiyev. 2007. *Khojaly Tragedy: An International View*. Baku: Anglo-Azerbaijani Youth Society.

Heywood, A. 2000. *Key Concepts in Politics*. Basingstoke and New York: Palgrave Macmillan.

HH Journal. 2008. 'To Catch the Moment between two Heartbeats'. Retrieved 3 September 2011 from http://journal.hautehorlogerie.org/en/from-our-correspondents/asia/to-catch-the-moment-between-two-heartbeats-161/

Hilton, I. 1982. 'Author of *White Hotel* in Storm over "Deception"', *Sunday Times*, 28 March.

Hirsch, M. 1997. *Family Frames: Photography, Narrative, and Postmemory*. Cambridge, MA: Harvard University Press.

———. 1999. 'Projected Memory: Holocaust Photographs in Personal and Public Fantasy', in M. Bal, J.V. Crewe and L. Spitzer (eds) *Acts of Memory: Cultural Recall in the Present*. Hanover, NH: University Press of New England, pp. 3-23.

———. 2001. 'Surviving Images: Holocaust Photographs and the Work of Postmemory', *Yale Journal of Criticism* 14(1): 5–37.

Hitler, A. (1925) 2004. *Mein Kampf*. Florissant: Liberty Bell Press.

Hodges, L. 2009. 'Hurricane Katrina: A View from New Orleans (2005)', in R.P. Ingalls and D.K. Johnson (eds), *The United States Since 1945: A Documentary Reader*. Malden and Oxford: Blackwell, pp. 218–21.

Hoskins, W.G. (1954) 1985. *The Making of the English Landscape*. London: Penguin.

Huffington Post. 2012. 'Eurovision Song Contest: Armenia Boycotts Event in Azerbaijan 2012'. Retrieved 28 May 2012 from http://www.huffingtonpost.co.uk/2012/03/07/eurovision-song-contest-armenia-azerbaijan_n_1327978.html

Hui, B. 2010. 'Mapping Historical Networks in *Die Ringe des Saturn*', in M. Zisselsberger (ed.), *The Undiscover'd Country: W.G. Sebald and the Poetics of Travel*. Rochester and Woodbridge, Suffolk: Camden House, pp. 277–98.

Hungerford, A. 2003. *The Holocaust of Texts: Genocide, Literature and Personification*. Chicago and London: Chicago University Press.

Huyssen, A. 1995. *Twilight Memories: Marking Time in a Culture of Amnesia*. London and New York: Routledge.

———. 2003. *Present Pasts: Urban Palimpsests and the Politics of Memory*. Stanford: Stanford University Press.

Iles, J. 2003. 'Death, Leisure and Landscape: British Tourism on the Western Front', in M. Dorrian and G. Rose (eds), *Deterritorialisations: Revisioning Landscape and Politics*. London and New York: Black Dog Publishing, pp. 234–44.

Imort, M. 2006. 'Eternal Forest – Eternal Volk: The Rhetoric and Reality of National Socialist Forest Policy', in F.-J. Bruggemeier et al. (eds), *How Green Were the Nazis? Nature, Environment, and Nation in the Third Reich*. Athens: Ohio University Press, pp. 19–43.

Ingold, T. 2000. *The Perception of the Environment: Essays on Livelihood, Dwelling and Skill*. London: Routledge.

International Children's Exhibition of Fine Arts Lidice. 2011. 'The International Children's Exhibition of Fine Arts Lidice'. Retrieved 30 April 2011 from http://www.mdvv-lidice.cz/en/

Jacobs, A. 2012. 'A Jewish Museum for Everyone', *Intermountain Jewish News*, 23 February.

Jacobson, M. 2010. *The Lampshade: A Holocaust Detective Story from Buchenwald to New Orleans*. New York and London: Simon & Schuster.

Jay, M. 2007. 'No State of Grace: Violence in the Garden', in D. Harris and D. Fairchild Ruggles (eds), *Sites Unseen: Landscape and Vision*. Pittsburgh: University of Pittsburgh Press, pp. 45–60.

Jennings, H. (dir.) 1942. *The Silent Village*. Crown Film Unit.

Jones, K. 2007. *Journeys of Remembrance: Memories of the 2nd World War in French and German Literature, 1960–1980*. London and Leeds: Legenda.

Jordan, J. 2006. *Structures of Memory: Understanding Urban Change in Berlin and Beyond*. Stanford, CA: Stanford University Press.

Kabachiy, R. 2010. 'Ukraine's Stolen Money'. Retrieved 3 April 2012 from http://www.opendemocracy.net/od-russia/roman-kabachiy/stolen-memory

Kaes, A. 1992. *From Hitler to Heimat: The Return of History as Film*. Cambridge, MA: Harvard University Press.

Kappeler, A. 2009. 'From an Ethnonational to a Multiethnic to a Transnational Ukrainian History', in G. Kasianov and P. Ther (eds), *A Laboratory of Transnational History: Ukraine and Recent Ukrainian Historiography*. Budapest: Central European University Press, pp. 51–80.

Kasalicka, I. 2011. 'The International Children's Exhibition of Fine Arts Lidice'. Retrieved 30 April 2011 from http://www.mdvv-lidice.cz/en/

Katchmar, M. 2008. 'Interview', Ukrainian Canadian Research and Documentation Centre website. Retrieved 3 March 2011 from http://www.holodomorsurvivors.ca/Video/video/Files/Maria%20Katchmar_video.html

Kattago, S. 1998. 'Narrating the Histories of Buchenwald', *Constellations* 5(2): 266–82.

Keil, C. 2005. 'Sightseeing in the Mansions of the Dead', *Social and Cultural Geography* 6: 479–94.

de Keizer, M. 2012. 'The Thread that Binds Together: Lidice, Oradour, Putten and the Memory of World War II', in E. Langenbacher, B. Niven and R. Wittlinger (eds), *Dynamics of Memory and Identity in Contemporary Europe*. Oxford and New York: Berghahn, pp. 120–35.

Kembayev, Z. 2007. *Legal Aspects of the Regional Integration Processes in the Post-Soviet Area*. Berlin and Heidelberg: Springer Verlag.

Kiernan, B. 2007. *Blood and Soil: A World History of Genocide and Extermination from Sparta to Darfur*. New Haven and London: Yale University Press.

Kilbourne, R.J.A. 2007. '"Catastrophe with Spectator": Subjectivity, Intertextuality and the Representation of History in *Die Ringe die Saturn*', in A. Fuchs and J.J. Long (eds), *W.G. Sebald and the Writing of History*. Würtzburg: Königshausen & Neumann, pp. 139–62.

Killen, B. 1992. 'Atrocity Reports Horrify Azerbaijan', *Washington Times*, 3 March.

Knigge, V. 2012. Press conference statement. Buchenwald.de. Retrieved 24 July 2013 from http://www.buchenwald.de/en/752/

Kocharian, E.A. and Y. Tam. 2008. Unpublished data (interview with J. Rapson, 8 April).

Koonz, C. 1994. 'Between Memory and Oblivion: Concentration Camps in German Memory', in J.R. Gillis (ed.), *Commemorations: The Politics of National Identity*. Princeton: Princeton University Press, pp. 258–80.

Koshar, R. 2000a. *From Monuments to Traces: Artefacts of German Memory, 1870–1990*. Berkeley, Los Angeles and London: University of California Press.

———. 2000b. *German Travel Cultures*. Oxford and New York: Berg.

Kramer, A.E. 2012. 'Armenians Are Shunning Song Contest in Azerbaijan', *New York Times*. Retrieved 29 May 2012 from http://www.nytimes.com/2012/03/08/world/asia/armenia-shuns-eurovision-hosted-by-azerbaijan-a-rival.html

Krüger, H. 2010. *The Nagorno-Karabkh Conflict: A Legal Analysis*. Heidelberg, Dordrecht, London and New York: Springer.

Kuznetsov, A.A. (1966) 1972. *Babi Yar: A Document in the Form of a Novel*, trans. D. Floyd. London: Sphere Books.

Kyiv Post. 2010. 'Yanukovych: Famine Of 1930s Was Not Genocide Against Ukrainians'. Retrieved 29 May 2012 from http://www.kyivpost.com/content/ukraine/yanukovych-famine-of-1930s-was-not-genocide-agains-65137.html

LaCapra, D. 2001. *Writing History, Writing Trauma*. Baltimore: John Hopkins University Press.

⸻. 2004. *History in Transit: Experience, Identity, Critical Theory*. Ithaca: Cornell University Press.

Lamb, H.H. 1977. *Climate: Present, Past and Future*. London: Meethuen & Co.

Lancaster, O. and A. Scott-James. 2004. *The Pleasure Garden: An Illustrated History of British Gardening*. London: Frances Lincoln.

Landsberg, A. 1997. 'America, the Holocaust and the Mass Culture of Memory: Toward a Radical Politics of Empathy', *New German Critique* 71: 63–86.

Lang. B. 2003. 'The Moral Space of Figurative Discourse', in N. Levi and M. Rothberg (eds), *The Holocaust: Theoretical Readings*. New Brunswick, NJ: Rutgers University Press.

⸻. 2005. *Post-Holocaust: Interpretation, Misinterpretation, and the Claims of History*. Bloomington, IN: Indiana University Press.

Langer, L. 1993. *Holocaust Testimonies: The Ruins of Memory*. New Haven, CT and London: Yale University Press.

Laub, Dori. 2003. 'September 11, 2001 – An Event Without a Voice', in J. Greenberg (ed.), *Trauma at Home*. Lincoln and London: University of Nebraska Press, pp. 204–15.

Lekan, T.M. 2004. *Imagining the Nation in Nature: Landscape, Preservation and German Identity, 1885–1945*. London and Cambridge, MA: Harvard University Press.

Lennon, J.J. and M. Foley. 2000. *Dark Tourism: The Attraction of Death and Disaster*. New York and London: Continuum.

Lepenies, W. 2006. *The Seduction of Culture in German History*. Princeton, NJ and Woodstock, Oxfordshire: Princeton University Press.

Levene, M. 2004. 'A Dissenting Voice: Part 2', *Journal of Genocide Studies* 6(3): 431–45.

⸻. 2010. 'The Elephant in the Room? Anthropogenic Climate Change, Genocide Studies and the Challenge Before Us', *International Conference of Genocide Scholars: Genocide as Actuality and Artefact, Conversations between Past and Present in the Prevention and Punishment of Genocide*.

⸻. 2011. 'The Reality and Urgency of Human-created Climate Change', *Rescue History*. Retrieved 3 November 2011 from http://rescue-history-from-climate-change.org/

Levy, D. and N. Sznaider. 2006. *The Holocaust and Memory in the Global Age*, trans A. Oksiloff. Philadelphia: Temple University Press.

Levinas, E. (1991) 1998. *Entre Nous: Thinking-of–the–Other*, trans. M. Smith and B. Hershaw. London and New York: Continuum.

⸻. (1969) 2007. *Totality and Infinity: An Essay on Exteriority*, trans. A. Lingis. Pittsburgh: Dequesne University Press.

Lewis, S. and A. Appelfeld. 1984. *Art Out of Agony: The Holocaust Theme in Literature, Sculpture and Film*. Montréal: CBC International.

Lidice Memorial. 2012. 'Wedding Ceremonies in the Lidice Rose Garden'. Retrieved 10 February 2012 from http://www.lidice-memorial.cz/marriage_en.aspx

Lisle, D. 2006. *The Global Politics of Contemporary Travel Writing.* Cambridge and New York: Cambridge University Press.

Lochner, L.P. 1942. *What About Germany?* New York: Dodd, Mead & Co.

Logan, P. 2011. *Humphrey Jennings and British Documentary Film Movement: A Re-Assessment.* Farnham and Burlington: Ashgate.

Logan, W. and K. Reeves. 2009. *Places of Pain and Shame: Dealing with Difficult Heritage.* Abingdon and New York: Routledge.

Long. J.J. 2007a. 'A Bibliographical Essay on Current Research', in A. Fuchs and J.J. Long (eds), *W.G. Sebald and the Writing of History.* Würtzburg: Königshausen & Neumann, pp. 11–30.

———. 2007b. *W.G. Sebald: Image, Archive, Modernity.* New York: Columbia University Press.

Lorimer, H. 2005. 'Cultural Geography: The Busyness of Being "More-than-Representational"', *Progress in Human Geography* 29(1): 83–94.

———. 2006. 'Herding Memories of Humans and Animals', *Environment and Planning D: Society and Space* 24: 497–518.

Lower, W. 2005. *Nazi Empire Building and the Holocaust in Ukraine.* Chapel Hill: University of Carolina Press.

Lyotard, J.-F. (1983) 1988. *The Differend: Phrases in Dispute.* Minneapolis: University of Minnesota Press.

MacDonald, S. 2009. *Difficult Heritage: Negotiating the Nazi Past in Nuremberg and Beyond.* London and New York: Routledge.

Magnus, R. and G. Schmid. (1906) 2004. *Goethe as a Scientist.* New York: H. Schuman.

Magocsi, P.R. 2010. *A History of Ukraine: The Land and Its Peoples.* 2nd ed. Toronto, Buffalo and London: Toronto University Press.

Mandel. N. 2006. *Against the Unspeakable: Complicity, the Holocaust, and Slavery in America.* Charlottesville: University of Virginia Press.

Marcus, P. 2011. 'WTC Steel Makes Strong Statement in Denver', *Colorado Statesman.* Retrieved 2 April 2012 from http://coloradostatesman.com/content/992983-wtc-steel-makes-strong-statement-denver

Margalit, A. 2002. *The Ethics of Memory.* Cambridge, MA and London: Harvard University Press.

Markle, G. 1995. *Meditations of a Holocaust Traveller.* Albany: State University of New York Press.

Martin, D. J. 2007. 'Lynching Sites: Where Trauma and Pastoral Collide', in A. Merrill Ingram et al. (eds), *Coming into Contact: Explorations in Ecocritical Theory and Practice.* Athens and London: University of Georgia Press, pp. 93–108.

Marx, L. 1964. *The Machine in the Garden: Technology and the Pastoral Ideal in America.* Oxford and New York: Oxford University Press.

Mauch, C. 2004. 'Introduction: Nature and Nation in Transatlantic Perspective', in C. Mauch (ed), *Nature in German History.* Oxford and New York: Berghahn, pp. 1–9.

Meneker, E. 1992. 'Living With Lidice', *Chicago Tribune.* Retrieved 20 April 20 2012 from http://articles.chicagotribune.com/1992–06–09/features/9202210339_1_monument-memorial-event-lidice-czechoslovakia

Merewether, C. 1997. 'Traces of Loss', in M. Roth et al. (eds), *Irresistible Decay: Ruins Reclaimed.* Los Angeles: Getty Publications, pp. 25–40.

Merleau-Ponty, M. (1942) 1962. *Phenomenology of Perception.* London: Routledge and Kegan Paul.

Mikesell, M. and P.L. Wagner (eds). 1962. *Readings in Cultural Geography.* Chicago: University of Chicago Press.

Milchman, A. and A. Rosenburg. 1998. *Postmodernism and the Holocaust.* Amsterdam and Atlanta: Rodopi.

Mitchell, W.T.J. 1994. *Landscape and Power.* London: Routledge.

Mizel Museum. 2012a. 'Contact Us'. Retrieved 3 March 2012 from http://mizelmuseum .org/about-3/

————. 2012b. 'Welcome to the Mizel Museum'. Retrieved 3 March 3 2012 from http:// mizelmuseum.org/home-2/hours-and-admission/welcome-to-the-mizel-museum-3/

Morrison, B. 1994. 'From Denver to Moscow: The Colorado Committee of Concern for Soviet Jewry, Part 2', *Rocky Mountain Jewish Historical Notes of the Rocky Mountain Jewish Historical Society* 12(3).

Moses, A.D. 2010. *Empire, Colony, Genocide: Conquest, Occupation, and Subaltern Resistance in World History.* New York: Berghahn.

Moses, A. Dirk and M. Rothberg. 'A Dialogue on the Ethics and Politics of Transcultural Memory', in L. Bond and J. Rapson (eds), *The Transcultural Turn: Interrogating Memory between and Beyond Borders.* Berlin: de Gruyter, pp. 29–38.

National Geographic. 2012. *Human Lampshade: A Holocaust Mystery.* Nat Geo TV Blogs. Retrieved 12 July 2013 from http://tvblogs.nationalgeographic.com/2012/09/27/ human-lampshade-a-holocaust-mystery/

NineMSN. 2010. 'Holocaust Holidays: Girls, Grog and Genocide?' Retrieved 13 April 2010 from http://travel.ninemsn.com.au/blog.aspx?blogentryid=616908&showcom ments=true

Nelson, S.M. 2008. *Denver: An Archaeological History.* Boulder: University of Colorado Press.

Nevada Mail. 1950. 'Illinois Reborn: Lidice Is Now a Memory Too'. Retrieved 20 April 2012. http://news.google.com/newspapers?nid=1908&dat=19500527&id=zWAfAA AAIBAJ&sjid=ltQEAAAAIBAJ&pg=1376,5158208

News.az. 2010. 'Azerbaijan's Khojaly and Czech Lidice Sign Protocol of Cooperation'. Retrieved 1 March 2010 from http://www.news.az/articles/10376

Nigmatulina, A. 2015. 'Tensions Reignite In The Nagorno-Karabakh Conflict'. Retrieved 1 May 2015 from http://www.aljazeera.com/indepth/features/2015/03/tensions-reig nite-nagorno-karabakh-conflict-150303121751335.html

Niven, B. 2007. *The Buchenwald Child: Truth Propaganda and Fiction.* Rochester, NY and Woodbridge, Suffolk: Camden House.

Nixon, R. 2011. *Slow Violence and the Environmentalism of the Poor.* Cambridge, MA: Harvard University Press.

Nora, P. 1989. 'Between Memory and History: Les Lieux de Mémoire', *Representations* 26(1): 7–25.

————. 2001. *Rethinking France: Les Lieux de Mémoire, Volume 1: The State,* trans. M. Trouille. London and Chicago: Chicago University Press.

Norman, R.J. 2004. *On Humanism.* London and New York: Routledge.

Novick, P. 2000. *The Holocaust in American Life.* New York: Houghton Mifflin.

O'Neil, R, and M. Tregenza. 2007. 'Archaeological Explorations: A Review by Historians'. Retrieved 1 March 2010 from http://www.holocaustresearchproject.org/ar/modern/ archreview.html

Panorama.am. 2012. 'Mayor Veronika Kellerova: Lidice, Khojaly Not Sister Cities, No Street Named Khojaly in Lidice'. Retrieved 1 April 2012 from http://panorama.am/ en/politics/2012/03/02/xocali-lidice-kellerova/

Parr, A. 2008. *Deleuze and Memorial Culture: Desire, Singular Memory and the Politics of Trauma*. Edinburgh: Edinburgh University Press.

Patraka, V.M. 1999. *Spectacular Suffering: Theatre, Fascism, and the Holocaust*. Bloomington: Indiana University Press.

Pearson, C. 2009. 'Creating the Natural Fortress: Landscape, Resistance, and Memory in the Vercors, France', in C.E. Closmann (ed.), *War and the Environment: Military Destruction in the Modern Age*. College Station: Texas A&M University Press, pp. 150–70.

Peck, H.D. 1992. 'The Crosscurrents of Walden's Pastoral', in R.F. Sayre (ed.), *New Essays on Walden*. Cambridge and New York: Cambridge University Press, pp. 73–94.

Podol's'kyi, A. 2008. 'A Reluctant Look Back: Jews and the Holocaust in Ukraine', trans. S. Lang. *Osteuropa* 8(10).

Pogue Harrison, R. 1993. *Forests: The Shadow of Civilization*. Chicago and London: Chicago University Press.

———. 2003. *The Dominion of the Dead*. Chicago and London: Chicago University Press.

Pohl, F. 1987. *Chernobyl: A Novel*. New York: Bantam.

Prague Real Estate. 2012. 'Lidice'. Retrieved 9 April 2012 from http://www.praguereales tate.cz/lidice/detailid-27216162/

Presner, T.S. 2007. *Mobile Modernity: Germans, Jews, Trains*. New York: Columbia University Press.

Radio Free Liberty. 2010. 'Communist Ukrainian Institute Head Denies Famine Was Deliberate'. Retrieved 3 April 3 2012 from http://www.rferl.org/content/Commu nist_Ukrainian_Institute_Head_Denies_Famine_Was_Deliberate/2112870.html

Radstone, S. 2011. 'What Place Is This? Transcultural Memory and the Locations of Memory Studies', *Parallax* 17(4): 109–23.

Rapaport, H. 1997. *Is There Truth in Art?* New York: Cornell University Press.

Raykoff, I. and R.D. Tobin. 2007. *A Song for Europe: Popular Music and Politics in the Eurovision Song Contest*. Aldershot and Burlington: Ashgate.

Reuters. 2015. 'Deadly Clashes Near Azerbaijan's Breakaway Nagorno-Karabakh Region'. Retrieved 1 May from http://www.reuters.com/article/2015/04/21/us-armenia-azer baijan-conflict-idUSKBN0NC1ZO20150421

Rich, V.A. 1998. *Cursing the Basil and other Folklore of the Garden*. Victoria: Horsdal and Schubart.

Rickels, L.A. 2011. *Aberrations of Mourning*. Minneapolis: University of Minnesota Press.

Rigney, A. 2008. 'Divided Pasts: A Premature Memorial and the Dynamics of Collective Remembrance', *Memory Studies* 1(1): 89–97.

Riordan, C. 2007. 'Ecocentrism in Sebald's *After Nature*', in A. Fuchs and J.J. Long (eds), *W.G. Sebald and the Writing of History*. W rzburg: Königshausen & Neumann, 45–47.

Rohdewald, S. 2008. 'Post-Soviet Remembrance of the Holocaust and National Memories of the Second World War in Russia, Ukraine and Lithuania', *Forum for Modern Language Studies* 44(2): 173–84.

Rose, G. 1996. *Mourning Becomes the Law: Philosophy and Representation*. Cambridge and New York: Cambridge University Press.

Rose, M. and J. Wylie. 2006. 'Animating Landscape', *Environment and Planning D: Society and Space* 24: 475–97.

Roth, M. et al. (eds). 1997. *Irresistible Decay: Ruins Reclaimed*. Los Angeles: Getty Publications.

Roth, S. 2003. 'Goethe and Buchenwald: Reconstructing German National Identity in the Weimar Year 1999', in P.M. Daly et al. (eds), *Why Weimar? Questioning the Legacy of Weimar from Goethe to 1999*. McGill European Studies Series 5: 93–106. New York and Baltimore: Peter Lang.

Roth, J.K. and M. Berenbaum. 1989. *Holocaust: Religious and Philosophical Implications*. Minnesota: Paragon House.

Rothberg, M. 2009. *Multidirectional Memory: Remembering the Holocaust in the Age of Decolonization*. Stanford, CA: Stanford University Press.

Russell, E. 2001. *War and Nature: Fighting Humans and Insects with Chemicals from World War I to Silent Spring*. Cambridge and New York: Cambridge University Press.

Russell, E. and R. Tucker. 2004. *Natural Enemy, Natural Ally: Toward an Environmental History of Warfare*. Corvallis: Oregon State University Press.

Rymaszewski, B. 2003. 'The Limits of Intervention in Museum and Conservation Practice at the Auschwitz Memorial and Museum', in *Preserving for the Future: Material from an International Preservation Conference, Oświęcim, June 23–25, 2003*. Oświęcim: Auschwitz-Birkenau State Museum, pp. 24–34.

Samuel, R. 1994. *Theatres of Memory: Past and Present in Contemporary Culture vol. 1*. London: Verso.

Santner, E. 2006. *On Creaturely Life: Rilke, Benjamin, Sebald*. Chicago and London: Chicago University Press.

Sauer, C.O. 1963 (1923). 'The Morphology of Landscape', in John Leighly (ed.), *Land and Life: Selections from the Writings of Carl Otwin Sauer*. Berkeley: University of California Press, pp. 315–50.

Scarry, E. 1985. *The Body in Pain: The Making and Unmaking of the World*. Oxford and New York: Oxford University Press.

Schama, S. 1995. *Landscape and Memory*. London: Harper Collins.

Schein, R. 1997. 'The Place of Landscape: A Conceptual Framework for Interpreting an American Landscape', *Annals of the Association of American Geographers* 87(4): 660–80.

Schlesinger, P. 2004. 'W.G. Sebald and the Condition of Exile'. *Theory, Culture and Society* 21(2): 43–67.

Schmidt-Hannisa, H.-W. 2007. 'Abberation of a Species: On the Relationship between Man and Beast in W.G. Sebald's Work', in A. Fuchs and J.J. Long (eds), *W.G. Sebald and the Writing of History*. Würzburg: Königshausen & Neumann, pp. 31–44.

Schneider, D.L. and W. Wette. 2006. *The Wehrmacht: History, Myth, Reality*. Cambridge, MA: Harvard University Press.

Seamon, D. 1978. 'Goethe's Approach to the Natural World: Implications for Environmental Theory and Education', in D. Ley and M. Samuels (eds), *Humanistic Geography: Prospects and Problems*. London: Croom Helm, pp. 238–50.

Sebald, W.G. (1995) 2002. *The Rings of Saturn* [*Die Ringe des Saturn*], trans. M. Hulse. London: Vintage Books.

Semprun, J. 1963. *The Long Voyage* [*Le Grand Voyage*], trans. R. Seaver. Paris: Gallimard.

———. 1983. *What a Beautiful Sunday!* [*Quel beau Dimanche!*], trans. A. Sheridan. London: Abacus.

———. 1997. *Literature or Life* [*L'écriture ou la Vie*], trans. L. Coverdale. London: Viking/ Penguin.

The Sentinel. 2010. 'Politician Honoured for Role in Rebuilding Czech Village Massacred by Nazis'. 17 November.

Shapiro, P. 2008. 'Foreword', in P. Desbois, *The Holocaust by Bullets: A Priest's Journey to Uncover the Truth Behind the Murder of 1.5 Million Jews*, trans. C. Spencer. Basingstoke and New York: Palgrave Macmillan, pp. vii–xiii.

Sharpley, R. and P.R. Stone. 2009. *The Darker Side of Travel: The Theory and Practice of Dark Tourism*. Bristol, Buffalo and Toronto: Channel View.

Shaw, P. 2006. *The Sublime*. London and New York: Routledge.

Shefler, G. 2011. 'Jewish Museums to Sprout Up in Kiev Next Year?' *Jerusalem Post*. Retrieved 3 January 2012 from http://www.jpost.com/JewishWorld/JewishFeatures/Article.aspx?id=239736

Silk, S.M. 1992. 'Writing the Holocaust/Writing Travel: The Space of Representation in Jorge Semprún's *Le Grand Voyage*', *CLIO: A Journal of Literature, History, and the Philosophy of History* 22(1): 53–65.

Smith, M. 2005. 'On "Being" Moved by Nature: Geography, Emotion and Environmental Ethics', in J. Davidson et al. (eds), *Emotional Geographies*. Aldershot and Burlington, VT: Ashgate, 219–30.

Snyder, T. 2010. *Bloodlands: Europe between Stalin and Hitler*. London: Bodley Head.

Sontag, S. 2007. *At the Same Time: Essays and Speeches*, ed. P. Dilonardo and A. Jump. New York: Farrar, Strauss.

Soper, K. 1995. *What Is Nature? Culture, Politics and the Non-Human*. Oxford: Blackwell.

St. Vincent Millay, E. 1942. 'The Murder of Lidice', *Life* 13(16): 90–100.

Stehlik, E. 2004. *Lidice: The Story of a Czech Village*. Lidice: Lidice Memorial.

———. 2007. *Memories of Lidice*. Lidice: Lidice Memorial.

Stephenson, J. 2006. *Hitler's Home Front: Wurttemburg Under the Nazis*. New York: Hambledon Continuum.

Stern, G. 2000. 'Echoes of Exile: The Literary Response to the Exiles by American Women Writers', in E.P. Frederiksen and M.K. Wallach (eds), *Facing Fascism and Confronting the Past: German Women Writers from Weimar to the Present*. Albany: State University of New York Press, pp. 153–69.

Stewart, S. 1998. 'Garden Agon', *Representations* 62: 111–43.

Stokes, M. 2004. 'Place, Exchange and Meaning: Black Sea Musicians in the West of Ireland', in Simon Frith (ed.), *Popular Music: Music and Identity vol. 4*, pp. 101–19. New York and London: Routledge.

Stross, B. 1942. *Lidice Shall Live*. London: Czechoslovak-British Friendship Club.

Sturken, M. 2007. *Tourists of History: Memory. Kitsch and Consumerism from Oklahoma City to Ground Zero*. Durham and London: Duke University Press.

Subtelny, O. 1991. *Ukraine: A History*. Toronto, Buffalo and London: Toronto University Press.

Suleiman, S. 2004. 'Historical Trauma and Literary Testimony: Writing and Repetition in the Buchenwald Memoirs of Jorge Semprun', *Journal of Romance Studies* 4(2): 1–19.

———. 2006. *Crises of Memory and the Second World War*. Cambridge, MA: Harvard University Press.

Tantillo, A.O. 2002. *The Will to Create: Goethe's View of Nature*. Pittsburgh: University of Pittsburgh Press.

Theisen, B. 2004. 'Prose of the World: W.G. Sebald's Literary Travels', *Germanic Review* 79: 163–79.

Thomas, D.M. 1981. *The White Hotel*. New York: Viking Press.

Thompson, I. 2009. *Rethinking Landscape: A Critical Reader.* London and New York: Routledge.

Thrift, N. 2008. *Non-representational Theory: Space, Politics, Affect.* Abingdon and New York: Routledge.

Thurston, M. 2001. *Making Something Happen: American Political Poetry Between the World Wars.* Chapel Hill: University of North Carolina Press.

Tidd, U. 2005. 'The Infinity of Testimony and Dying in Jorge Semprún's Holocaust Autothanatographies', *Forum for Modern Language Studies* 41(4): 407–17.

———. 2008. 'Exile, Language and Trauma in Recent Autobiographical Writing by Jorge Semprun', *Modern Language Review* 103(3): 697–714.

Tilley, C. 1994. *A Phenomenology of Landscape: Places, Paths, and Monuments.* Providence, RI and Oxford: Berg.

Time. 1942. 'Illinois: Hail Lidice'. Retrieved 10 April 2012 from http://www.time.com/time/magazine/article/0,9171,795994,00.html

The Times. 1992. 'Corpses Litter Hills in Karabakh', in T. Heydarov and T. Bagiyev (eds), *Khojaly Tragedy: An International View.* Baku and London: Anglo-Azerbaijani Youth Society.

Today.az. 2010. 'Azerbaijan's Khojaly Is Twinned with Czech Lidice'. Retrieved 1 March 2010 from http://www.today.az/news/society/62772.html

Tolia-Kelly, D.P. 2010. *Landscape, Race and Memory: Material Ecologies of Citizenship.* Farnham and Burlington, VT: Ashgate.

Truswell, J. 2010a. 'Talks Planned on Lidice Link-up', *The Sentinel,* 19 August. Retrieved 10 February 2011 from http://www.thisisstaffordshire.co.uk/news/Talks-planned-Lidice-link/article-2545769-detail/article.html

———. 2010b. *Lidice Lives.* Retrieved 3 May 2011 from http://www.youtube.com/watch?v=j-V-wUkgeQw

Tumarkin, M. 2010. *Otherland: Travels with My Daughter.* Melbourne: Random House.

Uekötter, F. 2006. *The Green and the Brown: A History of Conservation in Nazi Germany.* Cambridge and New York: Cambridge University Press.

Urry, J, 1990. *The Tourist Gaze.* London, Thousand Oaks and New Delhi: Sage.

Vaughan, R. 1979. *Twentieth-Century Europe: Paths to Unity.* London: Croom Helm.

Verlinden, A. 2008. 'Global Ethics and Dialogism', in R. Commers, W. Vandekerckhove and A. Verlinden (eds), *Ethics in an Era of Globalization.* Burlington, VT: Ashgate, pp. 187–216.

Vice, S. 2000. *Holocaust Fiction.* London and New York: Routledge.

Vlk, M. 2006. *The Lidice Memorial: The Guide,* trans. L. Kábrt. Nymburk: VEGA-L.

Von Plessen, M.-L. et al. (eds). 1999. *Walking through Time in Weimar: A Criss-cross Guide to Cultural History – Weaving between Goethe's Home and Buchenwald.* Ostfilden-rui: Hatje Verlag/Marie-Louise von Plessen.

Waal, T. de. 2003. *Black Garden: Armenia and Azerbaijan Through Peace and War.* New York and London: New York University Press.

Walders, D. 2006. 'Two Glimpses of History', in D. Farley and J. Sholl (eds), *Travelers' Tales: Prague and the Czech Republic.* Palo Alto: Travelers' Tales, pp. 281–88.

Walkowitz, R.L. 2007. *Cosmopolitan Style: Modernism Beyond the Nation.* New York: Columbia University Press.

Wanner, C. 1998. *Burden of Dreams: History and Identity in Post-Soviet Ukraine.* University Park: Pennsylvania University Press.

Wechsberg, J.. 2003. *Trifles Make Perfection.* Jaffrey: David R. Godine.

Weichart, E. 1947. *The Forest of the Dead [Der Totenwald].* London: Victor Gollancz.

Weissman, G. 2004. *Fantasies of Witnessing: Postwar Efforts to Experience the Holocaust.* New York: Cornell University Press.

Welsch, W. 1999. 'Transculturality – the Puzzling Form of Cultures Today', in M. Featherstone and S. Lash (eds), *Spaces of Culture: City, Nation, World.* London: Sage, pp. 194–213.

Wheeler, E. 1957. *Lidice.* Prague: Orbis.

Whiston Spirn, A. 1998. *The Language of Landscape.* New Haven and London: Yale University Press.

Whitehead, A. 2003. 'Geoffrey Hartman and the Ethics of Place: Landscape, Memory, Trauma', *European Journal of English Studies* 7(3): 275–92.

Wiesel, E. (1966) 2011. *The Jews of Silence: A Personal Report on Soviet Jewry.* New York: Schoken Books.

Wild, J. 2007. 'Introduction', in E. Levinas, *Totality and Infinity: An Essay on Exteriority.* Pittsburgh: Dequesne University Press, pp. 11–20.

Wilson, W.D. 2001. '"Humanitatssalbader": Goethe's Distaste for Jewish Emancipation, and Jewish Responses', in K.L. Berghahn and J. Hermand (eds), *Goethe in German-Jewish Culture,* Rochester, NY and Woodbridge, Suffolk: Camden House, pp. 146–64.

Winstone, M. 2010. *The Holocaust Sites of Europe: An Historical Guide.* London and New York: I.B. Taurus.

Wolschke-Bulmahn, J. 1997. 'Introduction', in J. Wolschke-Bulmahn (ed.), *Nature and Ideology: Garden Design in the Twentieth Century.* Washington DC: Dumbarton Oaks.

———. 2001. 'Introduction', in J. Wolschke-Bulmahn (ed.), *Places of Commemoration: Search for Identity and Landscape Design.* Washington, DC: Dumbarton Oaks.

Wylie, J. 2005. 'A Single Day's Walking: Narrating Self and Landscape on the South West Coast Path', *Transactions of the Institute of British Geographers* 30: 234–47.

———. 2006. 'Depths and Folds: On Landscape and the Gazing Subject', *Environment and Planning D: Society and Space* 24: 519–53.

———. 2007. *Landscape.* Abingdon and New York: Routledge.

Yates, F. 2001. *The Art of Memory.* Chicago and London: University of Chicago Press.

'Yerevan' 2011. 'Azerbaijani Soldier Killed Near Karabakh, Says Ministry', *Hurriyet Daily News and Economic Review,* 24 March. Retrieved 8 January 2012 from http://www.hurriyetdailynews.com/n.php?n=azerbaijani-soldier-killed-near-karabakh-says-ministry-2011-03-24

Young, I. 2000. *Inclusion and Democracy.* Oxford: Oxford University Press.

Young, J.E. 2003. 'Writing the Holocaust', in N. Levi and M. Rothberg (eds), *The Holocaust: Theoretical Readings.* New Brunswick: Rutgers University Press, pp. 335–38.

———. 1994. *The Texture of Memory: Holocaust Memorials and Meanings.* New Haven and London: Yale University Press.

Yuhas, A. 2015. 'Russia's Action In Ukraine Conflict An Invasion', *Guardian.* Retrieved 1 May 2015 from http://www.theguardian.com/us-news/2015/mar/04/victoria-nuland-russia-actions-ukraine-invasion

Zajac. 2003. 'Grey or Green? Problems with the Maintenance of the Vegetation on the Museum Grounds', in *Preserving for the Future: Material from an International Pres-*

ervation Conference, Oświęcim, June 23–25, 2003. Oświęcim: Auschwitz-Birkenau State Museum, pp. 57–62.

Zelinksy, W. 1973. *The Cultural Geography of the United States*. Englewood Cliffs, NJ: Prentice Hall.

Zilcosky, J. 2004. 'Sebald's Uncanny Travels: The Impossibility of Getting Lost', in J.J. Long and A. Whitehead (eds), *W.G. Sebald: A Critical Companion*. Seattle: University of Washington Press.

————. 2008. *Writing Travel: The Poetics and Politics of the Modern Journey*. Toronto, Buffalo and London: University of Toronto Press, pp. 102–20.

Zuroff, E. 2010. 'A Dangerous Nazi-Soviet Equivalence', *Guardian*. Retrieved 3 April 2012 from http://www.guardian.co.uk/commentisfree/cifamerica/2010/sep/29/seco ndworldwar-holocaust

INDEX